CORMAC McCARTHY'S HOUSE

SOUTHWESTERN WRITERS COLLECTION SERIES
The Wittliff Collections at Texas State University–San Marcos
Steven L. Davis, Editor

CORMAC

McCARTHY'S

HOUSE   Reading McCarthy Without Walls

PETER JOSYPH

UNIVERSITY OF TEXAS PRESS, AUSTIN

The Southwestern Writers Collection Series originates
from the Wittliff Collections, a repository of
literature, film, music, and southwestern and Mexican photography
established at Texas State University–San Marcos.

Portions of this book have been delivered as keynotes for the
Cormac McCarthy Society and have been published in the *Cormac McCarthy
Journal, Appalachian Heritage,* and *Intertextual and Interdisciplinary Approaches
to Cormac McCarthy: Borders and Crossings,* edited by Nick Monk.

Exhibitions of *Cormac McCarthy's House* were mounted in the Centennial Museum
in El Paso, Texas, in the fall of 1998; in the CAPITAL Centre in Warwick, England,
in the summer of 2009; in the Kulturens Hus in Luleå, Sweden, in the fall of 2009;
and in the Loyal Jones Appalachian Center in Berea, Kentucky, in the spring of 2011.

Requests for permission to reproduce material from this work should be sent to:
Permissions
University of Texas Press
P.O. Box 7819
Austin, TX 78713–7819
http://utpress.utexas.edu/about/book-permissions

♾ The paper used in this book meets the minimum requirements
of ANSI/NISO Z39.48–1992 (R1997) (Permanence of Paper).

LIBRARY OF CONGRESS CATALOGING-IN-PUBLICATION DATA

Josyph, Peter.
Cormac McCarthy's house : reading McCarthy without walls / by Peter Josyph.
— First edition.
p   cm — (Southwestern writers collection series)
Includes bibliographical references and index.
ISBN 978-0-292-74429-5 (cloth : alk. paper)
1. McCarthy, Cormac, 1933–
—Criticism and interpretation. I. Title.
PS3563.C337Z748 2013
813'.54—dc23   2012032973

doi:10.7560/744295

What is not underlined is worthless.

MILLER

. . . and if I'm not writing The Brothers Karamazov

while I read it, I'm not doing anything.

GENET

CONTENTS

ILLUSTRATIONS

CORMAC McCARTHY'S HOUSE

PART ONE

EXCURSIONS AND EXCHANGES

Come, shut your book, we're going to have lunch.

PROUST

Judging

Blood Meridian Or The Evening Redness in the West

by Its Cover

1. The Haiku Rebellion

When I was first invited into the anniversary hearings for *Blood Meridian Or The Evening Redness in the West* at the Southwestern Writers Collection in San Marcos, Texas, McCarthy's Portuguese translator, my friend Paulo Faria, had recently embarked on his second offensive against the translational fortress we were going to celebrate, so I thought it might be interesting to follow up Paulo's per diem queries to me with counter-queries of my own, as if I too were translating the novel—which I was, and always am, from pages of ana-morphic Panavision to a brain of less spectacular proportions. In the matter of McCarthy, I am never shy of enlisting the aid of better minds.

Paulo did not resist: his responses were based on the closest scrutiny and nearly a decade of pondering.

"Translating *Blood Meridian* is the supreme ceremony," he has told me. "I will do it for the rest of my life, always rewriting, always polishing, always from scratch, always the same but always different. I will burst into the temple again and again like Kafka's leopards until my irruption will be part of the ritual of reading *Blood Meridian* in Portuguese. I will do it until I die."[1]

I had one impediment. I was on strike against producing another work of prose until certain conditions in my professional life were met, and under this injunction I was writing a series of novels in haiku. As I am not a poet, and am disinterested in haiku beyond the Rule of 17, this, to me, was not actual writing—it was writing, so to speak, with the left hand. By the time three of these oddments were under way, with hundreds of haiku each, I started to reason, remember, read, even to see in haiku, fingers ever on the move

> unclenching to count
> my imprisonment in the
> number seventeen

Still, the notion of giving a talk on *Blood Meridian Or The Evening Redness in the West*, fashioned to reflect a Q&A correspondence and yet consisting of haiku exclusively, seemed too perilous a stunt even for a Broadway prestidigitator such as myself. When Harold Bloom said: "All that Hamlet, Falstaff and Cleopatra require of you is not to bore them" (*Genius*, 21), he posed a standard for literary intercourse that's easy enough to follow—*if you are Harold Bloom*. Can a scrappy New York vaudevillian engage with Judge Holden in a manner that would amuse the Judge himself? Haiku might be absurd enough to turn the trick for him, but would it for you? Probing the novel in haiku is barely a step above probing it in mime and, as with mime, haiku is annoying enough without it Zenning up a monument in Western literature. I envisioned a jetlagged McCarthy enthusiast on pilgrimage from, say, Barcelona, calling his wife and being asked how it's going at the conference. "Well, Maria—I just heard a guy giving a talk in haiku." "So then," Maria says, "I was right— we should've taken the boys to Disney World." As my self-assigned strike was not general, only against prose, I proposed an exhibition: new works on paper called *The Lost Blood Meridian Notebook*. For its title alone, how could the home of the McCarthy archive refuse me? I don't know how, but it did. I was stranded in haiku.

The haiku restriction might work better if I confined myself to the dust-cover, a notion that had tempted me ever since I first adventured into McCarthy: to meditate the novels through their dustjackets—not as an opening into McCarthy's picture plane or his framing devices. . . his use of black as a metaphysical color of depth and variety. . . his landscapes that are always dispatches from the interior—in other words, portraiture. . . or other paths of legitimate inquiry for readers who have legitimate minds—including the issue of whether McCarthy's delicious lexiphantism asks you as much to *hear* his sentences as to picture their anecdotal content—in other words, whether he isn't as much a musician as a painter—no, I would see what was there in the jackets themselves. In discussing what is between the covers of a book, can't we carve out at least a little time for the covers? They are the first things we see when we sit down to read, the last that we see when we stop. *Clothes make the man*, Mark Twain famously said, but we forget, or never hear, the punchline: *Naked people have very little influence on society.* A stroll through any mass-market bookstore will show you how intensely, almost hysterically, this is now applied to the world of the book. Graphic novelists have been enlisted to illustrate and, really, to author covers and bookflaps for every kind of classic, from Tolstoy to Kerouac, and many of these are more than mere monetary charmers—the best of them have captured the spirit of the book as well as, or better than, decades of fine photography, inventive graphics, and pretty Impressionism from the Musée d'Orsay. On the other hand, for my own book *Adventures in Reading Cormac McCarthy*, after supplying my publisher with a range of images from paintings of McCarthy's former home in El Paso to photographs of Suttree's trolley token or kid McCarthy on the steps of his elementary school, I was shocked to see an ugly mushroom of a tree as the prominent feature of the design. It wasn't me, wasn't the book, wasn't anything. A jacket can make and *un*make the man, and a jacket can make and *un*make a book. *Un*make an author, too. If there is one thing I *don't* write and *don't* care about it is nature—certainly not these brown stalks of wood with leaves on them sprouting out of the ground. Tough guys don't dance and my books don't wear trees. Whose book is it now? Mine mostly—but that's not enough. Luckily, that's me and my own chickenscratch. What happens when we turn to *Blood Meridian Or The Evening Redness in the West*?

2. *Or The Evening Redness in the West*

We cannot escape the fact that the name of the novel and the name of the author appear on both the boards of the book and on its dustjacket, so for me the dustjacket is inseparable from the text of *Blood Meridian Or The Evening Redness in the West,* and from the broader—one might say the global—phenomenon and cultural commerce of the novel. . . in the same way that, once it sold one of its souls to cinema, the contracts for options, the preproduction plans for the film, the film itself, its promotions and its reviews are also a part of it, as will be emblemized by a frame from the film on future editions of the novel which, if it is defamed or distorted by that image, must abide it as its progeny the way that it abides the likes of us; or, in the same way that the novel's exact title—so seldom said that my using it here might savor of the pedantic, even the contrary—is only dispensable, subsidiary, invisible, because we have made it that way.

Well, wait—stop for a moment. Why do we make it that way?

Do we think that McCarthy wrote it his way in order for us to ignore it?

Would it change our perception of the novel if we never again severed seven words off its title?

Is it of no significance that this novel, which was written with an authority seldom seen in American letters, has an act of indecision built into its title?

Have we made the mistake of viewing the word *Or* in *Or The Evening Redness in the West* as existing outside the title itself, as if it were added by publishers who couldn't make up their minds what to call it?

Is the habit (not mine) of adding commas and colons to a title that has neither a cry of help from a world of grading one too many papers?

Out of years of misunderstanding Derrida, have you confused deconstructing a title with dismembering it?

Now that I have shifted from a *we* to a *you*, let me ask you another question: By expecting me not to bother you for stealing the complexity out of McCarthy's title, are you warning me not to bother you for stealing the complexity out of McCarthy's book?

In his stimulating *No Place for Home: Spatial Constraint and Character Flight in the Novels of Cormac McCarthy,* my pal Jay Ellis at least remembers and discusses the rest of the title, and does so as early as Chapter 1, in which he calls it a "subtitle" (17), which it is in every respect: beneath the words *Blood Meridian*, beneath whoever can't be bothered to say it. But Jay also labels it a "second" or "secondary" title (188). If there *are* two titles, can I choose the other? And are you inviting me to say: "When did you first discover *The Evening Redness in the West*?" or: "Did you read *The Evening Redness in the West* before you read *All the Pretty Horses*?" Is reading *The Evening Redness in the West* like going to the polls to vote for Spiro Agnew, Dan Quayle, Dick Cheney, or Joe Biden? In Dianne Luce's thoughtful *Reading the World: Cormac McCarthy's Tennessee Period*, Dianne's list of abbreviations gives "BM" for *Blood Meridian*—really, an abbreviation of an abbreviation. My old friend John Sepich's book is not called *Notes on Blood Meridian Or The Evening Redness in the West*. Even John's revised and expanded edition, published under what we could call the moral sponsorship of the McCarthy archive, does *not* expand to include the title. Shane Schimpf's book is not called *A Reader's Guide to Blood Meridian Or The Evening Redness in the West*, and Shane never acknowledges the phantom limb until it is thrown the bone of a sentence on page 58. It is dropped from the front flap of the original dustjacket, and mispunctuated for the Library of Congress in the book's front matter, as it was in the Ecco Press paperback and has been in McCarthy criticism dating back to the issue of the *Southern Quarterly* that became Dianne Luce and Chip Arnold's groundbreaking *Perspectives on Cormac McCarthy*, where none of the three authors who contemplate the novel even squeak out its title in passing. It is mispunctuated in both editions of Rick Wallach and Wade Hall's *Sacred Violence: A Reader's Companion to Cormac McCarthy*, where it is never once said by any author, including me, and only appears in "Works Cited" at the end, as in Barcley Owens' *Cormac McCarthy's Western Novels*, where the book is poked and prodded for seventy-five pages as if McCarthy's title doesn't exist—or as if, because it's at the east end of the title, what is West in the title can be lost to what is West in McCarthy. This woefully neglected baptismal name is nowhere in either the contents or the index of Rick Wallach's *Myth, Legend, Dust*, in which none of the authors critiquing the novel bother to say its name, and in Neil Campbell's otherwise intelligent "Liberty Beyond Its Proper Bounds: Cormac McCarthy's History of the West in *Blood Meridian*," Campbell commits the logical gaff of calling the second half of the title a "qualification of the novel's title" (221), as if its seven dwarfs have decamped from the fiction to which they are attached and exist in some critical ether from which we can summon them if we need them. Rick has revered, discoursed, and broadcast the novel since buying it off a rack in an Australian railway depot in May 1991; he is currently writing a book about Judge Holden; and chatting in my livingroom the other day, he stated as true a half-truth as anything I've heard about the novel: "It doesn't valorize *anything* about us." But even Rick mispunctuates the title in his summary on the website of the Cormac McCarthy Society, where for decades now the title in full is rarely spoken and is excluded from the body of Rick's entry. On the back of Rick's old original Picador paperback, the heading over six quotations from reviewers reads: "*Blood Meridian* by Cormac McCarthy."[2] How do you like that? The title couldn't survive the three-quarter-inch divide of the spine—on which, of course, there is the usual amputee. Harold Bloom has told me that he bows to no one in his admiration for the novel, but a reader of his *Novelists and Novels* would never know its title because it is not given anywhere, not even in the index. Neither the title of the anniversary hearings on the novel, nor any of the talks on its roster, represented the title as written by McCarthy and as printed on, and in, the book. When McCarthy—the man himself, in the flesh, our contemporary—packed his papers for the archive and handwrote thumbnail descriptions of each packet, for *Blood Meridian Or The Evening Redness in the West* McCarthy printed two words: *Blood Meridian*. If you think I am suggesting that you ought to feel bad about cleaving those sad seven words, you are justified in feeling that I ought to be indicting McCarthy as well. I am indicting him. Because McCarthy doesn't mind the redaction doesn't mean that his novel doesn't mind. If you amputate one of your kid's toes, doesn't matter to me if you are the mother or the father. I indict me too: in the book that I, as a woodpecker, apparently wrote about trees in McCarthy, the truncated title is all over the place, as it is in this book. To argue that to say or to write *Blood Meridian* is simply a convenience, Peter (and can we move on?), begs the question, which is this: What has become of us that, in referring to a 337-page masterpiece of 116,900 words around which some of us have built our own work, words to which we return again and again to be seduced into its brawls and tournaments of sweet brutality with renewed admiration, wonder, delight—and, at times, with endoscopic penetration—we are all too lazy to say its actual name because nine words are too many for us?

3. The Other McCarthy

To contemplate a title's entitlements is more than to contemplate a cover, it is to contemplate an author. Is McCarthy saying of his novel *You can call it this or you can call it that*? Is he saying that *The Evening Redness in the West* is just another way of saying *Blood Meridian*? Is he signaling that his book won't make up your mind about anything—that it will be polysemous even as it announces itself? Had he reread *Twelfth Night, Or What You Will*; *Frankenstein; Or, The Modern Prometheus*; *Pierre; Or, The Ambiguities*; *Moby-Dick; Or, The White Whale*, and decided it would be fun to have an *Or* of his own? As with Stanley Kubrick's *Dr. Strangelove, Or: How I Learned to Stop Worrying and Love the Bomb*, does the chutzpah with which McCarthy encumbers the title of his tale reflect the chutzpah with which he tells it? Of Joyce's first book of poems Anthony Burgess said: "We can take *Chamber Music* in good heart when we have taken its title" (87), and I would say the same for McCarthy's first Western, for the chamber of Joyce's title was a kind of privy, and the music (Joyce was a urolagniac) was a woman relieving herself—in other words, when a genius first opens the window and calls out the name of his book, he is still composing it even as he advertises.

My own reading copy of *Blood Meridian Or The Evening Redness in the West* is a first edition with a terribly toned reproduction of Salvador Dali's *The Phantom Wagon* on the recto of the jacket. On the verso is the author, his hairline receding but looking healthy, youthful, slouched comfortably in a chair in front of small collection of books stacked against a woodpaneled wall. My dealer in Heidelberg, Winfried Heid, is a cool guy who tends to inform me *after* an exhibition has closed—"Yah, I give you exhibition Baden-Baden, very nice"—and who surfaces in New York now and then and, over a cappuccino, passes me an envelope for the sale of a painting he can no longer describe and I can no longer recall. Winfried is a specialist in Dali who has curated many exhibitions of his work, so I asked him where the original *La Charette Fantôme*, a 1933 oil on wood, might be found, for I was more or less bound, now, to sniff around it for clues about the evening redness we love to contemplate but dare not speak its name. The imperfect English of Winfried's response seemed perfectly apposite to a Dali motif.

"Dali's intention, almost," Winfried wrote to me, "introduction: pictures of concrete irrational are not with a rational mechanism explainable. For my opinion this painting is a symbol for his 'fall in love' with Gala, which started at this time. Dalí shows us how the love coming together (as a fragile part—see the old and rattly cart). He paint as an old master, but he show things *behind* the figures."

When the novel appeared, the Dali was in the mansion of the Edward James Foundation at West Dean College not far from Chichester. Since then it has moved to a private collection in Geneva, where I have yet to be invited. This is no great loss. It's an okay cover—Dali's wagon on its way to a big city is a bit cartoonish and a bit too much of a longshot for me—but covers can be worse—at least it's not a tree—and the luminescent lipstick font against a dark red ground is effective. As for what sort of image would invite the reader in while forcefully suggesting the feast of beautiful nightmares to which we are invited, that is not a challenge that I, as a visual artist, would undertake without trepidation. For Paulo Faria's first *Meridiano* his publisher in Lisbon chose a horse. They do ride horses, but this was not a Comanche horse, a Toadvine horse, a *tragic mount* of any kind; it was a horse—the head of a horse—from another novel—the next one. Pondering my first edition, I was captivated more by the portrait of McCarthy, taken by Mark Morrow, than the lame reproduction of a Dali that was not among his best. This makes sense. In *A Plea for Eros*, Siri Hustvedt says: "In every book the writer's body is missing" (102), and it would be nice if that were true, but it is characteristic of authors who are in my personal pantheon of able torturers, such as William Trevor, Joyce Carol Oates, Don DeLillo, Annie Proulx, Philip Roth, A. S. Byatt, Thomas Pynchon, that I never see a world when I try to read their work, I see a man or a woman in a chair, writing with a degree of fraudulence—I call it literary jerking off—that makes me hate even the word *literature* and hope that I am in another profession. When I read McCarthy at his best I do see a world, I don't see a man in a chair, so it's an interesting project for me to find him in one.

And I did, in fact, write about Mark Morrow's photograph in two pages of haiku. . . until it occurred to me to find out something about the photographer. Who *is* this Mark Morrow? How was *he* elected to point a lens at McCarthy when he was at the height of his powers, burning the darkest light in American literature? How did Mark Morrow come to be the other name, along with Cormac McCarthy, to be featured on the cover of this verbal sublimity? For all I knew he was a guy next door to whom McCarthy handed a camera:

"Mind taking a shot?" If he was a photographer, had he freelanced his way to the twisted keyboard that had hammered Harrogate and Lester Ballard into existence, or was he working for Random House when it was taking over half the world? Did he use a flash, or was the metered light off McCarthy brilliant enough to flare the lens and close down his aperture? Beyond his activity with the camera, was there more that he gleaned of his subject during the time that he was writing a masterpiece? What was it like to shake the hand that was forging the liquid iron of his prose? Did they toss down a few in a Knoxville snug? Did they, bachelors both without herselves to hinder them, sample some of the sluts on Magnolia Avenue, or a hundred-a-nighter working under Hazel Davidson out of Knoxville's Meadows Condominiums? Might this Morrow have sacrificed a morrow of his own after his subject devoured him in a South Central privy? Did McCarthy mention his Western? Had he needed to lift chapters, maps, notebooks, sketches, obscure depositions and shards of Anasazi off a chair for Mark to sit—or was there not a second chair? Is there, in a cardboard box or a metal file cabinet, an Ilford or Kodacolor envelope of proofsheets filled with more Morrow versions of McCarthy? Are there clues in them as to what Harold Bloom called "the mystery of why this astonishment was possible for him only that once" (Josyph, *Adventures*, 89), or as to how it was possible at all, and if there are no clues, what might the fact that there aren't tell us about the elusive, often invisible nature of genius? Adorning the best book, the First Folio, is an engraving by Martin Droeshout the Younger in which a cartoon head above a whaleboned supportasse and collar is too big for the body in the laced-up doublet, so that Shakespeare resembles more a Mayberry barber than the author of our humanity. No clues there, and yet the cover has not hurt the author's reputation, despite that it does not say much for Martin Droeshout other than to have kept his name alive for four centuries. Still, if the discovery of a hitherto undisclosed portrait of Shakespeare when he was writing, say, *Measure for Measure, Othello,* or *King Lear* on Silver Street in London's Cripplegate would constitute a seismic event, why should we wait another four hundred years before the *Antiques Roadshow* excavates and celebrates a lost Cormac McCarthy?

I looked up this Mark Morrow and I ordered his book *Images of the Southern Writer*, a five-year project that features Mark's portraits of Walker Percy, Eudora Welty, William Styron, Tennessee Williams, Robert Penn Warren, Shelby Foote, James Dickey, Erskine Caldwell—and Cormac McCarthy. The

portrait of McCarthy is not the one taken in the Colony Motel at 5102 Kingston Pike in the Bearden district of West Knoxville, and that was used by Random House for the jacket of the novel. It is an equally interesting—perhaps more compelling—portrait of McCarthy from around the same time, late spring of 1981. I wrote to Mark, proposing a conversation about the shoot, or shoots, and I wrote a version of the following passages for that book with the tree on the cover.

> In *Images of the Southern Writer*, McCarthy is pictured behind the ticket window of the old Southern Railway Terminal in Knoxville. "This is the window where you get a ticket with the destination left blank," McCarthy told Morrow (52), and of course *Blood Meridian Or The Evening Redness in the West* is, itself, a ticket with the destination left blank. It's an arresting photograph. When I taped a cropped copy of this picture to the original dustjacket—an act that would send any rare books collector into fits of apoplexy—the effect was so disorienting that I became nauseated, a reaction that I have whenever the universe appears unnaturally tampered with. McCarthy, smiling at the window, his striped shirt open to three buttons down, looks as if he has climbed out, or climbed up, to gaze at us for a moment before descending again into the depth of his narrative. What's disturbing is that he is more looking at me than I am looking at him. . . looking at me trying to pierce the darkness behind him. . . bemused by the sight of a joker like me prehending this impossible object, this seanachie séance he has chosen to call *Blood Meridian Or The Evening Redness in the West*. It makes me want to say: "Don't look at me like that—*I* haven't used the word *gnostic* even once!"
>
> Of course to Mark Morrow this would have to be falderal: McCarthy is looking at the young man with a camera. Yes, but that was then, this is now. Today, the black behind McCarthy is no longer a room in an abandoned train station, it is the interior, or a passage to the interior, of something inscrutable, something that is, to this day, known only to the author. Susan Sontag identified art photography as "an enterprise of notation" (126), a good way of viewing either of Morrow's images: for me they are both—to borrow that titular phrase from John Sepich—notes on *Blood Meridian*. If it is true that Judge Holden is a devil, or *the* Devil, or that there is, at least, a devil *in* the Judge, no need to look any farther than this image: there he

is, a big-eared handsome devil with a Warren Beatty mouth but a devil nonetheless.

Perhaps many devils. According to railroad historians in Knoxville, McCarthy's ticket window is really a taxi window under the stair to the second floor, a window that you passed before exiting into the parking lot beneath Depot Street. Wesley Morgan, indispensable aid to me in all things McCarthy, has sent me photographs. It is closed, all its glass is gone, but there it is, and it is not where you bought your tickets, it's the booth from which the taxi caller signaled your ride and organized the loading of your luggage from the baggage room.[3] The ticket counter was up on the second floor. Ticket indeed. Imagine—fiction from a novelist.

Was McCarthy misremembering?

Was he playing pretend and didn't care what the window was for?

Was he banking on a Nikon not knowing the difference?

Was he accurate in that a taxi in Knoxville would have no choice but to take you to a blank destination, especially now that he had channeled it into a novel with such capacious ferocity that a man could no longer get there by going there?

Here's what he was doing: he was setting up a shot, orchestrating a career. No one else was doing it for him. The publishing industry, the critical establishment, the mainstream readership could as easily have killed him as build him a reputation. Self-promotion, one of the least attractive phrases in English, is also one of the least understood. We have abused it for so long that we no longer see that it denotes the most difficult and necessary skill for any artist to master honorably. Around Concord, Henry David Thoreau—a fellow New Englander born less than 75 miles from McCarthy—planted arrowheads that he could "find" when walking with a visitor. The butterfly perched on Walt Whitman's finger in the famous photograph—Whitman's favorite, taken in 1877 by W. Curtis Taylor (of Phillips & Taylor, Philadelphia)—a butterfly Whitman liked to say that he had tamed, was in fact an Easter novelty made of cardboard on whose wings were printed lines from a Christian hymn written by John Mason Neale. However allegedly uninvolved McCarthy was in the sales of his books, it is silly to think that he wasn't engaged in shaping his image. We should also remember that a master of picturing world upon world for his readership is, of course, all the time, picturing himself.

In 1971 a magazine—I believe *Esquire*—published a set of remarkable photographs of leading filmmakers, giving each one a credit line for the image, not as its photographer but as its director. Federico Fellini, in a shot taken by Carlo Bavagnoli, posed with Styracosaurus, and it made such sub-liminal—you might say autographical—sense that I never again pictured the Maestro on a set without Styracosaurus as a persuasive a.d. All of us who are in, or expect to be in, the public eye can be directors too—even when we know not what we do. Now, when I picture McCarthy, I often think of Frank Lloyd Wright because Wright's *Autobiography* sits directly behind McCarthy's head in Mark Morrow's portrait in the Colony Motel. Filed as "McCarthy has read Wright," it is a mildly interesting, potentially efferves-cent memorandum for the critical enterprise, but for me it is a moment, an image, complete in itself: McCarthy in the farthest back unit of a Knoxville motel, surrounded by the Appalachian Mountains, plunged into a bit of the old ultraviolence O my brothers in the old Southwest with Frank Lloyd Wright at his back—reminding me of something that Wright wrote to a cli-ent: *All of the details are mine*, in Wright's case about houses but not a bad rule for a writer to remember when dealing with editors, agents, art direc-tors, perhaps even photographers. In Richard Pearce's *The Gardener's Son*, McCarthy, under an alias, appears in the silent part of a tophatted investor being toured through the Gregg cotton mill in Graniteville by its manager, James Gregg, played by Kevin Conway. McCarthy is only a few frames of extra work—when I worked as an extra, I thought of myself as breathable furniture—but I have always liked the notion of McCarthy as an investor, for it is not only the mill in which he is invested, it's the success of his own enterprise and its reputation. In preparation for making the film, McCarthy drove the South with Richard Pearce, collecting observations, exchanging ideas, and members of the cast and crew recalled to me fondly McCarthy's positive presence on the set, much the way the director of *The Road*, John Hillcoat, appreciated the long conversations about the novel and the film in which McCarthy participated, as well as the fax that McCarthy typed up and sent to him suggesting quite specific alterations to the final cut of the film.

In the matter of one's image, as in the matter of one's images, a writer cannot *not* be involved. At one time or another all writers are busy tam-ing their cardboard butterflies. Even Salinger and Pynchon are tied to images that are indelible, and confining their visages to a few photographs intensifies the few beyond measure. My favorite biography of Poe is not a biography at all, it is Michael Deas's remarkable *Portraits and Daguerreotypes of Edgar Allan Poe* (which, as with Mark Morrow's book, is sadly out of print, overdue for a new edition). As Sontag said: "To live is to be photographed," and, as she shrewdly added: "to live is also to pose" (134). When Anaïs Nin said: "Nothing exists until it is on paper" (Fitch 4), she was speaking about her diary and other inventions, but photography is paper too. If you take a photographer to a railway station at which you are, for the moment, gainfully employed in striking a pose and telling a tale, that's publicity—and it's being a novelist.

4. Mark Morrow

None of this was haiku, but it was an insert into a finished manuscript, not a new work, so I had kept to my resolve. Given that, for me, dialogue is *not* prose—not exactly—I was hoping that Mark Morrow was alive and that he would speak to me. Fortunately Mark, no longer a photographer but an editor for hire, had plenty to say about McCarthy.

"We became friends," Mark told me. "I visited him twice in Knoxville and once or twice in El Paso. We corresponded regularly for several years, and he gave me advice about writing and handling girlfriends, and mused about the success of *Blood Meridian*." When Mark was in Santa Fe recently he tried to reach McCarthy but nothing came of it. "Knowing Cormac, I suspect that he's left our relationship behind—without malice, of course, but as part of the natural ebb and flow of friendships and relationships."

Opposite the depot picture of McCarthy in *Images of the Southern Writer* there is a brief text from which I have quoted McCarthy's remark about the ticket window.

"Someone else was to write the essays for the book," Mark told me. "I took the pictures and made only a few notes. When I was finished with the photographs, the writer had not written a word, so I dropped him, I called the authors after the fact, propped the picture up on my desk, and I weaved the interview and other facts and comments into the picture and environs. Then I sent it to the author, who edited my essay for accuracy or additions.

So you *could* say that Cormac McCarthy was my editor, as were Robert Penn Warren and Tennessee Williams. I don't recall McCarthy having many changes."

In spite of the fact that Mark's account of going to shoot McCarthy was proofed and approved by McCarthy, it misidentifies the Colony Motel on Kingston Pike as the Colonial Motel on Kingston Street, a street that doesn't exist in Knoxville. There was in fact a Colonial on Kingston Pike but McCarthy wasn't there in 1981 because it was torn down in the mid-1960s. More fiction from a novelist? By now, both of these one-story roadside motels have been demolished, but one can find them in archival postcards. In a card of the Colonial calling it "A Home Away from Home," it is clearly the less depressing of the two, the sort of foliated, lounge-chaired court in which Faulkner might have stayed when he was working, or drinking, for Hollywood. Despite the motto "Pleasing You Pleases Us," despite AC, TV, pool, and maid service, McCarthy's motel, the Colony, doesn't look like a home of any kind—it looks like a place to be drilled full of holes in *No Country for Old Men*. To those of us begging for the word, a genius in a small room can look like an act of charity, but it *was* home for McCarthy when Mark found him renting it for sixty dollars a week, pleased with its location near the two-story house that was Draper Books, the Capri multiplex with three films a day, affordable restaurants, and

working well on the Western he had started seven years previous, years in which we tend to imagine him writing *Suttree*.[4]

Why didn't McCarthy make the corrections? If you have written *Suttree* you are Mister Knoxville and you sure as hell know there is no Kingston Street and you don't forget the difference between a Colony and a Colonial. Could McCarthy have left or added the error intentionally, perhaps as a strategy of avoidance—say, the way a woman, in a moment of hesitation while giving out her number, might alter one of the digits?

"Cormac did edit the piece," Mark said, "and maybe he did do that deliberately, or maybe he kept it for fictional purposes."

Mark showed me another shot from the Southern Railway Terminal: McCarthy with a plaque of four lines from Robert Burns in stanza 2 of "Is There for Honest Poverty."

WHAT THO' ON HAMELY FARE WE DINE,
WEAR HOODEN GREY, AND A' THAT,
GIE FOOLES THEIR SILK, AND KNAVES THEIR WINE,
A MAN'S A MAN FOR A' THAT.

The horrible engravure could have been done by one of the drunks in *Suttree*, and these lines—the entire poem—could be taken as an epigraph to *Suttree*. Who exactly in the Southern Railway had them bolted over the fireplace in a waiting room of light pink Tennessee marble for *colored passengers* in segregated Knoxville, where Robert Burns feels like Emma Lazarus on the Statue of Liberty: *Give me your tired, your poor*, of which there were plenty in anybody's version of Knoxville? McCarthy's hands are in pockets of what is *not* hooden grey, his eyes are piercing, and to say that he looks relaxed is an understatement: he looks transcendent. He certainly doesn't appear to be looking at Mark or Mark's Nikon, or to care whether he's dining on homely fare. Every author writing a great book is, of necessity, an exile: wherever you find him, he is not really there. To paraphrase Alex in *A Clockwork Orange*, in this picture McCarthy is *in the land* all right, pregnant with a tangle of profane contingencies without a hint of the hidden reservoir of resentment that has made him a master of the novel as vendetta; and, too, without a trace of the bookhound creating his authority from years of doggedly tenacious research. Here is only the poet, the galliard in whose voice the marginalia, the scraps of rejectamenta, the napkins, the notebooks, are lifted into a score. In this picture, McCarthy is all nascency: his face is becoming what his novel is becoming. When I asked Mark whether McCarthy brought him to the Burns—for he must have known it was there—Mark's memory was that they just happened to stumble upon it, but he also reminded me: "I really don't remember who suggested what." Having photographed Paulo Faria with McCarthy, who recommended a pleasing angle that included two Santa Fe icons—St. Francis Cathedral and a sign for the La Fonda Hotel—I would guess that the choice was McCarthy's. Clearly, *he has an eye.*

The other day I said to Wesley Morgan: "You should steal the McCarthy Burns. Go in there and pry it off. Better you than someone else."

"Someone already took it," Wesley said. "I went hunting all of the plaques. The five others are still there. That particular Burns has. . . disappeared."

5. War Time Souvenir Shop

At exactly this time I was renewing my studies of Bertran de Born, the twelfth-century Provençal troubadour known for his meddling in royal succession and his lyric expressions of love for bloody war. With wonderful lines in my lap like: "I am always fighting and making war and fencing and defending myself and moving about" (49), or: "They shall see how my sword can cut, for on their heads will I make a broth of brains mixed with links of mail" (49), or: "When there is peace on every land, let there be a strip of war left for me. . . . I agree with war, for I neither hold nor believe any other law" (51), or: "Not so much joy in sleep have I/Eating and drinking please me less/Than hearing on all sides the cry/'At them!' and horses riderless/Among the woodlands neighing/And well I like to hear the call/Of 'Help!' and see the wounded fall/Loudly for mercy praying/And see the dead, both great and small/Pierced by sharp spear-heads one and all." (59)—with such lines aplenty, I wanted to situate de Born in relation to Judge Holden—to posit him as a model for the Judge. . . not for McCarthy in composing the Judge, but for the Judge in composing himself. After all, de Born moved Dante to the most amusing conceit in the *Inferno*: de Born turned into a cephalophore who not only carries his own severed head but, like Paul of Tarsus, speaks out of it, a Hell that would have to appeal to the Judge who, even as a corpse, would never quit talking.[5]

The Judge and de Born. . . This was not one of those whisper connections of sequence and character or tone and atmosphere that give you an intellectual smile when they occur. . . such as when, in rereading *A Portrait of the Artist*, Stephen's departure from Cranly circulates—like a faintly perceptible odor or current—around John Grady's farewell to Rawlins. . . or when—to stay with Joyce for a moment—you read, in "A Portrait of the Artist," the story-essay of 1904 that preceded *A Portrait* and *Stephen Hero*, "An impulse had led him forth into the dark season to silent and lonely places where the mists hung streamerwise among the trees; and as he had passed this amid the subduing night, in the secret fall of leaves, the fragrant rain, the mesh of vapours moon-transpierced, he had imagined an admonition of the frailty of all things" (Joyce, "Portrait," 262), and you realize that you are being rowed up the Tennessee River by Cornelius Suttree. . . no, this was more like the theatre exercise in which you render some offstage action that is implied or discussed but never seen in the play, or compose a biography or improvise a scene that gives your character a life before he or she walks under the floods. When, recently, I found a scrap from September 2004 filled with notes from my Ground Zero project, I was puzzled and surprised to find this disembodied sentence: "What does Suttree do when we aren't looking at him?" If we can imagine the Judge as a youngster—and I am not sure that *young Judge Holden* isn't a contradiction in terms—and if we can envision that tall young eitherhanded buck reading the afternoon away under a willow, what book can we place in his hands that would make good sense to his appearance in a rain-soaked oilcloth slicker under a Nacogdoches Bible tent in which—while smoking a cigar, and sheerly for the hellraising of it—he accuses a preacher of fucking a goat in Arkansas? Can we not at least consider de Born's *The Joys of War*? And under his knee, or in his other hand, might not the Judge have had, as second best, those 241 decasyllabic verses in which an international fury of religious maniacs turns the beautiful countryside of Spain into a swirling sewer of blood, guts, and brain—I mean the *Chanson de Roland*, which appears to have been composed during de Born's century? In an excellent introduction to the poem, Harold March says:

> Roland, aided by the relics in the hilt of his sword Durendal, specializes
> in the down-stroke through helmet, skull, body, saddle and horse's back;
> this operation is performed three times by him. . . and once by Oliver. . .

who, though just as brave as Roland, went in for brains more than brawn; besides, his sword had fewer relics than Roland's. Some of the warlike materials are in the epic tradition extending back into classical antiquity, but the surgical details are not: entrails or broken spine protruding (lines 1201, 2247), the bared viscera (line 1278), brains bubbling down over forehead (line 2248). These matters are not for the squeamish, but the poet seems to be enjoying himself, as no doubt did the early hearers of his chanted lines. (xix)

It is that line *the poet appears to be enjoying himself* that puts me in mind of the Judge. Certainly whatever arguments we have about *Blood Meridian Or The Evening Redness in the West*, we would all have to agree that *the poet appears to be enjoying himself*. The poet of *Roland* even has his own savage ex-priest who is not even an ex, he is an archbishop, and with a name that reminds us of Tobin: Turpin, who impales the fierce pagan Abisme like a pig on a spit and tumbles him into a ditch for the love of "Mary's holy son" (58). I said that I don't mean to propose Bertran de Born or anyone else as a possible inspiration to McCarthy, but I can't help thinking about a dream of the poet H.D. when she was in psychotherapy with Freud in Vienna: *she was salting her typewriter*. "So I presume," she wrote, "I would salt my savorless writing with the salt of the earth, Sigmund Freud's least utterance" (148). What a question to apply to McCarthy's Olivetti: if he were salting it, *with whom*?

Ah, but such probes were superficial to my task, concerning which *not* the Judge and war and his formative literature or the savoring of keys but photography was all. Lenses. Flashes. Dodging. Cropping. Memory motels and lost horizons in railway depots. And now listen to this from Mark: forty-five minutes of Mark in conversation with McCarthy in the Colony Motel, a living document with impossible sound that has me leaning into speakers, pressing headphones into my eardrums, at one point sobbing, not for its profundity— it's just a chat—but for this seat in a time machine to where I should never be, that closet in the Colony, the growlery that knew that book before its tranks of Kid were finally cut, before the Judge was settled law, before it had an end and then another. . . knew that book when it was thickening with every drive in the mountains, every sit with a book in Emily Scott's easy chair at Draper's, every spark that flashed off a line in Chamberlain, every foray into fourth and fifth meanings in the microfont thickets of Webster's unabridged, every bolt of hubristic confidence daring him out of the corner and back into the ring with *The Sound and the Fury* or *For Whom the Bell Tolls*, every apparition at his seafoam blue Olivetti Lettera 32. . . a room that is knowing the novel that way now, today, because Mark and McCarthy are still there—we have this parachronic recording to prove it—for nothing that happens is ever not happening. . . and now look at this from Mark—O boy—a contact sheet with twenty shots of McCarthy in his Bearden scriptorium, with more books stacked up on the table behind McCarthy and me going blind as a monk trying to make them out—John McPhee's *Giving Good Weight*, an old John Player Motor Sport Yearbook, Ernst Cassirer's *Substance and Function* and *Einstein's Theory of Relativity*, Banesh Hoffmann's *The Strange Story of the Quantum*, Harold Blumenthal's *Sacco and Vanzetti*, Hans Reichenbach's *The Philosophy of Space & Time*, Carolyn Kolb's *New Orleans*, Gregory Bateson's *Mind and Nature*, Peter Forbath's *The River Congo*, Freeman Dyson's *Disturbing the Universe*, a book on Kant, John Locke's *Essay Concerning Human Understanding* in two volumes, F. Max Muller's translation of the Upanishads, *also* in two volumes, John R. Cooke's *The Border and the Buffalo*, Weston La Barre's *The Human Animal*, George F. Ruxton's *Adventures in Mexico and the Rocky Mountains*, T. E. Lawrence's *Seven Pillars of Wisdom*, the novel *Silence* by Shusako Endo—and, beyond that, views of McCarthy's bed with the Hudson's Bay point blanket on which he toned and tinted the shadowed land and convulsed the eternal discords of the novel, a Sony transistor radio, a cowboy belt, the motel phone, McCarthy's shirts, a bathrobe—good God, McCarthy and I were practically living together![6] No, the beautiful sirventes of a twelfth-century Provençal apologist for war would have to wait. Do you see what happens when—to borrow a phrase from the samurai—you attack the corners? Trust me: attack the corners, there is always something there.

Looking at these proofs, I think of number 29 of Kerouac's slogans for the "Belief and Technique of Modern Prose": "You're a Genius all the time" (Ginsberg, 137). Yes, but few artists show it in their work, even fewer in their appearance, Picasso being the most compelling exception in both cases. What Mark's recording and proofsheet tell me is what McCarthy's first house in El Paso used to tell me before I, as a painter, let the paint see it differently: that when he isn't impressing ink into paper, McCarthy—with exceptions, such as we have seen—impersonates an ordinary American. One sees this in his correspondence, where he is not a master of the epistolary art—he is not

Flaubert, not Henry Miller—so that if McCarthy *is* a genius all the time, he's a genius at hiding it.

Do you want an anecdote to back that up? In Paulo Faria's correspondence with McCarthy, the one time that Paulo could not resist posing a truly interpretive question, he asked McCarthy what happens between the Judge and the Kid in the privy at the end of the novel. McCarthy answered him. It was simple and clear. Two words, handwritten beside Paulo's question: "Don't know."

Speaking of Dante the Florentine reminds me that when he was fine-tuning his tour through the sadistic, subterranean vengeance of Christianity, Dante was living in the Palazzo degli Scaligeri in Verona, whose viceroy, Can Grande della Scala, decorated Dante's walls with murals of the Muses. Glorious. Audly David White, proprietor of the Colony Motel—well, I don't need to finish that sentence. It doesn't matter. I know this room at the Colony: I've spent much of my life in it. This is the room in which there is nothing on the walls because there are no walls. This is the room Henry Thoreau had in mind when he said that we live outdoors and we duck behind a panel. This is the room in which nothing is interesting until it burns to the ground. This is the room from which only your characters don't wish to escape. This is the room in which Picasso hangs an invisible sign: **NEVER GO DOWN TO THE BEACH**. This is the room in which once you have written the first word you would have written them all, although you will be the only one never to know that. This is the room in which you pick up the phone and it's Hemingway telling you that being a writer means finishing things. This is the room in which you formulate your own Occam's razor: The number of obligations must not be multiplied beyond necessity. This is the room in which you have to be willing for everybody who loves you to hate you. This is the room in which you assassinate the man that the world would have you be, then you assassinate the world. This is the room in which you hear who you are and what you are making in the noise of the traffic, the caw of a crow. This is the room in which you do not swat flies, you swat jetliners with a broken tennis racket. This is the room in which you walk the plank backward and catch yourself before you hit the water. This is the room in which, as the pendulum swings from supreme self-confidence to kicking the shit out of your paragraphs, doubt is a luxury you can never afford. This is the room in which the dimensions of Manifest Destiny are measurable in inches: 8½" × 11". This is the room in which life, however close to the bone, can never be better. This is the room to which it is not the nine Muses but their wicked stepsisters who come to copulate, and the prostitute pounded on the bed next door hears in the clack of your typewriter keys not the sound of your book but the sound of *being* booked. This is the room in which you redefine the seven sacraments, condense them into one, and receive it every day. This is the room in which you can only glory in, and glorify, the god of the good sentence.

6. Shooting McCarthy

"I have ten long letters from him," Mark told me about McCarthy, "including one on a letterhead from Hotel Victoria, Chihuahua Chih, Mexico. He's talking about his editor pressuring him to finish the book, *Blood Meridian* I'm fairly sure. He did write about his travels researching the book in his letters. It's been a long time since I thought about those days so long ago. I should have written more down before I was 57. I can't be sure even if my memories are factual—such as driving around El Paso with Cormac in his convertible El Dorado. Did I spend the night? Or two? I will have to take a detective approach to figure this out: scraps of paper, notes from long ago. Keeping a journal would have been a good idea."

When Mark and I lunched in the Skyline Diner on 34th Street in Manhattan, I asked him to sign his book for me, then I asked him to sign his and McCarthy's dustjacket, which he did in the lower-left corner over his name, which appears in very small white print over the red of the jacket that borders his portrait of McCarthy and the Dali on the cover. I also gave him a poster I had painted for a 1998 conference on McCarthy, and I showed him the snapshot I had used as a motif, hoping that the image of McCarthy's old house on El Paso's Coffin Avenue might recall his visits there.

"I remember that he had a shop," Mark said, "and that he was building window frames for his house, by hand, from scratch, using mortise and tenon. I thought that was amazing."

As I want to give you the thrust of my exchanges with Mark, you can thank Mark Morrow for your not having to suffer six pages of haiku about *Blood Meridian Or The Evening Redness in the West*. As for Bertran de Born as an avuncular inspiration to Judge Holden, you should take him up. De Born's a good guy. A little bloodthirsty. But so is McCarthy. So am I. So are you or you wouldn't be reading this.

JOSYPH: *(Referring to* Images of the Southern Writer*)* This is an important book. Most of these writers aren't around anymore. You caught them in time.

MARK MORROW: It's a Book of the Dead.

JOSYPH: But McCarthy's star is still on the rise. How did you get in touch with him?

MORROW: I began this project in 1979 after my fiction teacher at the University of South Carolina, William Price Fox, told me that I was a better photographer than writer. So I determined to do a book on Southern writers. I am not sure whether McCarthy was on my initial list—I believe he was, and likely in the column of "unknown" authors or maybe even "minor" southern voices. This was all before email—thankfully, otherwise I wouldn't have these dozens of letters from authors—but it was also before spellcheck, and my letters had a lot of typos in them. This is why for the first letter or two I misspelled his name either as "Cormick" or as "MacCarthy." The first letter I wrote to him asking if he would let me photograph him for the book—it was so amateurish, I don't know why he wrote me back. I have often thought that one of the reasons he agreed to see me was my obvious inexperience, lack of polish: I was not a threat because I did not know anything.

JOSYPH: He might have found that charming, but he wouldn't necessarily have wanted to be involved with you. He must have seen something.

MORROW: I did treasure my friendship with him based on the fact that for some reason he liked me—and the fact that I had no idea he was such a genius. Of course after reading his books I was impressed, but it was only after all the attention to the trilogy that I recognized fully his position in world literature. I think part of our friendship was that he liked my honesty and near bumpkin-ness, and because I did not have an agenda. *And*, I read his books and I understood them. I was not just a photographer.

JOSYPH: Did you read his novels *after* you knew you were going to see him?

MORROW: Yes, I read all of his books.

JOSYPH: Which would have included *Suttree*.

MORROW: Yes, yes. I found them hard to read. *(Referring to* Blood Meridian Or The Evening Redness in the West*)* I really like that one. Is this a first edition? I can't remember if I had him sign it for me.

I have a letter here from Cormac postmarked May 13, 1981, indicating that he got a letter from me and some pictures. I always included a 5 x 7 of William Styron and Tennessee Williams to show writers that I was legit.

McCarthy's letter to Mark states that he wouldn't object to being in Mark's book, but that arranging the shoot might be difficult, "as my movements are uncertain and unpredictable." McCarthy wonders whether Mark will be traveling up east, as McCarthy must go to New York to meet with his editor. "Other than that," he says, "I will be in & out of Knoxville," and he closes by saying that he might be going to Europe in July.

MORROW: He's always been a very private guy, apparently. He doesn't like to do interviews.

JOSYPH: Well, my understanding is that he's extremely sociable—he just doesn't talk to critics and journalists because he doesn't want to interpret his work for them, and since they're the ones writing about him, he gets this reputation. But if he lived even a portion of what's in *Suttree*, you'd have to say that he was, at least then, strenuously sociable. It's funny that Faulkner wanted the work to speak for itself but there are at least two volumes of interviews with him in which he talks about how he doesn't want to talk about it. That was part of his self-image, part of his act. I get the sense that McCarthy has patterned himself after Faulkner in that respect, only McCarthy has stuck to it.

MORROW: Yes, his reclusive reputation has more to do with his honesty and personal integrity than anything else. He just knows that if you open the door to all, no one benefits: he loses work time and gets off track, and the supplicant-fan-researcher gets a minimally engaged experience. It's a practical decision. He really does like people and values relationships. He's a good guy who just knows what he wants.[7]

I must have taken two trips to Knoxville, but it's confusing because Cormac didn't date his letters and my only clue to the date of a letter is the postmark, and I might have mixed up the envelopes. I wish I'd kept better notes. I do have a taped interview with Cormac that I used to create the essay that's in the book.

JOSYPH: People will be after that tape like the raiders of the lost ark.

MORROW: We mostly talked about other writers and the nature of fame and what success means to other writers.

JOSYPH: In the shots of McCarthy in the Southern Terminal, he is wearing a different shirt than at the Colony Motel: one with a collar, one without.

MORROW: I am fairly certain that I took the depot picture on the second trip, after the first, failed attempt.

JOSYPH: You didn't like this motel picture?

MORROW: No, no I didn't. For one thing, there's a whole discussion in a letter of something which is embarrassing—

JOSYPH: Is it all the white of the shirt?

MORROW: No, he's sitting with his legs open and he's got his crotch right there in the foreground and it's vulgar looking.

JOSYPH: So you cropped it? Or they did?

MORROW: I must have suggested it to the editor.

JOSYPH: But if you didn't like the shot from which this one derived, how did it get to Random House? Did McCarthy submit it?

MORROW: Yes.

JOSYPH: That's interesting.

MORROW: I think he wanted to help me succeed. And he did.

JOSYPH: Do you remember what equipment you brought?

MORROW: Yes, my daughter has the camera now. It was a Nikon F2 with a motor drive. I recorded this entire session—it was about an hour sitting there before we got into his car and drove someplace—so you can hear it, this camera, click-click-click.

JOSYPH: Why did you record the shoot?

MORROW: I thought I might write an article about him, but I decided against it. I did write one about Walker Percy.

JOSYPH: Did you use a flash?

MORROW: I had a Vivitar type of flash and a silver umbrella to bounce the light back onto my subject. I could set up and take down quickly. I didn't have to plug anything in. I used a flash for all of them. (*Referring to the depot shot*) That one too. I like the effect of the black in the background. It focuses on him and everything else kind of fades away.

JOSYPH: It's a great picture. Was this one of the ones you sent to him out of the proofs?

MORROW: Yes, and he was wondering which one to use. I don't know why I did this, but I have all the letters that he sent to me, and I have all the letters that I sent to him, so I have the entire correspondence from introducing myself all the way up to the last letters we sent. In a letter to him I said, about the one in the motel, well, I've shown this to a bunch of girls and they didn't find it too vulgar, but you might get some calls from them—something really stupid like that. But he never said, well, you're an idiot or anything like that. He was fine with me.

JOSYPH: *(Referring to the depot shot)* Exactly the effect in the lighting that you've observed is why this one's almost too strong for the novel. *(Referring to the motel shot)* This is such a different image. This is an author photo. *(Referring to the depot shot)* This is like: "O, man—who *is* this guy?"

MORROW: That's true. I'd never thought about that.

JOSYPH: *(Referring to the motel shot)* So this was a wider shot?

MORROW: Yes, it took in the whole room, including the telephone and everything.

JOSYPH: *(Looking at the wider motel shot)* It certainly doesn't look as if he's there overnight.

MORROW: O no, he was living there. In fact this letter—the postmark is two twelve eighty-one—

JOSYPH: *(Reading the postmark)* Knoxville.

MORROW: Yes. I must've been sending my letters to one of his brothers.

JOSYPH: Did he handwrite to you, or did he type?

MORROW: O, *everything's* handwritten, just like this. There are no typed letters. So he says: *(Reading)* "Opinion seems to be divided as to the relative merits of the different black and whites. My brother, who is a photographer and serious amateur, expresses a preference for the one looking out of the Victorian hatcheck parlor. Actually, the one taken in the motel room when I was looking at the camera isn't bad. Maybe it could be cropped to be long vertically and omit the lamp, telephone, bed. Or, is that not ethical?"

(Laughter)

JOSYPH: So he's thinking consciously about what would make a decent photograph—he's participating.

MORROW: Yes, yes. *(Reading)* "Anyway, pick the one you like."

JOSYPH: This is prior to thinking about the novel, so he means for *your* book?

MORROW: Yes.

In that same letter, McCarthy critiques a first-person story that Mark had sent to him, saying: "I think you'll have to write some more before you're fully turned into the 'I' that writes."

MORROW: Interesting way of putting it.

JOSYPH: *Before you're fully turned into the 'I' that writes.*
MORROW: *(Reading)* "Some writers with a body of work behind them, and some considerable reputation, never have done it. It's a perilous thing."
JOSYPH: *(Reading)* "They can write an essay in good sensible English but as soon as they sit down to write fiction. . . something strange happens to them and they begin to—"
MORROW: *(Reading)* "—speak in tongues. Only literary persons can read their stuff. Children and dogs know immediately that it's bogus."

These comments are comparable to what McCarthy told Morrow in the Colony Motel. "Even people who write well can't write novels," McCarthy said. "They assume another sort of voice and a weird, affected kind of style. They think, 'O now I'm writing a novel,' and something happens. They write really good essays. . . but goddamn, the minute they start writing a novel they go crazy. . . I don't know what happens to them. . . but you know I just can't read the damn stuff." One exception with which McCarthy was impressed and recommended Mark to read is Ron Hansen's first novel, *Desperadoes*. Published by Knopf the same year as *Suttree*, 1979, it is a brilliantly detailed first-person narrative about the Dalton gang that must have been an ally to McCarthy's first Western, for they are both gangster yarns that make you feel the heat in both the blood that is spilled and the blood that spills it, and see some semblance of your sorry self in the victims, even as you root for their killers. . . in other words, they *could* both be viewed as highclass pulp sensationalism as morally concerning as anything in mainstream American entertainment to which they are otherwise superior.

Also in his letter to Mark, McCarthy shares some tasty tidbits out of McCarthy's Book of Love and, along with that, a critical piece of advice about women that would prove instrumental in shaping Mark's future: "Find one who wears sensible shoes."

MORROW: Yes, you see, we were friends, and I was complaining about this idiot woman I was going out with. She was driving me crazy, so he would give me advice on women, and I took his advice and used it when I met my gorgeous, wonderful wife.
JOSYPH: Was she wearing sensible shoes?
MORROW: She was wearing sensible shoes.

JOSYPH: Did you know what he meant by that?

MORROW: Yes. Somebody who was grounded, who had something going on besides being just pretty or—

JOSYPH: Flirtatious?

MORROW: Flirtatious. Something deeper than just the fact that you can't wait to spend another minute with her. So, it was good advice, actually.

JOSYPH: He's writing to you as a buddy. You became friends, really.

MORROW: O yes. I have dozens of letters like this.

JOSYPH: So: you shot for about an hour, you taped him on a cassette, you got into the car and took a drive, *then* you went to the Southern Terminal another day. That's when he said—or later, over the phone, you decided together that he might have said or could have said: "This is the window where you get a ticket with the destination left blank," but that was the taxi caller's window, and in this letter he knows it wasn't where you got your ticket, because he calls it a Victorian hatcheck parlor. While McCarthy was posing for you, or while you were working on the essay together, he was *playing*—he didn't necessarily mean it literally. He was playing with the abandoned train station—this is where, and how, a man or a woman got the hell out of Knoxville. In other words, he was using the Southern Railway Depot as a prop.

7. *Meridiano de Sangue Ou O Crepusculo Vermelho No Oeste*

I've been thinking about the fact that McCarthy gave Mark a chapter in Mark's book, gave Mark the key to finding his wife, and attached Mark's work to one of the great novels of the century—not bad for an hour in a roadside motel. And so I can no longer see one man in that room: Mark's image, for me, is now a double portrait.

One thing that Mark and I have in common is participation in dressing a book by McCarthy. I began this chapter with McCarthy's Portuguese translator, Paulo Faria. I would like to conclude with him. The cover of Paulo's translation of *Suttree*, published by Relógio D'Água in 2009, features a shot of the Tennessee River and the Gay Street Bridge, one of hundreds I had taken on the challenge to find a little of Suttree's Knoxville in what is there today, but with no expectation of appearing on the book—although it did occur to me

that it would be a thrill for that to happen purely by the accident of Paulo's American friend, who is also a visual artist, having a few hundred funk-filled shots of Knoxville. I had no such totally surprising accidents planned for Paulo's second *Meridiano*, but here's what happened.

When a Portuguese literary magazine, *LER* (Read), published a piece about Paulo's visit to Knoxville, it used a few of my Knoxville photographs, including one of the model for J-Bone—James Long—shooting check pool with Paulo at the Fraternal Order of Eagles on Walnut Street opposite the church in which Long and McCarthy had been altar boys together. When Paulo's publisher agreed to let Paulo translate *Meridiano* for the second time—from scratch, without consulting the first attempt—the deal was that Paulo would not be paid for the work and that he would travel to the McCarthy archive at the Wittliff Collections and write a piece for *LER* to generate publicity for the project. Among the pictures I provided for this second article, there was one that Paulo liked for the cover of his translation and that's the one that was used. Trouble is, it was not only my image that was cropped to fit the format— once again it was the title, only here it had happened *on the cover of the book.* There was room for Peter's picture, but *Ou O Crepusculo Vermelho No Oeste* could go screw itself. Now, because of us, all of Portugal has lost *The Evening Redness in the West.*

As for that image, it's a burntout waste of a church such as the Glantons might have passed in their travels across the Southwest. It's a pacific image, but with a flavor of bleakness, abandonment, destruction; it is, at least, a little more germane than a pretty horse. And I am, of course, delighted to have it there. The fact that it was taken just off Centre Street in the Jamaica Plain suburb of Boston does not seem to have hurt the enterprise.

we're *all* in fiction—
even those of us who are
merely the dressers

A Walk with Wesley Morgan

through Suttree's Knoxville

During three days in November 2010, Wesley Morgan was kind enough to let me record the latest of the many excursions on which he has taken me to celebrate the novel that is, for both of us, the best of Cormac McCarthy's masterworks, a book that continues to excite us and to inform our very different lives in very different parts of the world. About *Suttree* we have yet to disagree. In the novel our friendship was planted and has grown. Wherever we wander, to *Suttree* we return like brothers traveling home. As with the followers of Aristotle who were known as Peripatetics because of his habit of strolling as he taught, I am a Peripatetic in the School of *Suttree*, for with my learned master Wesley I am ever in motion through the streets, the alleys, the waterfronts, the railway sidings of Knoxville.

As a professor at the University of Tennessee in Knoxville, Wesley has not formally taught a word of *Suttree*, for officially his field is psychology, but for decades now he has devoted much of his time to tracking down the people and places out of which the novel was built, and this is more than an avocation. His website is called *Searching for Suttree*, and indeed he has searched for him in the streets of the city he and McCarthy have shared, in archival newspaper articles, in courthouse records, in personal snapshots and professional photographs, in obscure graveyards, in school yearbooks, in junkshops, in maps, in stashes of letters for the viewing of which he has sometimes negotiated for years, and in the memories of past and present Knoxvillians. And his detective work has not been confined to *Suttree*. "I went out to Twin Creek Road and the Harris Chapel Baptist Church again today," he wrote to me recently in a message that typified the spirit of his researches, in this case about *The Orchard Keeper*. "Nobody seemed to be around. Things look quite different with the leaves off the trees. It gave me some new ideas and perspectives on where Arthur Ownby's cabin and the Green Fly Inn might have been. I will have to go back to the deeds office and see what I can dig up on a couple of the properties." Four hours later there was this: "I got to thinking about what I have been told of the Green Fly Inn—that it was at Brown Gap. I have assumed that Brown Gap was right where the Orchard Road and Twin Creek Road intersect Martin Mill Pike. But now that I think of it, one could make the argument that the actual gap is maybe a hundred yards farther up the road nearer the top of the hill. There is still a steep drop-off by the side of the road there, as well on the Twin Creek and Orchard Road side. Coming up Twin Creek Road, I could see some stonework beside and above the road and below Martin Mill Pike, suggesting that something might have been there at one time. I will have to see who owned that land."

Wesley's presentations and articles are always interesting and free of academic jargon or critical theory, sticking strictly to the facts as he has discovered them. Whenever I have a *Suttree* question, he answers immediately out of a resource that is truly staggering, and yet he is never proprietary or overly confident and is, in fact, fastidious at correcting his mistakes. The book in which he has gathered his findings is ever on the verge of completion, so that often I have told him that he is like Darwin, who couldn't stop growing and tweaking his *Origin of Species* and might have continued to do so forever if Alfred Russel Wallace, another scientist who was onto something similar,

hadn't provided the impetus for Darwin to let go and to send his book into the world. Taking a psychological tack, the other day I said to him: "If you finish and publish the book, *you will not die*. In fact you will live a long life to write others." Wes wrote back: "Perhaps I have not fully analyzed my hang-up about finishing," but he thought that I *might* be mistaken. "I have material for *The Orchard Keeper* and *Child of God* waiting in the wings that should keep me going for quite some time."

There is no room here for our visit to the site of McCarthy's childhood home along Martin Mill Pike, of which a chimney in the trees is all one can see

after the fire that destroyed it. . . or to the freestone wall that McCarthy constructed for his home on Light Pink Road. . . or to the gate in front of Orchard
Road where—supporting Wesley's claim that the so-called water tower featured in *The Orchard Keeper* is, in fact, a Federal Aviation Administration facility—one can see on the chain a lock with the inscription **FAA**, and where one
can see, along Martin Mill Pike, the steep declivity in the woods where the
Green Fly Inn might have stood before it suffered the catastrophe that high-
lights the novel. . . or to the Presbyterian cemetery—the oldest in Knoxville—
that is memorably evoked at the start of *Suttree*, and in which Wesley told me
about the local bootlegger who left his moonshine whiskey under one of the
ancient stones where, on what Wesley called "the honor system," buyers were
expected to leave their money. . . or to the former S&W Cafeteria—now a
beautifully appointed restaurant and bar called S&W Grand that, although
it has just opened, is soon to close down to nothing again—where men once
left their flat straw hats on a counter, and where you could still weigh yourself
on the scale on which Suttree seems to have gotten his "free weight". . . or
to the Bijou Theatre on South Gay Street above which Suttree roomed in a
building that was owned by the Presbyterian Church when the theatre was a
porno house. . . or to the engravures of lines from Robert Burns that we discussed in the last chapter—"Time comes wi' kind oblivious shade/And daily
darker sets it"—"Be ye not unmindful to entertain strangers"—"If ye hae made
a step aside/Some hap mistake o'erta'en you/Yet still keep up a decent pride/
And ne'er o'er far demean you"—those encouraging Scotch oddments carved
in marble and framed over fireplaces now in private offices in what had been
the Southern Railway Terminal. . . or to Clancy's Service Stamp Co. for a chat
with Walt Clancy, one of the characters in the novel. . . but here is at least a
sampling of what it is like to walk the great old Southern city of Knoxville with
one of its most extraordinary gentlemen and, with every step, to be reading
yourself deeper into the great American poem of *Suttree*.

1. The Reality in Front of You

*(A restaurant on Kingston Pike in West Knoxville near the former location of the
Colony Motel, where McCarthy worked on* Blood Meridian Or The Evening
Redness in the West*)*

JOSYPH: You were in Knoxville when McCarthy was living here. Why didn't you hang out together? Did you blow it?

MORGAN: Yes, I really did blow it. We had a lot of mutual friends and must have crossed paths hundreds of times, but we never caught each other's eye.

JOSYPH: How did you learn that you had this genius writing in your backyard?

MORGAN: In the old apartment I used to live in, a friend who lived upstairs had been an ex-military corpsman, a blood technician at the hospital, a student at the university, an alcoholic—and an aspiring writer and musician. He was perpetually broke. One afternoon he said: "Why don't you come up with me to the mountains? I've got this friend up there living in a cabin I'd like you to meet. We can drink some, party some, and he's a writer—he's awfully good—he hasn't published yet, but he's going to be good." Well, my schedule was pretty full, and I knew that it wasn't my company he wanted—he wanted transportation up to the mountains. I begged off, but he did tell me that the guy's name was Cormac McCarthy. I had never heard of him, but the name stuck with me. A year later my mother had a birthday. She was a heavy reader. A review in the *Knoxville News-Sentinel* said that Cormac McCarthy had published his first novel—it was Wilma Dykeman's review of *The Orchard Keeper*—so I thought: "That'll be a good thing to get her."[1] Miller's Department Store had a bookstore on the Henley Street level, so I ran down and picked up a copy. When I started to wrap it up, I thought: "Well, maybe I'll read it first." I was captured by it.

JOSYPH: Of course that was a first edition. Did it make it to Mom, then back to you again?

MORGAN: I had reservations about giving it to her, but she read fairly widely, so there was a chance that she might like the writing style if not the content. She politely said that she liked it but the language was a little rough for her. Years later I did go back to her bookcases and look for it. It wasn't there.

JOSYPH: Was it the level of the prose or the raunch of the dialogue that put her off?

MORGAN: The dialogue was too raunchy for her taste. My mother was more than a bit proper and prudish.

JOSYPH: In *Suttree*, when he's looking for J-Bone, who's selling shoes in Miller's, McCarthy refers to the "perfumed and airconditioned sanctuary" of Miller's and a "cool opulence available to the most pauperized" (68). Is that the Miller's where you bought *The Orchard Keeper*?

MORGAN: Same business, different location. Rich's moved from Atlanta to

Knoxville and built the store that I bought the book in. They didn't do well, so Miller's bought Rich's and had two major stores within blocks of each other. The "new" Miller's, where I bought the book, is now the University Conference Center. The old Miller's on Gay Street is now offices. It still has signs calling it the Miller's Building.

JOSYPH: Where was McCarthy living at this time? To a New Yorker, *cabin in the mountains* sounds woodsy, bearful—isolated.

MORGAN: That's what it was. It was in a fairly remote area at the time called Waldens Creek, between Townsend and Sevierville or Pigeon Forge. He moved there with his first wife sometime in 1961 or '62. It's a beautiful spot. The creek runs along it, forming a valley. Recently, I went up looking for the cabin because I had heard that it was about five miles from a particular intersection. It was a road through the valley with a couple of cabins along the way. Some of them look like they could have been there when McCarthy was there, but I took some pictures and my source didn't recognize any of them, so McCarthy's place might be gone.

JOSYPH: Is that neck of the woods in the early novels?

MORGAN: That's pretty much where *Child of God* is set.

JOSYPH: So when Lester Ballard is running through the snow with a mattress on his back—

MORGAN: That's right nearby. I believe the book's "Frog Mountain," better known as Bluff Mountain, with the turnaround where Lester gets his women, is not too far from there. Fox's General Store is at the intersection where I was told to measure from. There's an old sawmill site up there where they take Lester after he's been captured. And you can trace his route down that road to the store where Lester tries to sell the watches.

JOSYPH: You feel strongly that the route of *The Road* reaches here.

MORGAN: It's from McCarthy's descriptions that I've been able to have a mental picture of these places and drive the route myself. The first place that touches on his early novels is when the man and the boy go through Knoxville. They cross the Henley Street Bridge. The ragpicker in *Suttree* lives under that bridge. Then they go out to the McCarthy house, the family house on Martin Mill Pike, which is not linked with any of the earlier novels but is certainly linked with McCarthy. Then he goes along the highway to Sevierville, which is pictured in *Child of God* where the floods took place and the sheriff tells some stories. Then they go up to Gatlinburg, which is where Suttree takes his girl

Joyce when they drive through the mountains. *The Road* continues through Newfound Gap, which is where Suttree travels with Joyce while drinking in the back of a taxi. When the man and the boy come down in North Carolina, there's a pretty good chance that they go through Bryson City, which is where Suttree ends up after his transformative sojourn in the mountains.

JOSYPH: Two years ago, when McCarthy's childhood home on Martin Mill Pike went up in smoke, you witnessed the fire and you spoke to me from the ruins. Is that the home that the man and the boy in *The Road* visit?[2]

MORGAN: Yes, it is. I think *The Road* is the only novel in which it appears.

JOSYPH: It never occurred to me to make the connection. You've trained yourself to pin these places down.

MORGAN: That's why I was so interested in the yellow firebrick.

JOSYPH: This is the artifact that found its way onto the seat of your Volvo. In New York we say that things fell off a truck. Here, a brick fell *into* a "truck." I remember encouraging you to curate the remains. What was the significance of the yellow brick?

MORGAN: It's a heavy yellowish facing brick for the outside of the fireplace under the mantelpiece, facing the room. So it's kind of a fancy brick. In *The Road*, McCarthy describes a yellow firebrick—"They walked through the diningroom where the firebrick in the hearth was as yellow as the day it was laid" (26)—but I don't know whether he means the actual high-temperature-hardened brick for inside the fireplace. Those I couldn't get to: they were still cemented in, holding up the chimney.

JOSYPH: Either way, you have a piece of the novel now. This has been one of my themes as a reader of McCarthy: how do you touch a novel beyond the book that's in your hand—how do you walk it, live it, beyond the walls of your study and the armchair experience, enacting or reenacting it as a way of savoring it, absorbing it, understanding it beyond the verbal or the conceptual. Miller has a nice line in *Tropic of Capricorn*: "My understanding of the meaning of a book is that the book itself disappears from sight, that it is chewed alive, digested and incorporated into the system as flesh and blood which in turn creates new spirit and reshapes the world" (221). That's more a Millerean than a Morganesque perspective, but it's essentially the reader on his or her feet, taking the gloves off.

MORGAN: I also have some charred oak flooring I'd like to work into frames for some of my pictures of the fire and the remains.

JOSYPH: To me this is more than a kind of fetishism, or being a fan. From reading McCarthy, you see that he knows what he's talking about. Your researches establish that authority in other ways. To be able to go see it, touch it, load it into your truck, is additional verification—which is what you've been doing for years with McCarthy—showing that he's not making it up out of whole cloth.

MORGAN: Right. One of the things that struck me early on was something I had read in a review of *Suttree*: McCarthy's *colorfully imaginative characters*. I said: "They *weren't* imagined—most of them were people who were running around, identifiable." I wanted to point out the actual things that McCarthy described very, very well—not to take anything away from him—but it's a different kind of art when so much is based on—transformed from—the reality in front of you.

JOSYPH: The fact that, say, James Long—the J-Bone of *Suttree*—was a friend of McCarthy's doesn't make it easier for Long to come alive on McCarthy's page and to achieve the transcendence that makes him literature. But due to the fact that I was able to meet Jim when you brought Paulo Faria to play check pool with him at the Eagles Club, over on Walnut Street, I am even more moved when I find him in the novel, or the character who is based on him, being such a really good pal to Suttree.[3] It's J-Bone's name that Suttree gives to the bail bondsman—until he discovers that Long—

MORGAN:—is in the cell right behind him! And it's Long's mother who takes care of Suttree.

JOSYPH: Beautiful part of the novel, where Suttree allows himself a home for a while. You and I are privileged to be living at the time of the author, the time of the novel, the time of at least some of its characters, who we can meet in a poolroom and take a shot of rum with them—as we did with J-Bone, Big Frig, and Walt Clancy.

MORGAN: Jim smiled and said: "Well, I'll go get my stick."

JOSYPH: He was shooting so fast that it was only by taking 200 pictures that a few were in focus. He was playing beyond photography. "I guess sometimes you fall into a rhythm," he said. "I was always pretty fast. Maybe I'd do better if I wasn't." But he must've been a firstclass hustler.

I've always assumed that as you followed McCarthy after *The Orchard Keeper* there was a sea change with *Suttree*: you began to look for the novel in the city. Or were you scouting locations and characters before that?

MORGAN: One of the things that appealed to me about *The Orchard Keeper* was that I believed I had recognized some places in the novel, and built up a fantasy that I knew the locale. I was wrong. I was *way* off base. But the idea of trying to find the locations in his novels occurred to me early. When I read *Suttree* it knocked me over. I didn't have to search for those places. I was immediately aware of an awful lot, but I hadn't yet made a quest out of it. That came much later. It links up with my professional research in the history of psychology.

I was researching the Thematic Apperception Test, a personality test developed at Harvard by Henry Murray and his colleague Christiana Morgan in the 1930s.[4] You show someone a picture and you learn about his or her personality by the stories that are told about the picture. Murray was a psychiatrist whose major interest in life was Herman Melville. Reading *Moby-Dick* was a turning point for him. He believed that you could read some of Melville's works and determine a lot about Melville the man, and his goal was to write a psychobiography of Melville. The closest he came was an introduction to *Pierre; Or, The Ambiguities.*[5] It struck me that nothing was known about McCarthy, and I thought: "Why don't I select a novel of McCarthy's and see what I can learn about him?" One thing you discover about Murray's test is that the more imaginative the story, perhaps the more revealing it might be. So I thought it might be helpful if I looked at *Suttree* and identified those things that were a reflection of reality, and what I couldn't find would be imaginative and *perhaps* more revealing. I haven't carried that through, but that's what got me started in finding out how much of the novel is based on real people, places, events.

JOSYPH: You found more and more details that you could put your hands on.

MORGAN: Sometimes I think I can see Knoxville through 1950s eyes. Other times I'm lost. They've changed the streets around, torn down buildings, built new highways, developments—it's just so different. Where Suttree buries his son still remains a mystery. What might he have used to develop his description of it? Why might McCarthy have broken from his pattern, which was to have a place that was clearly identifiable? As far as I can tell, this McAmon Cemetery didn't exist anywhere. In one manuscript it was originally McCammon. Maybe that scene was more meaningful to him. He describes it as being in "mid Americas" (152). To me that's on the other side of the Mississippi. But why is he so vague about a location?

JOSYPH: It's a fascinating point, that everything else is made more real by setting it somewhere, and this is perhaps made *less* real to McCarthy by his not setting it *any*where. I've always felt that there's a father-son scene near the end of *The Gardener's Son* that is not in the film because McCarthy, who can write *anything*, avoided it, because being *able* to write everything doesn't mean that you can *bear* to write everything. But there's a lot of father-and-son-ness throughout *Suttree*. Where does Suttree go to jail and meet Harrogate?

MORGAN: That's on the other side of town. It was a workhouse. They have a new one now. The old building's still there.

JOSYPH: Early in the novel there's a foreboding of Harrogate blowing himself up using underground caves for criminal intent. Do they exist?

MORGAN: Yes, I've seen them. Knoxville's built on all kinds of caves and caverns. There's a popular one on the other side of the river, Cherokee Cave. It was under a couple of forts on the bluffs above the city. I brought Paulo out there and took his picture inside the cave.

JOSYPH: Harrogate's cave was meant to lead him to a bank. Is that possible?

MORGAN: Yes, there were caves under downtown too. The cave-in on the street that gives Harrogate the idea—that really happened, I've got newspaper pictures of that. The Cumberland Hotel was on Cumberland and Gay, across from the Bijou Theatre. The story is that when the hotel burned, bottles of whiskey from the bar broke and flowed down into the basement, through the caves beneath the town, and out through a spring near First Creek, so that people drank whiskey out of the spring. You can believe that or not.

JOSYPH: One of the themes of *Suttree* is that life has an underworld to which you connect at your own risk, but if you don't, that's also a risk. Suttree connects with it in every way possible. He really *wants* to put himself through it, even if he has to beat himself up—and here he's in a city that is built on all of these underground connections, so that even the psychological stream running through the novel connects to a physical reality.

MORGAN: Yes. Even the scene of Harrogate in the watermelon patch. I got contacted once by a writer about *Suttree*. He said that he knew where that story about Harrogate screwing watermelons came from. One of his old fishing buddies used to tell the story in bars around Knoxville. So I called this guy up. It was a challenge to know how to phrase my questions. I don't know how I had the chutzpah to ask him if it were a true story. Years of clinical practice, I guess. I said: "I've been told that you used to tell some stories in the bars around Knoxville." Yes, he liked to tell stories. I said: "There's one particular story about watermelons." "Yeah." "Can you tell me about that?" He said: "Wait a minute—let me see if my wife is around. Okay, she's in the other room." I said: "The story I had heard is about screwing watermelons." He said: "Yeah, it wasn't easy to get a piece in those days. I was raised out in the country. It was a long way between houses. We had to put our imaginations to work. Necessity is the mother of invention. It's just what I did." I said: "O—it was actually *you*?" He said: "O yeah. You know, it wasn't any easy kind of thing to do. You didn't want to get caught doin' that, so you didn't want to go out there in the middle of the day, screwin' watermelons. But if you go too late at night, the watermelons are cold." I said to myself: "*There's* somebody who knows what he's talking about." I'm pretty confident that McCarthy heard it either firsthand or secondhand from this guy.

JOSYPH: Talk about a writer not wasting anything!

MORGAN: One of the stories I've heard about McCarthy is that he constantly took notes.

JOSYPH: He *must* have. Every writer has to. But where the hell are his notebooks?

MORGAN: I was hoping to see some of them in the Wittliff Collections when I went to San Marcos. They're not there.

JOSYPH: If you read the early Whitman notebooks, you can find the exact page on which he begins to become Whitman: the first few lines of what we call "Song of Myself." Prior to that, that Whitman doesn't exist. In manuscripts for *Cities of the Plain*—the original screenplay, before the Border Trilogy— you can find the exact page on which the Wolf Trapper section of *The Crossing* begins. It's a shift in how McCarthy has Billy answer the question whether he's seen a live wolf: first it's a no, then an addendum is made in which Billy says yes, and clearly that's the origin of the story. Imagine having the notebooks for early *Suttree*.

2. The Wesley Track

(Next day, walking to Pete's luncheonette on Union Avenue, where Morgan often encounters McCarthy's brother Dennis)

JOSYPH: Here's my proposal about the cemetery. After he buries his son, Suttree is picked up by the local sheriff, driven to the bus station, and given five dollars to get out of town. Suttree gets off at Stanton, Tennessee, with three dollars left. Go westward, northward, southward from Stanton as far as you could for two dollars in 1951. How you find an old pricing chart—

MORGAN: Yes, that'll be a challenge. And that's assuming that Cormac did it, and didn't make it all up.

(Entering Pete's, Wesley is greeted by one of the waitresses)

TISHA: Is it Friday?

MORGAN: Not yet.

TISHA: Are you sure?

MORGAN: I hope not.

(At Morgan's table, second from back)

JOSYPH: Two dollars worth of distance on a bus. What do you think?

MORGAN: He bought whiskey out of the five too, didn't he?

JOSYPH: No, he bought whiskey out of the three. He travels on the two as far as Stanton.

TISHA: *(To Morgan)* What brings you out during the week?

JOSYPH: What brings him out is that I've dragged him out. The poor man is sick. His wife is sick. I'll be the death of him. If you don't see him again, it's because I wore him out. *(To Morgan, reading from* Suttree*)* "He left the bus in Stanton Tennessee with three dollars still in his pocket" (158). I'm now on the Wesley track: I *don't* think he made it up. Could be some small cemetery where the name wouldn't show, but if you find *the town*. . . and if you do, I'll drive there with you. We'll be the only two people to visit the cemetery who don't have someone buried in it. Here's the line that you mentioned yesterday: *(From* Suttree*)* "Peaceful and sunny in the mid Americas on an autumn day" (152).

TISHA: You all ready? I don't mean to bother you.

MORGAN: I'd like some sausage. A biscuit. And a bowl of grits.

JOSYPH: I'll have two scrambled eggs and two pancakes.

(Food arrives quickly)

JOSYPH: That was fast.

TISHA: We're quick around here.

JOSYPH: What'm I looking for?

TISHA: Butter and syrup—here you go.

JOSYPH: Boy, when J-Bone tries to get Sut to call home when he can't bear to tell him that Sut's son has died—what a scene. And that detail that tells you so much about the sheriff when he explains what a lowlife Suttree is: the sheriff starts the squad car that's already started. You *know* how agitated he is by the turn of a key and the grind of the engine. Interesting how critics are often more comfortable the farther they are from the facts of McCarthy's fiction. They love trying on philosophical systems. That's fine, but you've no idea how contented I am to read *Suttree* as *a book about a guy*—a guy who a guy like me has a lot in common with in what he's trying to do with the time that he's alive.

MORGAN: Yes, yes, I feel the same way.

JOSYPH: That's more than enough for me.

MORGAN: I think so too.

JOSYPH: I remember talking to Chip Arnold about figuring the date of *Outer Dark* based on a prohibition against hunting hawks. I can't recall whether we got an answer. Might have been early part of the last century—'20s, '30s, '40s.

MORGAN: I thought I dated it too: early 1800s.

(*Josyph is stunned into silence*)

MORGAN: Early 1800s.

JOSYPH: *Honestly?* (*Morgan nods*) Holy *cow! Really?* (*Morgan nods*) *1800?* That's *scandalous.* You should write that up and get that out there. That's really *agitating.* Wow!

MORGAN: I've been saving that. But now I'll have to look at the hawks, too.

3. It's Not Gnosticism

(*In a now-vacant area along State Street near Jackson Avenue*)

MORGAN: This is what I think was Marble Alley. It's where I picture Ab Jones being beat up by the police, and Suttree stealing the police car before he drives it over the Gay Street Bridge and ditches it in the river. It didn't look like this. There were buildings along here, and this was one of the alleys. It continued on to Summit Hill.

JOSYPH: It's an especially brutal beating for Jones *and* the reader.

MORGAN: There's an interesting thing in the archive about that scene, which is a little more detailed in one of the drafts that I read, and Suttree is more explicit in his feelings. When he's in the police car, he's talking on the two-way radio and the guy says: "Who is this?" Suttree says something like: "This is God. I want you to leave my niggers alone down there." That's the most explicitly antiracist thing that I've seen in the novel. But he cut it out.

JOSYPH: Interesting how many things he wanted to leave *im*plicit. He wrote to Paulo: "I think it's always better to assume some glimmer of intelligence in the reader." That's an understatement. He had a very strong sense of working against the obvious.

MORGAN: Yes. We're now on Jackson. Down here at the corner is Sullivan's Saloon.

JOSYPH: With all the painted ladies painted into the upstairs windows.

MORGAN: Right. Next to that is Annie's restaurant, where McCarthy's ex-wife Annie DeLisle used to be. She was a real pioneer down here in revitalizing the Old City. I didn't know that she had been married to Cormac. Frank Gardner, who used to run the saloon, has been down here a long time. My wife rented a booth for selling old things in the Jackson Avenue Antique Mall that Frank also owned. It was behind the saloon.

JOSYPH: That place had a great old barber's chair I would love to have owned—would've been perfect to write in. I fantasized shipping it to New York and settling in—for me, it would have been like buying a house. I remember talking to a barber here in town. He said that he knew Suttree personally.

MORGAN: Frank said he used to party a lot with the McCarthys. I've been meaning to talk to him about it. He used to buy up first editions, then ask Cormac to sign them for him. I guess it was okay for one or two, but Frank was making a business out of it and I think Cormac finally refused to do it anymore.

There's the Southern Station—you can see the old train cars. There is a club that rehabilitates and maintains the cars. I remember coming through Knoxville, riding the train to Atlanta and back to Washington, D.C., when I was a kid. We'd get on in Atlanta in the early evening and arrive in New York City sometime in the afternoon.

JOSYPH: That jagged steplike appearance of the station—is that some modern piece of hotass architecture?

MORGAN: No, that's the original architecture. It was Frank Pierce Milburn, the famous Southern Railroad architect, who designed it. Opened in 1903. Passenger service ended in 1970. It had a clocktower but I think it fell through and they had to remove it.

JOSYPH: So much for the famous architect.

MORGAN: Evidently he needed an engineer.

(*On Locust Street*)

MORGAN: This is the new Miller's Building.

JOSYPH: Where you bought *The Orchard Keeper*? Those were the days when you could buy books in department stores.

MORGAN: You could buy anything. And they're air-conditioned, as Suttree found out. And smelled good. I guess they still smell good.

(*On Main and Walnut*)

MORGAN: Here's the post office Suttree walks through. Those four big federal eagles were carved by Albert Milani in the early 1930s. Pink Tennessee marble, which is really limestone. You're right about the Burns inscriptions in the Southern Depot: pretty bad workmanship, but you look at this and you see that they *did* have some skill in this area. In front here is the lawn where the goat man keeps his goats in *Suttree*. They've planted some hedges. There used to be just grass. The courthouse is down to the left. This side was the city jail way back when.

(Walking toward the north bank of the Tennessee)

JOSYPH: I'm always aware of how steep the drop is on the last block to the river. I can't recall whether McCarthy mentions that in *Suttree*.

MORGAN: He mentions steps, I think, and cutting through some backyards.

(At the river)

JOSYPH: After the brief prologue, *Suttree* begins with an animated description of the worlds that are under and around these great old bridges over the Tennessee. You get the feeling that Suttree is always rowing under them. And the sense is that it's more than just bridges up there: it's civilization.

MORGAN: Yes. We're on the northern bank of the Tennessee between the Gay Street Bridge just east of here, and the Henley Street Bridge a little west. Suttree's houseboat would have been beneath us on the water around where Calhoun's restaurant is now. He set his fishing lines just below the Southern Railroad Bridge down west of the Henley. The ragman lived under the south end of the Henley, up in the embankment just under the deck. I've been in there—I climbed down and took a picture from his point of view, looking in this direction.

JOSYPH: So when Suttree visits the ragman early in the novel, he's rowing across to the south side of the river and climbing up the embankment under the deck?

MORGAN: Right. He brings the ragman a fish and has to avoid those awful charred taters the ragman will offer him.

JOSYPH: Would there have been industrial traffic?

MORGAN: Barges. There was a sand and gravel company nearby that had a lot of traffic. Today we have two ships docked here: the *Nina* and the *Pinta*.

JOSYPH: Columbus discovering Knoxville.

MORGAN: Somehow the *Santa Maria* didn't make it.

JOSYPH: What would have been here in 1951 that we're not seeing now?

MORGAN: Right across the river, where the gas company is now, was Rose's lumber mill. Farther down was a slaughterhouse. Baptist Hospital was here by the mid-'50s, but that was the one single building—all the rest have been added. On this side, the parkway was not here. This entire northern bank has been redeveloped. All that construction over on the south side is for the building of condos.

JOSYPH: Was it ever a residential waterfront?

MORGAN: O yes, there were people living here. There were houses up on the hill that had seen their better days by the '60s. Poor whites in shacks up on stilts. Some houseboats.

JOSYPH: So Suttree's houseboat wouldn't have been the only one?

MORGAN: No, there was a community of squatters.

JOSYPH: Suttree is often looking for someone but he's not thrilled to be sought out himself, least of all by family or people from town. And yet he's in a fairly conspicuous dwelling: he's right down below, on the water.

MORGAN: Yes, but I think these houseboats were invisible to most Knoxvillians.

JOSYPH: You're saying this was fairly off-limits, out of the way?

MORGAN: Correct. You'd go to one of the bridges, not down to around the houseboats. There were a couple of businesses down here, warehouses and such.

JOSYPH: There were a few deaths along the waterfronts and even a burial.

MORGAN: Leonard's father, you mean? Yes, that was right out here.

JOSYPH: And there's the jumper suicide at the start of the story.

MORGAN: The Gay Street Bridge is probably the most common for suicide. Some people jump off the Henley Street Bridge, but it's much more common off the Gay for some reason. Typically, people used to jump off the west side of the Gay Street Bridge, just like they jump off the east side of the Golden Gate. The tongue-in-cheek surmise is that, out of habit, one walks out on the bridge on the right side of the highway because that is where most people live, and when they go out to jump off they don't cross the road to the other side because they don't want to get hit by a car.

JOSYPH: What's this I've heard about the naming of a park?

MORGAN: There's some planned development on the south side of the river, there was going to be a riverfront park, and they were looking for a name. Somebody below my radar did a survey of potential names, usurping the power of the naming committee on the city council. The name that was

overwhelmingly chosen was Suttree Landing, so they made that survey public and, I think, partly froze the naming committee, because I think the committee likes to gain some political advantage in naming a place. Also, the economy tanked and the development was put on hold. I've tried to contact the naming committee, because I wanted to attend, but I've never gotten a response.

JOSYPH: So right now there's nothing to name—but it's kind of neat that there is, at least, a movement to honor Suttree.[6] There's a beautiful long quotation from *Suttree* embedded in Market Square, but how many Knoxvillians have read the novel itself?

MORGAN: It's more common now that McCarthy's name is more easily recognized, but I would think it's still pretty unusual.

JOSYPH: Do you meet Knoxvillians who feel about *Suttree* the way some Dubliners felt about *Ulysses*—that it's a putdown, a disgrace, dishonors the morality of the city?

MORGAN: I heard that early on it didn't get an especially warm reception because it pictured Knoxville in not the best light. Knoxville had a long history of trying to recover from the reputation of being an ugly city—which I think it didn't deserve. So, yes, of those in town who were familiar with it, there were a lot who didn't take to it in a terribly positive way—much the way you say that Joyce was received in Dublin. But I honestly don't think that there are many people who have read it—still.

Years ago I went to the Catholic High School library, looking for some old high school newspapers.[7] While the librarian was digging around, I went to the card catalogue to see what they had of McCarthy. I was wondering about *Suttree*, for in it McCarthy has some things to say about Sut's education in that school. The only thing they had was *All the Pretty Horses*. I was tempted to buy some other novels and donate them just to see whether they would keep them there.

JOSYPH: In 1993, during the first McCarthy Conference in Louisville, I drove here and went to the university bookstore. They had McCarthy, but it was Mary. Here's the town where it's set! What does it take to get that book its proper recognition? I would rate *Suttree* among the top five novels of its century, and I refuse to understand, sanction, pardon, forgive any claim or resentment against it—anything but the highest praise.

MORGAN: (*Laughing*) Yes!

Harrogate lived under the north side of the Hill Avenue Viaduct that spans the First Creek just east of us. We can walk over there. We'll go to Stinky Point first. That was a big fill going into the river where people dumped a lot of trash, and it was below the First Creek, which was also quite polluted and evidently had a well-deserved reputation as smelling quite bad.

(*Walking along Southern Railroad tracks*)

JOSYPH: When you were a student here, were there any old-fashioned whorehouses? Richard Selzer told me that in Troy, New York, there was a street, Sixth Avenue, on which the prostitutes were working. That was *their* street. Did you have that here?

MORGAN: I've been told that a couple of the old hotels downtown operated as whorehouses, and I remember reading in the papers of periodic raids—generally right before sheriff's elections—where the sheriff or the police would go out and pick up some people, and Magnolia Avenue was a common place for that, so I suppose there was a fair amount of activity there. And there were a couple of well-known madams in town, Hazel Davidson being one of them.

This is about where Stinky Point would be.

JOSYPH: What's that noise?

MORGAN: The gasworks across the river. Sound travels really well here in the valley. Suttree remarks about hearing the lumber mill across the river. I'm sure he could hear very well the whine of the band saws and such. We have an excursion boat that's based here now, and of course in *Suttree* there is the *River Queen* that Leonard tries to hold up.

JOSYPH: But that's not in the novel.

MORGAN: It's alluded to. I found a deleted episode about it in the archive.[8]

JOSYPH: Would the riverboat have been parked at the time of Leonard's terrorist attack?

MORGAN: No, it was in motion. But I haven't been able to find an excursion boat that was based here in the '50s, so I'm not sure that it isn't an anachronism—but we have one here now. We had boats that would occasionally visit and try to establish a route between here and places downriver, like Chattanooga.

JOSYPH: In Troy, Lucky Luciano used riverboats for prostitution. I think the main whoreboat was *The Paradise*. It was understood that that was where you went to—as Richard Selzer, the quintessential Trojan, put it to me—*get your ashes hauled.*

MORGAN: I hope it wasn't *all* of the boats. I made a trip on one of them when I was a little kid, from Albany down to New York.

JOSYPH: You were born in Albany.

MORGAN: Yes. I don't think my mother would have taken it had she known it was the whorehouse!

We're approaching First Creek. There's been a lot of development down here too. We're going to cross a pedestrian bridge that wasn't here then, and we can look upstream and see the Hill Avenue Viaduct, where Harrogate lived.

It's partially closed now for deck repair. Architecturally, it's much the same as the Henley Street Bridge, which is also due for renovation.

JOSYPH: It's disorienting, because it's not over the Tennessee proper, it's over a creek that runs into it, and so it's at a perpendicular to the Henley Street Bridge.

MORGAN: Right. There was a valley here. Up First Creek there was a lot of slum housing, particularly on the east bank. It now flows underground, but it used to be freeflowing. If we were really adventurous, we could get a canoe and go a mile or so up the creek, take a flashlight and drift down, hoping we didn't get hung up somewhere beneath the city. Sounds like something I'd've tried when I was younger. You can see the pollution in the creek.

This is the spur line of the Southern Railroad that Suttree crosses. It's where that freight train was that you were shooting a while ago. It services businesses farther down the track for maybe ten miles. I believe there used to be a spur that ran all the way down the other side of the river as well. That shed by the water tank houses an old, refurbished steam engine. Sometimes they run it with an excursion train or pull it with one of the diesels.

JOSYPH: (*Photographing the creek*) I can tell that my white balance is off because the polluted water is blue and it's not supposed to be.

Sut fishes the Tennessee and sells fish. Have you ever?

MORGAN: No, I've never fished. There are people who fish along the river. One gets the feeling that Suttree wasn't a great fisherman.

JOSYPH: What's the toxicity level?

MORGAN: I wouldn't knowingly eat anything that came out of it. But it's much cleaner now than in Suttree's day.

JOSYPH: If this is better, better's still disgusting. Well, it's all part of Appalachian history.

MORGAN: Sure is. If we look down the railroad tracks toward the city, toward the bridges, we can see all the way down what would have been the waterfront. Neyland Drive covers up what would have been parts of Front Street. Looking up First Creek, we can see the place where a young girl's body was discovered in one of the city's dumps—and found its way into the novel. (*From* Suttree) "And news in the papers. A young girl's body buried under trash down by First Creek. Sprout Young, the Rattlesnake Daddy, indicted for the murder" (416).[9]

JOSYPH: Down these tracks is it all built up, or would we see some old houses, traces of the old waterfront life?

MORGAN: Not a thing, no. Let's see whether we can walk over the Hill Avenue Viaduct.

(*On the Hill Avenue Viaduct, which spans First Creek*)

JOSYPH: So, McAnally Flats would not have been visible from here?

MORGAN: No, that's three or four miles away.

JOSYPH: Suttree must've been thin: he had some hell of a walk whenever he went there.

MORGAN: Yes, you wouldn't want to walk it more than once a day.

JOSYPH: What kind of existence would Harrogate have had under here? Would he have been protected?

MORGAN: Pretty well. There's a little concrete bunker that's in the bulkhead of the bridge, a rectangular hole that you could climb through, and inside you'd be very well sheltered. And then there's the deck of the bridge to provide shelter from the rain and the snow coming down. Cooling in summer. Not a bad place to hang out.

(Under the viaduct, near Harrogate's hole)

MORGAN: They took the fence down! Ah, great! It's still partially fenced in, but it used to be that to get to Harrogate's hole in the bulkhead you had to crawl underneath the fence, which was a really dicey and dirty thing to do. I guess because of the construction they've taken down a section of it. Of all the people I've taken in here, I don't think I've ever been up to the actual spot, the entrance into the concrete itself, so this is pretty exciting for me. In the past, I've just stuck my lens through the fence. I suspect they will fence this back in eventually. One of the first times I came down here was after a rain. I smiled to see clearly identifiable pigeon tracks. I could see Harrogate waiting for them to light on his electrocution device.

So. . . let's see what we've got. *(Looks into the hole)* Can't see back in there too well. It's a small little cave. Looks like there's some curtains that are hung and some bags and plastic on the floor where somebody's been sleeping. Somebody has been staying down here. My eyes are adapting. Yes, it looks like a couple of makeshift beds. Maybe some blankets. And a lot of trash. I'll bet you can take a flash. Pretty neat spot here. *Slick,* Harrogate calls it when he sees the ragpicker's place under the Henley. With the exception of the plastic bags, this could be a scene right out of the '50s. Harrogate might well have been here. They ought to put up a plaque: **HOME OF GENE HARROGATE: 1951–1954.**

JOSYPH: I thought this outer area is where he resided, just underneath the protection of the deck. That's really an apartment in there. You could theoretically survive in that.

MORGAN: O yes. This is really exciting for me.

JOSYPH: *(Shooting into the aperture)* I never use a flash. Oh wow, you're right. Well here's the $64,000 question: do you want to go in?

MORGAN: I could get in part way, but that won't. . .

JOSYPH: This aperture's caked in filth. If we had brought something, even a Hefty bag, to put down. . .

(Josyph climbs into the access hole)

JOSYPH: For once I'm glad for a flash. I'm getting most of what's in there. What is that hanging from up there?

MORGAN: I thought it looked like a curtain—maybe for privacy if you had to share the space.

JOSYPH: Let's do this. (*Handing Morgan the recorder*) Hang onto this for a second. Can you push me in?

MORGAN: (*Edward R. Murrowing*) So now Peter has gotten up in Harrogate's hole here and is just about to drop off into the inky blackness and is taking some pictures on the inside of the bulkhead.

JOSYPH: There's nobody *in* here, is there?

MORGAN: I hope not.

JOSYPH: (*Calling*) I'm not bothering anyone, am I? (*Stepping farther in*) Jesus. . .

MORGAN: Does it drop off on the other side too?

JOSYPH: There's some cardboard. God knows. It feels like there's a body under there.

MORGAN: Might be.

JOSYPH: It's a terrible sensation. It's very cobwebbed. As soon as you walk in—well, I can't walk in, but—

MORGAN: It's too low?

JOSYPH: Well. . .

MORGAN: You might not be able to get out.

JOSYPH: I'm using the red light of the camera to see by. . . Lot of Hefty bags. . . Beer cans. . . Tremendous amount of cobwebs overhead, suggesting that it hasn't been used recently, because if I went in the rest of the way I'd take them down on my head. It's like Poe in here—"The Cask of Amontillado."

MORGAN: I think you could live in there undetected for quite a while if you weren't seen coming and going. You sure couldn't tell that anybody was in here from the outside. It's shielded really well even today.

(*Josyph goes all the way in*)

MORGAN: Well, you're in.

JOSYPH: Jesus Christ. My God. O good lord. Christ. How did he know about this?

MORGAN: McCarthy? Well, he must have been here. If I were a young kid I probably would have poked around under bridges after school, but. . .

JOSYPH: Yeah, I'm in all right. Boy. It's upsetting. I realize. . . Huh. . . It's upsetting. . . Because Harrogate is fiction, but somebody was living in here for Christ's sake, so. . . it's. . . it's 2010 and. . .

MORGAN: *Still* somebody—

JOSYPH—somebody is *in* here.

(Josyph breaks down, tries to collect himself)

MORGAN: *(Supportive)* Yes. . .

JOSYPH: You see, that's. . . that's what. . . that's what all of these critics, these bullshitters, they just don't understand with their *gnosticism* and their. . .

MORGAN: Yup, yes. . .

JOSYPH:. . . it's just not about. . . Somebody has to *come in here* at the end of the day. I was homeless. . . once. . . and I know what it's like. . . It's not *gnosticism*, I'm telling you. . . they're just out of their minds. . . They have to get out of their houses and see this—this is what it's about, the whole book. . .

MORGAN: Yup. . .

JOSYPH: . . .and he found it, and he understood it, and he *nailed* it. . .

MORGAN: He sure did. . .

JOSYPH: . . .and *that's* where the genius is, not for any of that other. . . (*Collects himself*) Sorry to get so upset. I apologize. I don't know. . . I don't know why an inch or two should make such a difference.

MORGAN: Can you get out? Let me get around so I can catch you.

JOSYPH: I'm going out the wrong way.

MORGAN: Can you turn around?

JOSYPH: Sorry for getting upset.

MORGAN: That's a pretty powerful scene in there.

(*Josyph breaks down again*)

MORGAN: Yeah, it's amazing to think that somebody. . . Really. . .

JOSYPH: But that's how right he was—whenever he wrote that—'60s, '70s—this is 2010, the rich are richer, the poor are poorer, and people are still going inside the First Creek Bridge to really rot in there.

(*Trying to clean up*) Interesting: it doesn't smell too badly. It has a kind of a cool, cavernous smell. There's nothing rancid or foul, even with the bags, which I assume are—what—old clothes? I can't go to lunch with your daughter—

MORGAN: Sure you can—

JOSYPH: —with all this filth all over me. She's going to wonder who's this slob covered in shit. Just tell her I'm a guy you pulled out of the viaduct.

(*Still cleaning up*) Well, it's hopeless. . .

Imagine going in there every night?

MORGAN: Well, this has been an amazing trip already.

(*On Hill Avenue, above Harrogate's place*)

MORGAN: *Suttree* mentions this house, Blount Mansion, the oldest structure in town, late 1700s. Blount was a governor of the state. Another part of the contrast in *Suttree* is that Harrogate's place is just fifty yards away from one of Knoxville's oldest tourist attractions that every upperclass Knoxvillian was proud of. Right underfoot was Harrogate.

JOSYPH: Literally—

MORGAN: —yes, underfoot. It's a museum now.

JOSYPH: I don't want to go in there. . .

Believing in *The Sunset Limited*:

A Talk with Tom Cornford
on Directing McCarthy

Tom Cornford is a talented director and teacher who has worked at Shake-speare's Globe, the Royal Conservatoire of Scotland, the Guthrie in Min-neapolis, and the Fachhochschule in Osnabrück, Germany. His presentation of *The Sunset Limited* in June 2009 at the CAPITAL Centre in Warwickshire, England—a staged reading for which he had only a few hours of rehearsal, with Michael Gould as White and Wale Ojo as Black—impressed me with its vitality, intensity, and clarity of vision. No surprise, then, that Tom himself is vital, intense, clear. With the encouragement of Nick Monk, who organized and hosted the international conference on McCarthy at which the reading was presented, Tom and I decided to have a talk about the play and its theatrical potential. Rather than submerge my reservations about it, I thought it might be interesting to probe them with a director who had recently tackled it and had retained his enthusiasm. As with Ted Tally and Billy Bob Thornton when they spoke with me about adapting *All the Pretty Horses*, Tom did not need to trumpet his admiration for McCarthy as a writer: it was evident in everything he said.

1. Cornford Speaks Directly to McCarthy

JOSYPH: Are you descended from the Cornforths—those dwellers by the ford of the cranes—of Durham? Or are you of the Cornfords of York, or of London? I need to know whether you aren't, by chance, related to the Cornford who famously translated Plato's *Republic*. That would place a weighty pedigree on this dialogue.

CORNFORD: F. M. Cornford's wife, Frances, was descended from Charles Darwin, and she was a poet and close friend of Rupert Brooke. Their son was John Cornford, a communist and poet who fought and died young in the Spanish Civil War. He looked a bit like me, so naturally I was hopeful of a connection, but they are the Cambridge Cornfords and we are the London Cornfords, so I hoped in vain, I think.

JOSYPH: Well now we have to face the tribe of Cormac. . . so take a leap of imagination that I am Cormac McCarthy come to Coventry, knocking at your door, saying: "Tom—help me out, but don't treat me like a Pulitzer—what I *don't* need is a pat on the ass. If the play is fine, leave it. If it's not, tell me what will make it sing."

CORNFORD: The Russian actress Alisa Frejndlikh is reported to have said: "When I play a writer like Dostoyevsky, he holds me in the palm of his hand. When I act the work of some of these new writers, I feel as though I am carrying them on my back" [Cox, 76]. It's a feeling I know well from directing new plays. Often we come across a boggy patch where the dialogue moves awkwardly from one character to the next, or a character's purpose is unclear and we have to find a way of carrying the play to the next bit of firm ground. It wasn't a problem that we had very often with *The Sunset Limited*. There is a clear movement from line to line and the voices come easily off the page. In that sense, the play held the actors securely in its palm. The problem was that they didn't always know what they were *doing* there.

When I direct a play, we need to find a score for each of the roles. That score is determined, indirectly, by the dialogue, but it also *precedes* the dialogue. An example would be White's desire to leave, which is expressed in different forms, as a kind of musical theme, throughout the action. His discomfort in his surroundings will therefore be felt in his unconscious and expressed through his physical behavior before it is formulated in language, just as his subsequent decision to stay is expressed without words.

WHITE. I didnt leap into your arms.
BLACK. You didnt?
WHITE. No. I didnt.
BLACK. Well how did you get there then? (*The professor stands with his head lowered. He looks at the chair and then turns and goes and sits down in it.*) What. Now we aint goin?
WHITE. Do you really think that Jesus is in this room? (8)

This is a clear example of *an event*, a moment when each of the characters changes his intention. Initially, White wants to leave and Black is going to follow, then White decides to stay and asks Black if he thinks Jesus is in the room. For this short segment, I asked White a) to persuade Black to unlock the door, and b) to stop Black from leaving *with* him; and I asked Black a) to dissuade White from leaving, and b) to persuade White to take him along. These intentions become the driving force for each character, and their actions will be modified by the given circumstances.

JOSYPH: Where they are, for example.

CORNFORD: Yes, because White is in an unfamiliar tenement and Black has an unfamiliar guest. Also, the two only met maybe half an hour ago when Black prevented White from throwing himself under a train.

JOSYPH: It's an interesting premise, but it develops a little strangely, no?

CORNFORD: Well that's just it. The beginning of the play is very clear in its structure, and it's lively: both Black and the play soften up their targets with good jokes. It's a conventional opening and everyone feels secure. The play's development is much less conventional. We begin to realize that it is resolutely anticlimactic and not interested in narrative-rhetorical development. It is interested in *the characters'* rhetoric, *not its own*. The action does not form itself either into a story or into an argument. Instead, it plays with variations on its initial antithesis. The motif of White wanting to leave and Black wanting him to stay will be replayed again and again—almost, as I've suggested, like a musical theme. But unlike a classical theme, it won't develop in the sense of *changing into something else*. Instead, it *deepens*. We see a tension between two mutually conflicting conditions, and that tension is continuous but also shifting. The reiterated statement of that tension allows it to accrue resonance and to uncover complexity, but not *to progress*.

JOSYPH: After the performance you were asked about Marsha Norman's *'night, Mother*—a more famous two-hander about a suicide—and how it relates to *The Sunset Limited*.

CORNFORD: It was a good question, because *'night, Mother* does lots of things that we might expect *The Sunset Limited* to do. It explores the psychology of a relationship through a narrative progression toward a climax that is marked by a series of emotional cruxes. *Sunset* deliberately eschews that approach, and with great success. It is more interested in a character's spiritual condition than narratives of his psychology and relationships, and its emotion is indirect, even subliminal. This means that the play will always be flirting with formlessness. The dialogue can move smoothly back and forth, but the actors will still need *to carry* the play without clear changes to follow. Events are like gear changes. If they aren't there, the actors end up in the wrong gear and either the engine's screaming or they step on the gas and there's no power. In rehearsals, they will stop and say: "What am I *doing* here?" Then we have to go back and find the missing gear change.

What the play needs, then, is structural clarity, and its absence is most apparent in the middle. It doesn't need to be overt, but it needs to hold the actors in the palm of its hand.

JOSYPH: What if McCarthy were to say: "I understand what you mean about structural clarity. Now, give me *assignments*, Tom. Without completely rewriting the play, what could I, as a writer, do to help the actors, and you as a director?"

CORNFORD: Whatever you do, your script, if it ends up in my hands, will be turned into a sequence of events and segments of action or beats. If you were to do that to the play yourself, you'd have to ask two questions. First: When exactly does the change from this segment into the next segment happen? It has to be the same moment for both characters or the structure falls apart. Second: What is driving this character during this segment—what is he trying *to change* through what he does? Most writers find this a waste of time because they are so focused on the spoken words, but experience is not scripted in spoken language.

I use a kind of tabular format to score productions, which is derived from the script and then supplements—and at times replaces—the script in rehearsal. In one sense, this is a deliberate wrong move: going *away* from the script in order to return to it with different kinds of knowledge about the characters— knowledge about their pasts, the situation in which they find themselves, their bodily states, their behavioral and gestural languages—knowledge that will allow us to have a more useful attitude to it as a notation of action. If you work on the play in this way, I can foresee at least two outcomes. First, it will sharpen the changes in your characters' behavior. Second—this might prompt a little rewriting—it might encourage you to broaden the range of tactics for each character. Black seems limited in his range of tactical responses. Perhaps that's appropriate if you think of him as having, by the end, lost the battle. I'm not sure about that, though, and I wonder whether he might be allowed more variation and unpredictability. Finally, it would allow us to share a language for speaking about *the whole play* and not only its dialogue.

2. Cornford Speaks Shortly to Kazan

JOSYPH: It's interesting that you conceive a play in musical terms, but in deeper ways than thinking about sound. As an actor I have even scored my scripts—doesn't matter whether it's Pinter, Chekhov, or plays that I have writ-ten—so that for every line I know my intention, the obstacle to that intention, and how I, as a character, resolve to overcome that obstacle. In this, it's helpful to ask: "What would have to happen if I—my character—got *exactly* what I wanted?" So let me ask you: what, really, would have to happen for White to consider that he's gotten what he wants out of what he's been saying? Does he just want to leave? Does he want to disillusion Black? Or does he want to make some kind of social space in which he can simply exist between the past and the future—extenuating the now for its own sake, or out of fear, or indeci-sion? For me as an actor, such an answer *might* become a problem. One of my teachers used to say: "No one is going to pay top prices to sit in a theatre to see a play about *the rent*. Your objectives have to be life and death, and they have to be *hot,* and not just *hot—pistol* hot." Is there any such burning objective for White? Or is the lack of it a fault in the play, a reason for its being less theatrical than it might have been?

CORNFORD: The note that I gave Michael that made the biggest difference to his performance is that White is just as evangelical as Black. White wants his vision of life to convince Black. When they sit back down after White's first attempt to leave, White asks Black: "Do you really think that Jesus is in this room?" (8) This is to get Black to express a fundamental belief so that he, White, can chip away at it and destabilize the worldview that Black has built on it. It's a rhetorical maneuver that is more typical of Black, as in the debate about the Bible that starts with his question: "Have you ever read this book?" (10) But White is the first to use that maneuver. He also expresses a belief of his own: "I believe in the Sunset Limited" (14).

On one level we thought of White's suicide as a kind of baptism, a solution to his spiritual crisis. The problem, of course, is that it will only be a solution if he's right, and therefore he needs to prove it to himself—and to Black. That's the paradoxical position he expresses in his final speech: "Now there is only the hope of nothingness. I cling to that hope" [59]. I think the actor playing White needs to create a character that so desires to find meaning in his life, and whose life has offered him so few opportunities to do that, that he is left *only* with suicide. The first stage in developing such a character is to see that when White is attempting to convince Black, his objective is ultimately turned back on himself.

JOSYPH: Let's revise my question, then, about how the play might have been written differently and ask how Black might better have gone about "saving" White. Am I alone in feeling that the one kind of saving is followed too soon with the other, and that he might have had a more positive prospect if he had simply fed White, drank coffee with him, and hoped to see him again? Is there an urgency behind it for Black that we can see as a counterforce to White's urgency? You've hinted at this in saying that they are equally evangelical. Is Black *so* certain about his faith and its usefulness to White that he can't wait a moment to start converting him—or is he that *un*certain?

CORNFORD: Anyone who presents himself as that secure has got to be compensating for something, and we see, when he's alone, that Black is far from resolved. I think part of Black's trouble is that he needs to be right more than he needs to make White's day better. By giving White something to fight

against, he makes it easier for White to take the very course of action from which Black is trying to dissuade him. If I were Black, I'd liken myself to White implicitly. I'd try to establish solidarity rather than emphasize the contrast. But in that respect, Black's weakness is the play's strength.

JOSYPH: When I told you I didn't believe that White was going to kill himself again—once was probably enough—you said that you don't speculate on what occurs after the stage is dark, so let me ask a related question: Would it be interesting to you if McCarthy were to write a second act?

CORNFORD: I think it's best as it is.

JOSYPH: I used to love writing one-act plays that you couldn't possibly follow with another act—and then write the other impossible act.

CORNFORD: But here the old joke about condensing the action of plays into one short sentence—*Waiting for Godot*: Nothing happens—twice—comes to mind, because basically this play is existential, it's about the characters' spiritual condition. And I'm tempted by an autobiographical reading of that. When McCarthy was interviewed by Oprah Winfrey, he said that his answers to questions about religious belief would depend on what day he was asked, and the play expresses that movement back and forth. There are also coincidences between the play and McCarthy's life. White's father was a government lawyer, as was McCarthy's. Black is from the South, which is where McCarthy grew up. White has read the great works of European culture, as

McCarthy has. Black has no possessions, and McCarthy has lived ascetically. My understanding of the play, therefore, is that it expresses unresolved and even irresolvable tensions.

JOSYPH: Are you saying that it's built into the play that they more or less finish where they started?

CORNFORD: In narrative, characters have to resolve themselves to a course of action, but that would be inconsistent with this play. There's a similar feeling in *No Country for Old Men*, where the narrative is driven by chance, and in *Blood Meridian*, where events arrive like forces of nature. In both books, the characters' actions are usually procedural and reactive. They're driven by the need to manage a situation that already exists. White and Black find themselves in a similar predicament, so a second act would have to either repeat the first act with variations, as in *Godot*, or imply an agency that they don't possess.

JOSYPH: This reminds me of *The Crossing*, a case of repeating the first act in the second *and* the third in that Billy crosses the border and gets in trouble in Mexico, after which he crosses the border and gets in trouble in Mexico, after which he crosses the border and gets in trouble in Mexico.

CORNFORD: *The Sunset Limited* is a bit like the Prelude to *Tristan und Isolde*—if you will allow me a pretentious parallel. I remember in a lecture Daniel Barenboim played that famous chord on the piano, and instead of leaving it hanging, as it is in the score, he resolved it. What had been wonderfully, ineffably significant became just a trite little tune. It was a very good musical joke, and I guess I can't imagine a second act to *Sunset* that wouldn't be a philosophical joke in the same way. But I'm not a writer. What would you do in your second act?

JOSYPH: To say what I'd do would imply a way of writing that is alien to me, for I seldom have the slightest idea of what'll happen next. So let me more or less see it being written as we speak. White knocks at Black's door. Black says: "Who is it?" White says: "It's me." Black says: "Professor?" Silence. Black excitedly opens all of the locks and sees White at the door. "Professor. I . . . never expected. . . I mean. . . I *hoped*, but. . . *Look* at you. Ain't *this* somethin. You're not *a ghost*, are you?" White: "I *might* be. Is that a reason to keep me standing in this stinkhole of a hall?" Black: "Professor, I am so glad to see you, you can *be* a ghost, you can be *the devil*—any damn thing you please—come in, come in." White: *(Entering)* "Jesus—I still don't see how you can live in this dump." And it might well be that White is, in fact, a ghost, with a disturbing tale to tell

Black about life on what Black has thought of as "the other side." Or. . . more temptingly, and more challenging: Lights up on White's apartment. Books, notebooks, CDs, DVDs, coffee cups, magazines, piles of the *New York Times*, desktop computer with papers, folders, an electric cup warmer, coffee table with laptop, posters on the wall suggesting opera, theatre, ballet, the *New Yorker*, a widescreen TV, et cetera. A key turns in the door, White enters with Black, he seats Black on a sofa or a chair at the coffee table. As they resume their conversation, we discover that White has just saved Black from killing himself. White looks directly at Black. He speaks quickly. White: "Now listen. If you think, for one minute, that I'm going to talk you into the fact that life is worth living, or that suicide is somehow morally wrong, you've got the wrong man. What I *can* do is give you a cup of coffee and a croissant. I use a French press, it'll be good, I just have to boil the water. My croissants are from yesterday but so are we. There's jam, butter, eggs—I've never fed a suicide, I don't know what it does to your appetite, you might be starving, might be sick—I'm trying to get us to do something normal—so say yes. Yes? Good. I'll make the coffee. (*Pause*) Is that okay? As a plan? For the next ten minutes?" Black makes a sign of "okay," and Act Two proceeds as an inversion of Act One, as if the events of Act One have never taken place. Then, after you have seen two sides of the same coin so to speak, we have the tastiest of all: Act Three. Just don't ask me what it is: I'd have to write at least one of the Act Twos first.

CORNFORD: Damn! I was thinking I was right until you mentioned the one in White's apartment. The electric cup warmer is great—I'd no idea there *was* such a thing. Is White going to torture Black by keeping him alive? I think that might work.

JOSYPH: Incidentally, I don't know how he is on Wagner, but when I told McCarthy that Paulo Faria—his Portuguese translator—is big on Mozart, McCarthy said to him: "You are? *I'm* a Mozart man."[1]

CORNFORD: I wouldn't have guessed that. Did you ask him what it is about Mozart?

JOSYPH: No, but I gave him a great CD, *The Avatar Sessions*, by my friend Tim Hagans, a jazz genius who likes Black's reference to Coltrane. Cormac—whose son is a jazz musician—called Coltrane a very fine composer. You used a taste of Coltrane for the reading. How did you choose that piece?

CORNFORD: Well, *A Love Supreme* was an obvious choice for those who would recognize it from the brief blast that I played at the end, but I didn't choose it for the suggestion that Black has achieved "closure" or "peace," but because it wrestles with itself and struggles forcefully onward. It's a *supreme* effort of the will. I wanted it to underscore White's exit as much as Black's spiritual struggle. In breaking the bounds of the locked door, White is a kind of Christ figure. But his triumph, if he achieves it, is over life rather than death, and in that sense it resonates powerfully and disturbingly with Black.

JOSYPH: In the Steppenwolf Theatre production of the play that I saw in October 2006, it was in the 59E59 Theaters in Manhattan, where the stage was smaller than Black's apartment—in fact it was barely the size of his kitchen. White was played by Austin Pendleton, a fine actor whose work I have always admired. But it wasn't a great performance. Part of it had to do with the fact that his partner, Freeman Coffey, did not know his lines well enough and was slowing down the exchanges—literally hanging the play up. I also think that the work you'd have done with your actors to sharpen the beats was not evident. But there was something else: neither actor seemed to know what to do with himself physically. It's almost as if the director, Sheldon Patinkin, had thought: "Well, they aren't going anywhere, so there's not that much to do." Blocking the play more organically could have improved it by at least 20 percent.

CORNFORD: The problems of pace in the verbal exchanges, of clarifying events, and of movement and physical actions are all intertwined for me. I looked at pictures of the Steppenwolf production. It looked as though the table were stage center with Black and White on either side of it, slightly turned out toward the audience. That concerned me. I don't like seeing things falling on the centerline. It creates a balanced image that will tend to make the play feel settled, decided. It's hard to give characters a strong reason to move in a balanced space and therefore to maintain visual dynamism. Also, it seemed to imply that the characters were having a dialogue for the audience: expressing themselves outwardly, as if they were on a talk show. Both of these factors will compromise the physical-visual dynamic, which is generated, for me, by two things: intentions and the given circumstances.

There is a kind of thread, as I think Anne Bogart says, between the actors, and that thread needs to be kept taut. The situation that you describe is a slack thread. Often this can be caused by a technical difficulty, such as a poorly learned text, but often it's indicative of an attitude *toward* the text. I tend to counter this with an exercise on verbal impulses: picking up on the precise words, or information, in the other character's speech that prompts your reply, repeating that from your own point of view, then continuing with your own text. For example:

BLACK. What did he die of?
WHITE. [What did he die of?] Who said he was dead?
BLACK. [Dead?] Is he dead?
WHITE. [Is he dead?] Yes. (16)

This emphasizes the continual effort of each character, while speaking and while listening, to move the conversation in a direction that suits him. Gradually the exercise prompts gestures and movements in space so that you have a situation, kind of like boxing, where they each try to work the ring to gain an advantage. After the exchange that I just quoted, there's a stage direction: "They sit" (18). This happens after Black tells White that he can see the light in him and blesses him. What that tells me is that the blessing has to register as a significant event, for it changes the rhythm of the scene. It's one of a series of moments in the play where the tension between the characters is pulled very tight, then allowed to release.

JOSYPH: I see your point, but in this case I think "They sit" means that they continue to sit at the table but without speaking. One could translate "They sit" as "Pause," or "Beat," or "Silence." I use "They sit" that way in my own work. McCarthy uses it a lot when he tells you that a character is sitting the horse.

CORNFORD: Aha. Of course. I hadn't thought of that. Well, in a sense we're on the same page: the stage direction, or rather stage description in your version, marks a rhythmic change rather than functioning as an explicit instruction. I'd say the change can be achieved in any number of ways: sitting down if they've been standing; sitting in silence if they haven't; but it's not the kind of thing I'd explicitly prescribe. The actors did express concern about all that sitting, though, and I know what they meant, as I'm keen to keep altering the picture. But sitting *can* be very active. It's not one posture. There are infinite ways of sitting.

Speaking about ways of sitting: On page 16, White is described as "Looking around the room." This relates to another reason for wanting characters to move: the given circumstances. White is locked in an unfamiliar place and he feels vulnerable. This gives him reason to be taking in his surroundings, responding to simple stimuli: the locks and his memory of Black fastening them; noises from the street; and—we assume—the sounds of passing trains heard through a window. I encouraged both actors to reorient themselves toward, or away from, these stimuli at different times, and of course that has a multiple effect. It suggests physical actions, it opens them up to the audience, it changes the picture, and it helps to anchor their imagination of the scenario so that they can immerse themselves more deeply in it.

JOSYPH: Whenever I've acted or directed a one-man show, which are often on a practically bare stage, it has seemed to me that every slightest move and every seemingly insignificant prop (and, as well, every piece of wardrobe) carries that much more weight.

CORNFORD: Physical actions are always my first concern. I don't separate them from the text: I see speech as physical action. When I talk to the actors about what they're doing, I use the same language to describe their speech *and* their movement. Physical actions aren't any more or less important when there are only two characters and a few objects, but I do have to be more imaginative and thoughtful about how I *plot* the physical action. That's a question of finding variety. Plays with more characters and varied settings can make life easier, but every play has a built-in physical life, sometimes notated in detailed stage directions, sometimes in speech, or in a mixture of the two.

JOSYPH: How tied are you to McCarthy's stage directions?

CORNFORD: You need to have a very good reason to disobey a stage direction, but limiting your consideration of physical action to the action notated by the text (even in, say, Beckett's *Acts Without Words*, which are minutely detailed in their stage directions) is an abdication of responsibility on the director's part.

JOSYPH: That reminds me of a story about a discussion between a director and a scene designer working on Beckett. They couldn't agree on what would constitute a door being, as Beckett described it, imperceptibly ajar. They asked Beckett. He said: "Closed."

You mentioned condensing *Godot* into a sentence. I recall watching Elia Kazan in a director's workshop at the Actors Studio. It was the kind of scene where you wouldn't be surprised to see Norman Mailer across the aisle from you, sitting there with his bag of groceries from Gristedes. Despite this relaxed atmosphere in which no one was expected to say "Holy shit—it's Kazan! It's Norman Mailer!" I was impressed with how rigorous—one could almost say merciless—Kazan was about the director being able to summarize the theme, the through-line, the spine of the play in one compelling sentence. "This is a play about. . ." His view was that if a director couldn't be that clear about the point of it all, and thus to consider every moment as a contribution to that, he wasn't ready to clarify things with his actors. Not every director works this way, and not every playwright would want directors to, but if Kazan were on your case over *The Sunset Limited*, what would you say to satisfy that demand?

CORNFORD: This is a play about two men, in an inhumane environment, trying to make their lives mean something significant.

JOSYPH: Given that I've played McCarthy here, I shouldn't balk at playing Kazan, so I'm going to say that your initial formulation is too weak, abstract—*wishy-washy*—I can't get my teeth into it. "Tommy—you want your actors going on stage reminding themselves that *this is about making their lives mean something significant in an inhumane environment*? I can barely *say* it, let alone *act* it. I need you to send me out into the street in front of the theatre, calling people in to see a play about. . . *what*? 'Best show in town! Get your tickets to the search for significance in an inhumane environment!' No. Give me some meat and potatoes."

CORNFORD: "Search for significance" might be an improbable pitch, but it works for churches—or at least it did this Sunday morning as I drove through Brixton and passed half a dozen minibuses pulled up at the side of the road to collect people for services.

3. Cornford Addresses the Locks on the Door

JOSYPH: After the presentation, you said that you might prefer to cast Black with an actor who has a larger, more imposing physical presence. I understand that that would make Black an outward, visible representation of everything about which White is uncertain in these unusual circumstances, but I refuse to believe that Black represents a danger to White, other than that he wants to save White's life and convert him to Christianity—which is of course a danger of its own. In the New York production, Freeman Coffey was an imposing physical figure but I never once felt that White was afraid of him or that the play would have made more sense if he were—in fact, the opposite.

CORNFORD: The casting of Black is more about going with what he tells us (which I see no reason to disbelieve) about his previous life and his time in prison. When he questions White's method of putting on his coat, White asks if he means it's effeminate. White also asks if he's a prisoner, and Black flips the question off, saying: "You know better n that" (16). White *sees* Black as physically imposing. Not huge or frightening, but stronger and more conventionally masculine. I don't think that's ever the real reason he stays, but it gives him pause for long enough to keep him there at moments when, if they were in a bar, say, or on a park bench, he might just walk away.

JOSYPH: It is too far a stretch for me to believe that a man who has saved my life will not respond to my request that he unlock his door.

CORNFORD: Given that Black responds to White's direct request at the end, the locks function really as a delay mechanism: they force White to want to leave *enough* to be direct and make Black do something he'd prefer not to do. Since White is almost always indirect, the requirement that he be direct to get the door unlocked helps to give him pause at crucial moments.

4. Cornford Addresses His Actors

JOSYPH: During the very short rehearsal that you had with your actors, what troubled them the most?

CORNFORD: The biggest complaint was that they didn't know where it was going. There are long passages that tend to meander if they are not tightly controlled, and everything starts to sag.

JOSYPH: Poor White has practically no physical activities, and the play doesn't encourage you to invent many, either. You can't have a guy cutting carrots for the stew after he's just tried to step in front of a train.

CORNFORD: Right, and actors instinctively *anchor* themselves with actions—the fight, the kiss, whatever—and there aren't many *at all* in this play. They had no trouble with the sections where speech and action go together, such as Black going to get his coat and trying to persuade White to take him along. Or the conversation about the food as they eat. Or working out the sums. Where the speech starts to float *away* from action—like those moments in Chekhov when they all say, "Let's philosophize," and off they go—they started to get frustrated. I had to say, "Look, this must be *really* significant to these men or they wouldn't go on at such length about it," and

I would suggest character-driven reasons for that. Sometimes that means big emotional things—Black clearly feels that he *must* save others to atone for what he has done—but also simple things: perhaps neither of them has had a proper conversation with anyone for days or even weeks.

JOSYPH: Black doesn't even have a Coltrane solo—he's like Johnny, the West Indian trumpet player in *The L-Shaped Room* who, when Leslie Caron gives him a jazz record, apologizing for the fact that there's no phonograph, holds it up to his ear and tells her he can hear it. Nowadays, with CD players costing practically nothing, is that believable?

CORNFORD: Occasionally an actor would complain that such and such *wouldn't happen*, or they would ask: "Why the heck doesn't he do this or that?" I have no patience with those kinds of questions: the characters do what they do *and that's that*. One of the actors balked at the initial situation—he couldn't accept the premise—so I helped to realign his thinking so that he could believe in it. Often that kind of complaint is really just shying away from doing the hard work. It was telling that that complaint came before we really got started and it didn't come up again. Later complaints about verbiage that isn't well anchored to action were much more genuine and serious, and that's where clear and tight direction makes the difference.[2]

5. Cornford Compares *The Stonemason* and *The Godfather II*

JOSYPH: Would you like to direct *The Stonemason*?

CORNFORD: I'd love to, but I'd need a fairly long leash. I'm drawn to it because it takes a documentary-realist story and molds and blurs it to explore its mysteries. Papaw, Big Ben, and Ben almost become a part of each other, not reliably distinct selves. Their stories and natures are twined. I was watching *The Godfather II* last night, which does a similar thing. The significant difference, though, is that Coppola has the confidence to do it with very simple montage. He dissolves from young Vito to middle-aged Michael and back again, and he juxtaposes the revelation of Fredo's betrayal with Batista's resignation and the ensuing disorder. McCarthy's staging, on the other hand, seems clumsy.

JOSYPH: To me it's worse than that, as if he never bothered to *think* about theatre. When I read those stage directions, or look at Ben *at the podium*, I suspect that John Grady Cole has seen more plays than McCarthy.

CORNFORD: I see what he means in his note about placing the events in "a completed past" (5) and allowing the drama "its right autonomy" (6), but his double Ben isn't the best way of achieving that—there is a more elegant solution, although I'd need to try out a few options before I could say what it is. But I think his novelist's eye for actions and images that capture larger stories serves him very well.

JOSYPH: How so—by asking for a real stone wall on the stage?

CORNFORD: I *love* the "wall of actual stone" (9). Next to that, the lectern and the podium and all the other scenic stuff in the stage directions sound like clutter to me. But I think the action in *The Stonemason* is eloquent and economical. Another option is, of course, to film it.

JOSYPH: *The Sunset Limited* is filming as we speak, so it may yet happen.

CORNFORD: Or to make a film about the process of staging it.

JOSYPH: What Pacino did with *Richard III*? It'd be nice to do that with McCarthy participating.

CORNFORD: Yes—let's do it.

JOSYPH: Is there an appreciable similarity between Black and any of the characters in *The Stonemason*?

CORNFORD: Yes, there are a lot of echoes. Black has a good deal of Papaw in him. Ben has learned from him that "true stone masonry is not held together by cement but by gravity. That is to say, by the warp of the world. By the stuff of creation itself" (9–10). If Black were on a building site, he'd be saying that. He'd have been similar to Soldier as a kid. He must have gone through Big Ben's despair. And he has Ben's evangelical urge. Ultimately, he's most like Ben in that Ben feels that he, too, has lived the lives of his family, and he has the demanding, godlike example of his grandfather to live up to.

JOSYPH: In both *The Sunset Limited* and *The Stonemason*, a story is told that is, for me, the best thing in the play. In *The Stonemason* it's Papaw's account of Uncle Selman's murder. I once wrote that this was the true kernel of the play, or of a play that McCarthy didn't write. In *Sunset*, it's Black's story of beating the daylights out of the guy who attacked him in prison. You hear that and you think: "O. . . this guy can really write." For me these bits are especially interesting because they are, in fact, short stories—passages of prose, if you will—set within the context of a play, and yet they both stimulate interesting dialogue—Ben's reaction to Papaw is *very* interesting, and White is most interesting in his reaction to Black's story. It's just that in both cases McCarthy has other fish to fry and he moves on. You probably don't agree with me that if McCarthy had taken each of those stories and trusted in their power to generate a better play than the one he'd had in mind, he might have had a pair of minor masterworks. But I'm wondering whether those two anecdotes leaped out at you as well?

CORNFORD: Yes, they did. The jailhouse story is particularly good because it is introduced at a time when we've had witty repartee and a good set piece— the sums—and it shocks the play into darker and more revealing areas. And yes, McCarthy is clearly more confident in shaping and editing prose than dramatic action. I don't think, though, that using the stories for other plays is the answer. I think the answer is to allow the characters to tell more stories. The stories mustn't be allowed to *detach* themselves from the drama, but, as you say, both of these emerge from the drama and feed back, deeper, into it.

JOSYPH: Have you seen characters in any of McCarthy's novels who resemble Black and White, or are they unique in kind within the McCarthy canon?

CORNFORD: I can't think of a close similarity in *Blood Meridian*, although White has a project not entirely at odds with Judge Holden's. I read the Judge—and here I'm borrowing heavily from shooting the breeze with Nick Monk—as a figure of modernity, as Chigurh is a figure of chance.[3] That desire to categorize and disenchant the world is similar to White's spiritual attitude, but I don't think that's useful to an actor because they go about it in such incompatible ways. From my knowledge of the novels, I can't think of a particularly apt parallel, although both Black and White's relationship to a world that has a palpable but unfathomable presence, and yet is distant and carelessly hostile, is reminiscent of the novels. White jumping in front of the train, and Black praying aloud once White has gone, both remind me of the mules vanishing into the ravine in *Blood Meridian*.[4]

JOSYPH: I have an approach—I'd almost call it a rule—in directing an author's work. It's that I don't believe an author's characters exist in any other author's world. Authors do not write generically: the more one has a sense of Pinter the playwright and the world of Pinter's stage, the closer one can come to freshly interpreting a play or a part without turning Pinter into someone else. Tennessee Williams' characters are in Tennessee Williams' world, Mamet's characters are in *his* world, Beckett's are in Beckett's and so on. Each of those worlds might suggest unlimited potential and variation, but they aren't interchangeable. On Broadway, I saw John Malkovich as Biff in the Dustin Hoffman *Death of A Salesman*. It was a compelling performance, but it wasn't a Miller Biff, it was a Sam Shepard Biff, and it disrupted the unity and overall force of the production. One could argue that since Miller was involved in the casting, my theory is bilgewater—but I would argue that either the choice was a mistake, or that Malkovich was underdirected to partake in Miller's world. I mention this because it seems to me that if an actor were to study, say, *Blood Meridian*, *Suttree*, *Child of God*, *Outer Dark*, he could have a sense of what might constitute a Cormac McCarthy character, at least insofar as he would have a strong sense of McCarthy's world—the world of McCarthy's prose. But if he were then to read *The Stonemason* or *The Sunset Limited*, he would see that those characters would never find their way into any of the novels. The two worlds seem set apart. There might be themes or concerns and even literary approaches that cross over, but McCarthy is *a very different writer* for the stage. Do you find that to be true?

CORNFORD: I absolutely agree about directing *within the author's world*, and thank you for clarifying my uneasy feeling about Malkovich's Biff.

Yes, McCarthy is a different writer for the stage. The dialogue is noticeably fuller in the plays, although parts of *The Stonemason* have something like the novels' economy of speech because there is more scope for action and behavior to do the work. The characters in the plays feel softer, less *hewn*. On the page they don't have the piercing otherworldliness of the novels, although

I think some of that quality should find its way onto the stage. I often find myself frustrated in the theatre that a novelist's care hasn't been taken to imagine, edit, and creatively distort "reality" to fit the world of the play. Often they have only adhered to the conventions which seem to gather like barnacles on playwrights. I try to avoid that by beginning with simple clues in the dialogue. Black's clothes aren't described, but we know that he was on his way to work, so what kind of job does he do? Apparently the people he works with will know he's not coming if he hasn't turned up and won't be too worried, so perhaps it's a casual kind of work. When I first read the play I was midway into *The Wire* on DVD, so I pictured the ex–drug dealer Cutty out of jail and doing yard work before he sets up his boxing gym. Looking like that, Black could conceivably not have met a professor before and could therefore be "studyin the ways of professors" (7), and he could conceivably not know what *primacy* means. He also has to reassure White that "everthing in here is clean" (40), so the apartment must look shabby. After I've gathered this kind of information, I start to think more widely about the kind of world we're in. Here I used the novels as a guide. They have a rich, symbolic texture. Simple things resonate powerfully, like the coin in "A Drowning Incident" that is clutched by the boy while he runs to see the puppies—puppies that he exchanged for the coin—vanish into the water after they have been shot. We can learn from that in designing the plays in the way that we select objects, and in the ways they are handled by actors.

JOSYPH: Can you learn from the novels in creating the mood or the climate of the piece?

CORNFORD: Yes, the novels can be very helpful. While preparing *Sunset*, I thought of the unbearable tension of episodes such as *The Wolf Trapper* in *The Crossing*, the insistence on violence as a natural law, the harsh landscapes, the wind, the rags of plastic wrapping in *Cities of the Plain*, and McCarthy's attraction to other writers who deal with issues of life and death, as Richard B. Woodward reports in "Cormac McCarthy's Venomous Fiction." All of that clarified for me the image of the train coming through a deserted station at 80 mph, it began to reverberate through the characters, and it helped set the stakes for the play. I suspect it sets them much higher than they would be if you hadn't read the novels, and that may be a failing of the play. But the clues for a director are there. "A black ghetto" (5) might be strictly inaccurate and/or out of date, but it communicates the atmosphere. The clues might be clearer if

McCarthy had seen more theatre and had consequently gained a more liberated sense of its possibilities, but they are there.

JOSYPH: What do you make of the fact that throughout the stage directions, in both published editions of the play, McCarthy refers to "the professor" and "the black"? It reminds me of *The Prince and the Pauper* or *The Princess and the Pea. The Professor and the Black.* One wonders that an editor didn't say: "Do yourself a favor: say *Black* instead of *the black*. Referring to *the professor* and *the black* just doesn't cut it these days." When someone writes a treatise on McCarthy and race or racism, and someone certainly will, he or she will be all over that. It will probably be an *unfair* treatise, and slanted assways—in writing about *Suttree*, I have extolled what we might call McCarthy's *integrative* spirit in that novel—but isn't *the professor* and *the black* rather a lapse? It's almost as if it were written for McCarthy's own reference in his initial draft and then never altered to Black and White—something a good editor should have argued for. Did you, or Wale and Michael, notice that particular terminology?

CORNFORD: I did notice it, although I think it wasn't mentioned in rehearsal. Then again, one of the things that Wale and Michael did that was so successful was to accept the types they were given by the script, and then to play *with* them, not *against* them. Michael played "the professor": he was socially awkward and uncertain in his manner, though rigid in intellectual

conviction. Wale played "the black" in that he played up to some aspects of the stereotype: the streetwise patter, the capacity for violence, the capacity for religious intensity and evangelizing. But I think that both of them succeeded in being ambiguous. It was suggestively unclear to what extent they were consciously or unconsciously performing their racial-social types for the "other," and that seemed true, and not just in the naturalistic sense. We didn't go far enough to do what I think Anne Bogart calls *burning through* the stereotype. She talks, for instance, about male and female actors performing stereotypical gender roles with the genders reversed. I couldn't really see a way of doing something like that, apart from trying to finish the play with White occupying the position of faith (in death) and with Black in a position of doubt. But there I was trying to give a sense that faith and doubt are a part of each other and can't be separated. Of course the same is true of race, but I wasn't making that point.

6. Cornford Comes to America

JOSYPH: When you are using an English actor, how American do they need to sound if the part has been written with an ear for local speech that's as good as McCarthy's?

CORNFORD: Very. When I directed David Mamet's *The Shawl* at the Gate in London, I asked an American actor I knew to read for me. It was dumb of me to ask him, because I was never going to get three American actors, so he was always going to make the others sound inauthentic. I cast an English actor instead. An audience's ear will attune itself comfortably to stage American, providing it is reasonably consistent. But it's not so simple. The other thing I noticed about my American friend was that he *looked* American. It was unmistakably in his body before he opened his mouth. It drives me mad when the people in, say, *The Cherry Orchard* or *Blood Wedding* are *so English*. Their behavior just doesn't match the play. I have a similar feeling when we visit my wife's family in the Yorkshire Dales. I'm a Londoner: I do things quickly. People in rural communities have an entirely different pace, and it registers in their accent, their movements, their body rhythms—everything that expresses their relationship with the world. *They fit the landscape.*

Also, it's not simply a case of *how American* my actors have to sound in the sense of their correspondence to "the real thing." That notional "real thing" keeps moving out of reach. White is American, but he grew up in Washington, he's the son of a lawyer, he's a university professor, he's lived in New York for some time—and so on. You can't consciously manipulate that kind of specificity, but you can move toward it by thinking not of *an accent* but of a character's relationship with the world, of which his accent is a part. *No Country for Old Men* is brilliantly cast in this respect. Tommy Lee Jones and Josh Brolin fit the landscape so well, and Javier Bardem is perfectly out of place. So while I might have to accept compromises with the odd vowel sound, the characters have to *belong to the play.* Learning the accent and finding McCarthy's speech rhythms would be part of the actors' process, but the ability to absorb them deeply into the body is what ultimately counts for me.

JOSYPH: Despite a world of reservations about *The Stonemason*, I once offered to direct it in the Kentucky town in which it is set, at the Actors Theatre of Louisville. Would it interest you to direct a full-scale production of either play in the States?

CORNFORD: Yes, I'd love to direct them both anywhere, and doing them in America—such as *The Stonemason* in Kentucky—would be a felicity I'd want to exploit. It would allow me to get to the meat of the piece more quickly. I've taught acting to third-year students from the Guthrie–University of Minnesota's BFA program in London for the last five years. We've talked about my going out there to direct, which I'd love to do—I'm waiting for the invitation—especially with the students I've taught. Teaching a system is great, but they can't really get it into their bones until they've felt it in rehearsal and a run of performances. These students are basically Meisner trained, which I have found to be an enormously helpful foundation, and it's not common in this country. Many English actors are used to being asked to reproduce an effect, and that generates a kind of acting which I find arid, self-conscious and, frankly, distasteful. It often exploits the character to tell us *what the production thinks of them.* And there is certainly more a culture of *practicing* in America. I teach at the Actors Centre in London, which offers marvelous opportunities for actors to develop their craft, but it is scandalously underused by the profession because we've all allowed ourselves to become demoralized by funding cuts and commercial cynicism. My advice to a young actor is to move in with a musician or a dancer and practice as much as they do. Whatever the dangers and excesses of the Method, the Actors Studio is a landmark and that in itself sends out a message. We don't have that.

JOSYPH: I have speculated that it might help me to solve, or prove unsolvable, the problems of *The Stonemason* if I undertook to play the part of Ben, a character who annoys the hell out of me. As a director, one is always, in some sense, playing all the parts, but as a director who also acts, would it interest you to perform as either Black or White? As a heathen and heretic, I'd like to play Black. I'd like to see whether—to paraphrase *The Godfather*—if I used all of my powers and skills, I could convert White to the Good Book so that he, like Billy Bob's character in *The Apostle*, falls to his knees and prays with me at the end. McCarthy, in the audience, would say: "Wait. . . that's not in the script. . . what the hell's happening?"

CORNFORD: That's interesting. Your idea of playing Black to see if you can convert White is actually one of my most common notes: *I want you to go on and make sure that today you get what you want—try to change the ending*. It has the most profound effect on a play if the actors take that idea seriously. So often I go to the theatre and watch a bunch of people auditioning alongside each other for their next job, or trying to convince me that this play is funny or moving or that their character is clever or a victim or sexy or goofy—it's like watching a very long advert, and I think: *Don't give me the advert, I've paid for the play*. Part of that play is the continual tension between *what could happen and what ends up happening*. My religious instincts, like McCarthy's I guess, move back and forth between Black and White, and I frequently find myself at both ends of a spectrum, so I suppose I should play them both.

JOSYPH: Do you believe that Jesus is in this room with us?

CORNFORD: No, but I believe it could be a useful thought.

JOSYPH: For an all-out production of *Sunset*, would you encourage your actors to improvise, take the play in different directions, in order to come back around to the page?

CORNFORD: Yes. I always ask actors to improvise, and continue to do so even at the stage of verbal accuracy and repeating detailed actions. I think of acting like a sport. Rehearsals have to train actors to play instinctively, with shape and intelligence and purpose. Asking an actor to do that without basing the work on improvisation is like asking a boxer to go into the ring having only punched the bag.

7. Cornford Defends the Oomph in *The Sunset Limited*

JOSYPH: You've mentioned boxing, so, let's go a couple of rounds. Every time that I see the play, or reread it, I have this gnawing sense that it's not really a play. It's called "A Novel in Dramatic Form," but it isn't a novel either, not a McCarthy novel.[5] It's a dialogue, but so is Galileo's *Two World Systems*, so is Wilde's *The Critic as Artist*. If *Sunset* were submitted to me as an artistic director, I'd say: "Cut it to shreds and use that as the basis for starting the play again." I'd have said the same about *The Stonemason*. For me, *Sunset* is too much glibness and banter—not enough theatrical *oomph*. There's more *oomph* in one exchange—*any* exchange—in *No Man's Land* than all of *Sunset*. All the more impressive that you managed so much *oomph* in your reading.

CORNFORD: I honestly feel that the *oomph* is there. Yes, Pinter is more availably dramatic—usually—and the introduction of two further characters in *No Man's Land* takes that play beyond its initial premise on a trajectory that *Sunset* declines. But that is partly to do with Pinter's chosen themes and with his experience of the theatre and the theatrical. *Sunset* is, in some ways, a challenge to the theatre because it *eschews theatrics*. But it does that with a purpose. That purpose is in some ways novelistic, in that watching it is more like sitting down to read a boxing match than to watch it. But in its construction it is nothing like a novel; it's more of a dialogue in the philosophical sense. That doesn't disqualify it from being a play, though. As for the glibness and banter, it is the director's job, as it is in, say, *'night Mother* or *The Importance of Being Earnest*, to discover what's *driving* that. I've seen Wilde, tediously, given *the style* treatment (you know, all that *wit*) and, on rare occasions, I've seen that handbag and the name "Earnest" *really matter*. And I can imagine a *'night Mother* that fails to deliver *the heart* in the wit of the play.

Sunset has the feeling of trying to be long enough to justify the ticket price, but it's a meditative piece and therefore we *need* the time to get into its rhythm. I remember seeing a beautiful production of *Death and the Ploughman* by Johannes von Saaz at the Gate in London. Medieval ploughman argues with Death, who has taken his wife, then he comes to terms with it—*the end*. I was rapt. And I've been bored out my mind by plays you would think could not possibly fail. I'm not saying the script isn't important—it's very hard to be better than your script—but still, it's what you do with it that counts.

JOSYPH: If you were to cast me as White and we had a first reading around the table and you asked us to air our opinions, I would say: "As a New Yorker, I find it annoying that McCarthy, Master of Research, didn't bother to get the fundamentals of New York subways. No New Yorker would refer to a subway station or a subway stop as *a train station* or *a train depot*. And despite the fact that commuters ride the subway, they aren't *commuter trains* (49): that term is reserved for trains coming in from the outer boroughs or from Jersey, Long Island, Connecticut. As for White saying 'There wasn't any post' (13), if there weren't any posts, then we weren't in the subway. The fact that White refers to Bellevue Hospital as 'up' (47) suggests that McCarthy didn't even consult a Manhattan map. So I need some help here. I can accept the convention that we both refer to some express roaring through the 155th Street station as the *Sunset Limited*, but I need to know what happened, physically, in the subway. In Manhattan, if you want to kill yourself, you walk to the edge of the platform, wait until you see the lights of the train, and step down onto the tracks—it's only a yard or two drop—and the train will do the work. It's not pole-vaulting, it's not the broad jump—*you just step off the platform*. How did Black save my life? What was this 'amazin leap' (12)? If I were 'haulin ass' (13) and took some mighty leap that sent me 'off the edge of the platform' (14), Black would have to have been down there already if he were going to catch me—and that makes no sense."

CORNFORD: Exactly. The matters of terminology need a rewrite, unless the mistakes are deliberate, in which case I need to know why we are deliberately confusing New Yorkers in the audience but not anyone else. As for the backstory, I got images of trains and stations and laid out things on my desk and tried to work it out—and came to the same conclusion. McCarthy can only have intended that either a) White imagined the leap and was actually caught by Black, who was running behind him down the platform, or b) Black was on the tracks, or c) Black is an angel who appeared from nowhere, or d) the play takes place in a distorted dream-reality, which isn't made sufficiently clear. Or, I suppose, e) Black *is the train*. My solution with the actors was to ask them, apologetically, to say it as if it made sense, but I did also use it as evidence for the surreal atmosphere that I wanted them to capture. That's the only reason I can think of for McCarthy to present the story so unclearly—that he wants it to come across as mysterious, as not quite right. If that's correct, I think it needs to be done with more clarity. Whether or not it's a lapse, it has the feeling of one.[6]

8. Cornford Proves an Upstart Crow

JOSYPH: The reading that you directed took place in the shire of Shakespeare, where you are a man of the theatre in residence. As a teacher, writer, and director, you're working on something called The *Hamlet* Project, which entails excavating and tributing the craftsmanship of earlier directors and their approach to that play. I have referred to McCarthy as a Rhode Island Shakespeare, so let's end by connecting the two. You've worked at Shakespeare's Globe on the South Bank of London, a great venue for Shakespeare. When I tried to imagine *Sunset* there, I couldn't—it seemed as if it were the anti-Globe—until I tossed overboard that little apartment and all the stage directions and the actors started *moving* in a much wider choice of personal spaces. That set me wondering. You require a good reason to ignore an author's stage directions. Let's presuppose that a very good reason is to try something fresh and unique to make the play work in ways that the author hadn't imagined. Can you envision a production of *Sunset* in which McCarthy's stage directions would be thrown out the window and there are no locks because there isn't any door and they aren't stuck at the table because there isn't any table? Could a more abstract—perhaps, you could say, surreal—approach to the play be productive? Or, to go back to what set me off on this, could you find a way of doing it at the Globe?

CORNFORD: Yes. But abstraction takes us *away from action*, and therefore from acting. Surreal is a more achievable goal. We'd end up with a more Beckettian play, but it's an attractive idea. The difficulty with abstraction is that it has to be set *somewhere*. *Waiting for Godot* isn't nowhere; it's near a tree by a road, and there is a clear sense of time, of waiting and hunger and so on. Likewise, Hamm's parents, in *Endgame*, aren't notional beings: they are people who live in dustbins and eat biscuits. All drama must be realistic on some level because it is constructed from concrete actions. I can imagine a very bad *Sunset* at the Globe that would cut references to the original setting and turn the play into a philosophical dialogue. A good one would require a new setting

and, consequently, some rewriting. Characters can be confined in huge spaces as well as small ones. I'm thinking of Cary Grant at the crossroads in *North by Northwest,* and of all those McCarthy deserts. Setting *Sunset* in one would open the actors out and it would use the epic dimension of the Globe as well as giving them something simple and concrete to play. The Coen brothers do this very well in *No Country.* They capture the way the book yokes the bizarre and the mythic into its uninflected view. It's a testament to their craft as film-makers—and to their attentive reading of McCarthy—that they can match McCarthy's prose in doing this without self-consciously striving for effect. The encounters with everyday life—Moss and the guys by the border, Chig-urh and the suburban kids after the car crash—gently underscore the story's surreality without allowing it to settle comfortably into a genre or divorcing it *from* reality. That would be the challenge at the Globe, but in a sense it's always the challenge—I'm back to talking about the world of the author and of the play. What you'd need to do at the Globe is to match McCarthy's world to the building.

"Now Let's Talk about *The Crossing*":

An Exchange with Marty Priola

"Why not pick out a passage of Josyph and have a go at it?"

I was speaking to my friend Marty Priola about *Adventures in Reading Cormac McCarthy*. Marty has written charmingly—and concisely—about McCarthy's work, a rare thing to do, and it was Marty who created what became a home on the Web for the Cormac McCarthy Society.[1] When I prodded my Memphis friend to question my book and to challenge me about it, I added a provocation: "I am slogging through that horrible Priest's Tale in *The Crossing*," recalling that Marty had an equally strong feeling about it. "I have always loved the Priest's Tale in *The Crossing*," he had said, "and I think it dialogues rather well with *The Stonemason*, which, as you know, came out about the same time. There's a good deal in *The Sunset Limited* that speaks to that too."

In the world of criticism—a world in which I, as an artist, have been welcomed as a guest who isn't expected to be versed in the manners of the table—my evaluations, such as those of *The Stonemason* in a piece called "Older Professions," are sometimes atypically frank and unequivocal about certain flaws in McCarthy's artistry.[2] But in the last part of "Older Professions" I took the enjoyable liberty of countering myself, not by challenging the points I had made but by seeking other relations with the play that coexisted, however uneasily, with the beating I had given it. When a smart McCarthy scholar met me in Knoxville (on leave from service in Afghanistan), he made the mistake of having a pleasant conversation with me, after which he apologized for what he was about to do: take me to task in a paper about *The Stonemason*. "I'm looking forward to it," I said. "You're setting a good example." The attack was barely noticeable—more a tip of the hat—but this gentleman-soldier was sorry he hadn't met me before he wrote the talk. The truth is that if he had really known me better, he might have tried to please me by taking a tougher stance.

This afternoon I was browsing the mezzanine of Westsider Books on 80th Street and Broadway, an independent bookshop with a literary cast—a sweet old rummager—a type that is nearing extinction, even in New York. From the little platform mezzanine, one looks down at walls that are stacked to the ceiling with books, stacks that are negotiable only by ladder and a long and potentially treacherous reach, for the wall has the makings of an avalanche. Such a warming bookish view recalls the Manhattan of Bartleby, the London of Dickens, not the Broadway on which, a short walk away, the Apple store is open, and busy, twenty-four hours a day. While I was up there scouting for discoveries and maybe a first of McCarthy, I heard a young man asking whether the owner had seen a film starring Samuel Jackson and Tommy Lee Jones called *The Sunset Limited*, and wasn't it a book, and did they happen to have it? I called down that it was a play by Cormac McCarthy, available from Dramatists Play Service. "Wasn't it great?" the man asked about the film. I agreed that it was well made. I then extracted, from a shelf of antique counterculture, a very old *Partisan Review*, a symposium issue from 1953: "America and the Intellectuals." In it, a very young Norman Mailer—he was thirty and had published his first two novels—begins his contribution to the discussion by saying: "I think I ought to declare straightaway that I am in almost total disagreement with the assumptions of this symposium" (67). This reminded me of my dialogue with Marty, and of my sense that if the world of McCarthy criticism would like to make its way into a wider readership, it could do a lot worse than to include at least a few energetic exchanges between opposing points of view. Neither Mailer's reputation nor that of the *Partisan Review* appears to have been retarded by Mailer's note of dissension.

In the exchanges below, are Marty and I too tame with each other? At least they reflect two divergent perspectives that coexist within their admiration for, and enjoyment of, McCarthy's work, and perhaps we have paved the way for future antagonists to remove the white gloves. This afternoon, in an energetic mood, Marty said: "What are words for, if not to offend people? *All men are created equal* was radical in its day; so was the beginning of John's gospel, and Martin Luther King's 'I Have a Dream' speech, Tom Paine's *Common Sense*, Thoreau's 'Civil Disobedience,' and so I say *let's have a good deal more of offending people*. We get someplace that way. In our present censorious climate, we muddle around in the muck." I am also pleased that Marty, who is trained in the law, placed his trust in my encouragement to not perseverate whether *x* or *y* is perhaps too digressive for the case before the court. If McCarthy can be read impersonally, I hope that it is never done around me. Not that I haven't suffered some very dull, narcissistic recollections of how McCarthy's work has intersected a life, but I would not have invited Marty into this exchange if I were not interested in the Priolan enterprise. In an early letter to Henry Miller, Anaïs Nin tells Miller that "to persist in a theme without swerving is defective" (Miller and Nin, 90). As a caution against underestimating the range or the reach of one's subject, Nin's use of *defective* is delightful, but it also suggests a view of the essay that harks back to Montaigne's sense of his prose as a reflection of the process of thought *as it happens*—in other words, of personal memoir *as improvisation* and as an extension of the forms of dialogue and correspondence.[3] If this experience has deepened Marty's and my friendship, it is partly because we have listened to each other *as we thought*, and it has encouraged my conviction that criticism will not be hurt at all if it shows more directly what happens when you are out walking the world, living a life, with an author in your eyes.

Peter, Old Man,

Yes, I'm deliberately stealing that jovial phrase from Harry Lime, though why I'm not yet sure. For me, Harry Lime is always relevant.

I was looking again at your "How to Flunk the Final Exam on Cormac McCarthy," and I came across the statement that ends your fifth question.[4] You assert that the Dueña Alfonsa's history lesson toward the end of *All the Pretty Horses* is "a mistake" and that it "anticipates the stylistic quagmire of *The Crossing*" (203). Now, I know that your leading questions are not answered in that essay, and that device is part of its charm. But I'm frustrated by your gimmick in this particular case. You write with a kind of anger about McCarthy's historical dalliance there (and about *The Crossing*, which I don't think you've much addressed). Then you go off on some wild Josyphian tangent and leave those two comments lying there rhetorically unsupported, like two unexploded mines waiting for some hapless victim. Again, charming, but as a sort of barrister myself, when I encounter such a baldfaced accusation I want to say, in the posture of a downhome Southern defense attorney, "Your honor, if the prosecutor would like to testify, I'd ask that he come forward and be sworn." I would perhaps agree that the Dueña's speech in *All the Pretty Horses* is a mistake. But calling *The Crossing* a "stylistic quagmire"—frankly, that simply annoys me.
—M

My Dear M:

We are in accord about the ubiquitous relevance of Harry Lime and, more generally, *The Third Man*. They are among the motifs in the first novel I wrote. Nor is it inapt that I should be cast in the posture of Holly Martins, hack author of pulp Westerns who fails to convince a beautiful woman that her lover is slime. In critiquing a part of *All the Pretty Horses* I am, at least, hacking *at* a Western, and whatever I have written about McCarthy would have to be seen as pulp (if not pulpable) in relation to bona fide professional criticism. Although. . . I recently read Kenneth Lincoln's *Cormac McCarthy: American Canticles* and was shocked at how horribly written it is—shamefully bad. One would want to congratulate anybody who makes it into print, especially if he's chosen a serious subject and appears to be working against the scientifying of criticism, but it's a mess like this one—from a professor of contemporary literature at UCLA—that enlivens and encourages me about my own scrawls on McCarthy in relation to what escapes from the academy.

Now let's talk about *The Crossing*. I have always loved *The Wolf Trapper*, have always been sorry that it wasn't issued on its own, as is. When I was in my teens, short books like *Of Mice and Men, The Yearling, A Separate Peace, The Time Machine, The Call of the Wild, The Old Man and the Sea*, were taught in high school. Seems to me *The Wolf Trapper* would fill that need beautifully. Some books are eminently teachable and it's not a word against them. I recall first reading that condensation of its beautiful opening pages in the July '93 *Esquire* as part of its Summer Fiction Special, an issue that featured the model Vendela exposing her airbrushed thighs under a short white nightgown sitting atop a heap of mannequins ("What Every Man Should Know About Models," the cover reads, advertising an article on "the perverse allure and weird mythology of the new mannequin culture" by Philip Weiss). Well—that's the queer mix that comprises the mainstream glossy these days. I never read the stories by Richard Ford, James Salter, Ann Beattie, Peter Matthiessen—I don't need that much fiction in my life (unless I am writing it) and, as Oscar Wilde said, my tastes are simple: I always settle for the best. (I never read "What We Think About When We Think About Models" either. I have been a model and there's not much to think about.) I also recall what a delight it was to read aloud from *The Wolf Trapper* at the first McCarthy conference in Louisville, for which I directed those readings from each of the novels. I doubt that *The Crossing* was even out yet, for I recall having to xerox the pages of *Esquire*. With a scene like the one in which the rancher in the Model A happens upon Billy and the wolf, you would have to be a theatrical deadbeat not to score. With lines like: "What I'd like to do is try and save you the trouble of bein eat" (*Crossing*, 59), or, about the wolf coming up from Mexico: "I dont doubt it. Ever other damn thing does" (60), or, about holding the frightened horse: "I aint sure but what I'd as soon hold the wolf" (61), an actor needn't do much. I am never not moved when, after the old rancher touches the wolf, he steps back, looks at Billy, and says: "Wolf" (60). Even at his level of worldweary cynicism there is inescapable wonder. He and Billy are now equals in age and experience: for the first time ever in these two lives—one short, one long— they are standing beside a wolf they can touch. McCarthy's genius is to set it up so that all the Model A rancher needs to say is "Wolf."

The Wolf Trapper is McCarthy at the top of his form. Even the previous scene between Billy and the rancher *without* the wolf is exquisitely rendered.

In opposition to all of what I call *the rest* of *The Crossing*, I would give you this about the rancher's crazy lighter: "He put the pack away and took from his pocket a brass lighter that looked like something for soldering pipe, burning off paint. He struck it and a bluish ball of flame whooshed up. He lit the cigarette and snapped the lighter shut but it continued to burn anyway" (37). When he says "I had to quit usin the hightest" (39), it's hilarious—and revelatory, an opening into another book, one of many novels within the novel. When the Model A rancher reappears to help Billy with the wolf, he is already a character. Hemingway said that if you know it and you leave it out, it'll show that you know it, but if you *don't* know it and leave it out, it'll show that you don't know it. McCarthy has learned how to know it and leave it out and yet leave it in—a little—at the same time. What he knows about the Model A rancher is in the Model A's lighter, even more than in his dumbass joke about Texans being full of it—full of hot air, full of shit—before he says to Billy: "You aint from Texas are you?" (39)

When I heard the rumor—one that was never verified—that McCarthy submitted *The Wolf Trapper* as a finished piece and that his agent or editor encouraged him to write a longer book, I thought: "If that's true, he shouldn't have listened. He needed a break. *The Wolf Trapper* is all the Billy he ever needed." Before my last keynote, the one that you heard in San Marcos, when I referred to "McCarthy at his best," I had deleted the phrase "from *The Orchard Keeper* to page 127 of *The Crossing*," feeling that my talk would be obnoxious enough, no need to alienate lovers of *The Crossing, No Country, The Sunset Limited* or *The Road*. Whether anybody loves *Cities of the Plain* I cannot imagine, but there must be someone.

On the other hand, I vividly recall walking across campus at Appalachian State, where we had the second or third McCarthy conference, and chatting with Christian Kiefer. When I told Christian what I've just told you he surprised and enlightened me by saying that he preferred *the rest* of *The Crossing* precisely because it did not have the tightness and unity of *The Wolf Trapper*, and because he found it more challenging—intellectually stimulating. That ambulatory talk has been a touchstone reminder that in matters of McCarthy-taste there is no disputing; that what fails for me in every respect—e.g. *the rest*—can be *the best* for someone else. I have no need to be all that down on a book that is an inspiration to others. In San Marcos I reminded Christian of that conversation, and I believe he said that his perspective has changed.[5] If so, it would accord with my belief at the time that Chris found *the rest* more interesting precisely because he was young and perhaps unsophisticated in matters philosophical. This sounds condescending, but I didn't feel it that way—I felt that if you don't see *the rest* as a lot of flapdoodle, you might find it fascinating indeed.

It is also true that, in the same way that I used to keep trying to give *The Stonemason* chances to get good, I have entertained the thought that if I tackle *the rest* of *The Crossing* at exactly the right time, perhaps the flapdoodle will unflap itself. In an interesting monograph about painting called *A Lost Leadership*, John Russell wrote: "In ways that we recognize but cannot always account for, great art keeps something in reserve for each successive generation" (12). I have tried to be my own second generation and see whether I can't discover secrets in McCarthy that weren't available to me twenty years— a generation—ago, so that I can say to an old self, as Whitman said to Horace Traubel: "I seem to be right, you seem to be right: do you regard that as being impossible?" (Whitman, *Camden Conversations*, 126). Some of these experiments are plain and logical—listening to *The Road* as an unabridged audio recording—and they fail miserably. Some of them make no sense even to me, they just happen, and yet they might be successful, such as a recent rereading of *No Country* in sequences starting from the back and working my way forward to the beginning, *excluding all of Bell's monologues.* That, for me, was the best *No Country* to date. Just don't tell the author—or anyone else. If these are the most egregious of my earthly sacrileges, I should still be safe in one of the outer rings of Hell, no?

The other day you recommended the Priest's Tale. It sparked a flashback to that unforgettably long story by which Billy is molested on a break from his journey when he eats with the priest in Huisiachepic (*Crossing*, 139–159). Those pages were such tough going—again—that I found myself looking ahead to see where they ended. I can elaborate—which I suppose is what you are asking for. Before I do, tell me why you recommended that passage and what you find so appealing. We can use it as a starting point for clarifying our opposing views.

Best,

Peter

Peter, Old Man,

Thanks for the mini-review of *American Canticles*. Do you think that book suffers from problems other than the usual stylistic ones? Academic writing is, after all, its own peculiar genre, one where notions of style are all too often ignored. A law professor of mine once said that he didn't care how I expressed my thoughts as long as the relevant information was there. I was, and remain, shocked by that, as the clever use of language and rhetoric ought to be a lawyer's bailiwick. It ought to be a literature professor's too, but the professoriate seems to have forgotten that criticism—even difficult-to-grasp criticism— can be accessible. What's the point of writing a book if nobody understands it, or cares to read it?

McCarthy at his worst is fascinating, often brilliant, and generally better than most of the prose stylists writing today. *Cities of the Plain* may be the best example of bad McCarthy, but I have fond memories of the epilogue; there are moments throughout that work very well; and various sentences, paragraphs, and scenes work perfectly. The problem with *Cities of the Plain* is that there isn't enough *there* there. McCarthy was apparently in the midst of a stylistic transformation, paring down his language to the nub. *No Country for Old Men* and *The Road* show further evolution of that style, but when they do they disappoint me. I want more description, and perhaps more involvement from McCarthy in his landscapes. Maybe that's McCarthy's point, though. Perhaps the romanticism of the world is dead for McCarthy after a certain point, and the books are more sparse when they move toward the present because our times don't merit that baroque richness. Considering the Border Trilogy (excepting the epilogue, which stands on its own in some crazy McCarthian dreamscape), I might argue that the farther back in time one goes, the richer the prose gets. As you approach the end of the saga, it's all flat. That flatness might be McCarthy's way of highlighting and foregrounding the action, of making it seem mythic. Whether or not he succeeds might be worth thinking about. When I've gone back and reread passages from *Cities*, I've found myself liking them more. It's not that they're better, it's that *Cities* is a victim of the *Godfather III* Syndrome. It's not that bad a movie, there's just no way it can hold its own with the first two. That's probably true of all McCarthy's work post–*Blood Meridian*. Once that book is out there, you have to top it, or at least approach it, and nobody can do that.

This brings me back to your recollected conversation with Christian. I agree with his comment, but I would refine it. I encountered *All the Pretty Horses* at 21. That strikes me as the perfect time to read that book, so I suppose I will always find it peculiarly meaningful. And it was my first McCarthy. After it became a bestseller and award-winner, McCarthy's back catalog was slowly reprinted, but I don't think I'd read them all by the time of *The Crossing* in 1994. I went with my girlfriend to a bookstore in Memphis that was located in a former movie theatre and we each bought a copy of *The Crossing* on publication day. We returned to my place and read all day and half the night. *The Wolf Trapper* was much expanded from what we saw in *Esquire*, but no less perfect. And then. . . there's that sense of exhaustion and bewilderment I've encountered nowhere else. To enter into Part II of *The Crossing* is a peculiar sensation. You've been through such a cathartic moment with Billy that the next step in the plot is like a new and different book. Perhaps that's because Billy has been utterly changed. Perhaps it's that *The Wolf Trapper* is really that good. Where do you *go* after *The Wolf Trapper*?

I think *the rest* of *The Crossing* is the answer: you don't go anywhere. Or, if you do, you're so emotionally damaged by what happened to you and that wolf that you never recover. Billy grows up only by the hardest. In some sense, then, the Priest's Tale is a relief. It's not subjecting Billy to more pain, but offering him an opportunity to reflect on it, to learn and to grow from it. If not Billy, maybe *we* can do that. That's part of the reason I admire that section. It's quite dark, but it's told at some remove from the terror. McCarthy appears to have worked on that section for months. When we were in San Marcos I looked at *The Crossing* in manuscript. There is version after version of that story. Each version is more focused, tighter. McCarthy is dealing with some heady philosophy and metaphysics, but it's always humanized—notably by the eggs and the cat. Look at Annie Dillard's "Total Eclipse," in *Teaching a Stone to Talk*. There's something in that story about how eggs can bring a guy right back down to earth. I think McCarthy is playing with that device in the Priest's Tale. I have a few thoughts about the language of the priest, too, but I've already said too much for one missive. Does it even begin to answer your question? I'm not sure you answered mine.

—M

Dear M:

What was the name of the theatre in Memphis, and what was the bookstore?
Best,
Peter

Peter, Old Man,

The bookstore was on Poplar Avenue, one of the main drags in Memphis. It was a Bookstar, a chain. Used to be a theatre called the Plaza, where I saw *Bambi* for the first time as an adult. I was 18 and the gal I went with was too. The theatre had armrests that could be retracted so they were out of the way. It was a most pleasant way to watch *Bambi,* with a cute blonde leaning on my shoulder and the scent of peach shampoo permeating everything. She died later of "an untreatable disease of the blood."
—M

Hey Marty:

I have read to women, and they have read to me, and we have each sat and read our respective books, but I have never sat with a woman who was reading *the identical book.* I once sat beside a woman and read over her arm, but I was *pretending* to read because she had made the invitation to share with me, an offer I couldn't refuse for a reason you can imagine.

You mention the archive in San Marcos. As I was telling Wesley Morgan amidst the *Suttree* haunts in Knoxville, I believe that I located the moment in which *The Wolf Trapper* begins. In Box 69, Folder 9 of McCarthy's papers in the Wittliff Collection, there is a most interesting page—page 14—of the script for *Cities of the Plain.* John Grady says: "You ever seen a wolf, Billy?" For Billy's answer, McCarthy first typed: "Nope. Never did. They been trapped and poisoned out years ago. My daddy used to trap em up in the Oregon Mountains and they wasn't plentiful then." McCarthy lined that out and, in his own hand, changed it to: "Not a live one. Never did. I don't doubt but what there's still some in the Davis Mountains. My daddy used to trap 'em. Used them big old number four Blake and Lambs." This is all crossed out. Above it, McCarthy wrote: "INSERT PAGE 14 A & B." On page 14A, Billy's answer is: "Yeah. I seen one in a trap one time. My daddy used to trap wolves down in Hidalgo County for the government back in the twenties when we lived down there." The brand and number of the trap are transformed. "They were number fourteen Newhouse," Billy says, "and they looked big enough to hold a grizzly bear to me." When John Grady says: "How did you happen to see the one in the trap?" Billy's answer is the germ of *The Wolf Trapper*. McCarthy changed a no into a yes and wrote the outline for one of his masterworks. Seeing that reminded me of reading the early notebooks of Whitman. On this page he's a journalist-schoolteacher from West Hills, Long Island who aspires to be a poet. On the next page he is someone and *something* new: Walt Whitman, American, entering into *Leaves of Grass*. In the step between one page and the next he is entering history. McCarthy was McCarthy when he wrote that screenplay, but the wolf of *The Wolf Trapper* didn't exist on page 14, then there she is on 14A. That's the sort of discovery that opens the door to an author's workshop.

About those eggs from the priest. . . In my copy of *The Crossing* I find a slip of paper from 1994 on which I wrote: "I Thank You for the Breakfast: The High Cost of Free Food in *The Crossing*," the title of a piece I began but never completed, perhaps because I like to praise McCarthy more than not. . . and because *The Wolf Trapper* is more than enough book for me: I can disregard, or pretend to disregard, *the rest*. In the margin of the page on which the priest gives Billy his breakfast, I wrote: "Scrambled eggs & coffee = 16 pages of flap-doodle." So you see that I too had the eggs in mind. Then I wrote this:

> "To obtain your objects," said Wellington, "you must feed." This from
> the man who breakfasted on toast and tea before defeating the French at
> Waterloo. But his advice is applicable to our purpose. To properly—I won't
> say understand—to properly *read The Crossing*, it is necessary to contem-
> plate food; not chiefly in its etymological, ontological, entomological,
> metaphysical, or scatological ramifications. We must first consider food *as*
> *food*: prepared, eaten, digested. As we take this culinary tour of McCarthy's
> seventh novel, we should remember that Billy Parham's troubles begin
> when, like Pip with the convict in *Great Expectations*, he meets an outlaw
> Indian and brings him stolen food from home. It's this Indian who later
> kills Billy's parents and tries to lure his brother into the same fate, calling

him by name, a name the killer learned when Billy brought him to feed the Indians.

When Billy stops at a church and is fed four eggs, scrambled with butter and served without bread, it might read like Billy's first free Mexican meal, but he pays for it with an interminable narrative. This is worse than having a free bowl of soup in a soup kitchen and having to stay for the sermon. The old man's story runs sixteen pages. That's four pages—roughly twelve minutes—per egg. Poor Billy has to sit for nearly an hour for one plate of scrambled. McCarthy's jumpcut past Billy's response or non-response (for the next thing we see is Billy's departure) is perhaps the only thing McCarthy could have done, because Billy couldn't *have* a reaction to that story. It also suggests that the old man is not really yakking to the boy, it is McCarthy who is yakking to the reader. We are not asked to care about Billy's response because McCarthy hasn't cared: he is talking to us. He has lapsed as a novelist and, as in *The Stonemason*, picked up his pen as professor of flapdoodle. This is a very expensive meal.

I don't necessarily agree with myself, but my overall reaction is much the same, so do speak to me about *the language* of the Priest's Tale. Part of the quagmire of *The Crossing* is that McCarthy has become so habituated, if not addicted, to numinous, quasi-mystical turns of phrase that some of his people have started to sound exactly like his prose, a problem that, as you know, I have written about as hurting Ben's speeches in *The Stonemason*. Doubtless you will have a kinder interpretation than that McCarthy had written himself into a bad habit.

Best,

Peter

P.S. What was the name of the girl who died? Did you kiss during *Bambi*? Has there ever been another? Did the girl with whom you read, simultaneously, *The Crossing* ever ask—as in Joyce's "The Dead"—about the *Bambi* girl who died?

Peter, Old Man,

All right, since you asked, I have a vivid memory of leaving the Plaza with Heather one night, the whole area shrouded in thick fog, the night very cold.

That moment sticks with me: the night, the quiet, the cold, and the fog diffusing the light. Everything was all white with that building, and in my memory of it now, it beckons. Or exists as an island, alone, rising out of the night. The day we saw *Bambi* was utterly unlike the night I just mentioned. It was hot, Memphis hot. The theatre was cool inside, though. And no, I never kissed Heather—*Bambi* was just too cute for it—although I've regretted not doing so. She and I watched *The Name of the Rose* on an old VCR, and that would have been a good time. Why I didn't, I don't know. She lay on my bed and listened to the *Amadeus* soundtrack, the second movement of Beethoven's Seventh Symphony. . . and I *never* kissed her. Heather visited me in a dream once—but that's another story. And no, the other girlfriend, later, never knew or asked about Heather.

You ask about the language of the priest. He seems to have had some theological training. I take that from his diction. He's very precise, and I think that's partly owing to his character. McCarthy's always been good at dialogue, and it's revelatory of character here. From it, I think we can conclude that this man has been alone for a while. He has talked with his cats. They don't answer, so he has to carry the conversation. He has anticipated the questions because he has also been talking for the cats' side of the argument. And the cats, naturally, don't agree with him. This man is haunted by his past and he defends himself, too. Some notion of that sentiment is expressed by Ben in *The Stonemason*. In fact, *The Stonemason* often serves as commentary on *The Crossing*.

But consider a book called *The Beauty of the Infinite* by David Bentley Hart, a work of renown in theological circles. I'm intrigued by it, although I don't think I have all the background to fully understand it. Its first sentence is: "The rather prosaic question that initially prompted this long, elliptical essay in theological aesthetics, stated most simply, was this: Is the beauty to whose persuasive power the Christian rhetoric of evangelism inevitably appeals, and upon which it depends, theologically defensible?" (1) My point is that the priest talks like a theologian, and one ought to *expect* him to talk that way. McCarthy's revisions there are often small matters of diction: changing a word to affect the rhythm of the prose. But the reasoning had to be right, too. As did the things McCarthy lifted from folks like C. S. Lewis, from whose *A Grief Observed* the priest quotes directly.

I'm not sure I'm making my point all that well, so I'll send you this and wait for your comments.

—*Marty*

P.S. What did you mean by "Has there ever been another?" Another what? Why I'm up at 5 a.m. writing about McCarthy and an old dead not-girlfriend is beyond me.

My Dear M:

When I ask you whether there has ever been another, I mean a girl quite as perfectly loveable as Heather. Heather might seem far afield from *The Crossing*, but I will never be able to separate them. Opening day, you bought *The Crossing* in the place where you went to the movies with Heather, who died without your kissing her. Such a sad story.

I should have answered you about *American Canticles*. Its problem is more than stylistic. You can have sound ideas badly expressed, but you can't have a forceful argument badly made—the making *is* the argument. But that distinction applies to Lincoln's book marginally. At its core it is literary noise—an imitation of intellect and observation. Singing about another artist, even whistling about him (or her), is not that easy. To improvise it well, you have to be a genius yourself—otherwise, it has to be *composed*—*carefully*. If that man can think and if he can write, if he can whistle or if he can sing—and I assume that he can—it doesn't show in his book.

   Here's a line from page 17 of *The Crossing*: "Their father took down one of the jars and turned it in his hand and set it back again precisely in its round track of dust." That's the essence of McCarthy, and the reason why Lincoln isn't writing about McCarthy when he thinks that he is. If I were ever asked, in a public forum, what I think about *American Canticles*, I would have to say: "Their father took down one of the jars and turned it in his hand and set it back again precisely in its round track of dust." And if I were asked why I have an uncertain opinion about *the rest* of *The Crossing*, or why I have neglected to write much about it, I would say: "Their father took down one of the jars and turned it in his hand and set it back again precisely in its round track of dust." And if I were asked to step out and say something significant about Billy and Boyd, I would say: "Their father took down one of the jars and turned it in his hand and set it back again precisely in its round track of dust." And if I were asked to find some substantive intimation of *The Road* in *The Crossing,* I would say: "Their father took down one of the jars and turned it in his hand and set it back again precisely in its round track of dust." And if I were asked how it is that I can assert, with certainty, that the plaidshirted schoolboy standing on steps between St. Mary's school and the Church of Immaculate Conception in Knoxville knew, in advance—back then, in days of yore, when he was a cute Catholic kid amongst kind old Southerly souls, gamblers, killers and maniacs—that he *had* it, and knew, right then, that he was going to *do* it, I would say: "Their father took down one of the jars and turned it in his hand and set it back again precisely in its round track of dust." And if I were asked why I hated the 9/11 Administration—the Cheney-Bush years—I would say: "Their father took down one of the jars and turned it in his hand and set it back again precisely in its round track of dust." And if I were asked what's missing from American education, I would say: "Their father took down one of the jars and turned it in his hand and set it back again precisely in its round track of dust." And if I were asked why I've said that culture in the United States is falling faster than anybody can catch it, I would say: "Their father took down one of the jars and turned it in his hand and set it back again precisely in its round track of dust." And if you ask me why you are never not sitting next to Heather in the Plaza on Poplar Avenue, I will say: "Their father took down one of the jars and turned it in his hand and set it back again precisely in its round track of dust."

Having been so long away from *The Crossing,* I have wondered whether I was hallucinating when I tried, after my first reading, to compare it with *Great Expectations.* Now I see what I meant. When the Indian orders the boys to fetch food and other supplies, it really does echo the conwict Magwitch ordering Pip to bring him wittles and a file. Elsewhere I have compared McCarthy to Dickens. A lot in common. I wonder how much Dickens McCarthy has read? In talking to Mark Morrow, McCarthy said: "I was twenty-six years old, I'd never read a serious book." We know enough to take McCarthy's point without taking his statement too literally. But there is only so much time. Writers *can* have similar imaginings without adapting from one another. Nevertheless, the opening of *Great Expectations*—I mean *The Crossing*—has *Great Expectations* written all over it. It's extraordinarily done. You know that the Indian will kill you—or someone. As evil as it gets, worse than Judge Holden, who is at least having a grand old time at his malevolence, and has a spirit of largesse about him. The Indian's a witless homicidal thief: a deadzone jailbird—red trash. And quite the real thing.

The Crossing is like a woman who can't wait to argue when all you want to do is to keep kissing her cheek. Such exquisite pleasures in *The Wolf Trapper*. The touching compassion and complexity of the second rancher who helps Billy, a man to whose cattle the wolf is enemy, and yet he'd like to buy the wolf and he helps to administer first aid. Or his reaching up to adjust the brim of a hat that's not there—the way it suggests its near-permanence as outdoor appendage, as well as the pandemonian chaos that drew him out without it. Or, in the first paragraph after Billy and the wolf have headed for Mexico, the first plural form of the personal pronoun, a thrilling thing to read: "Midday they crossed through a low pass in the easternmost spur of the Guadalupes" (*Crossing*, 63), man-horse-wolf making a *they* such as we've known in *All the Pretty Horses* and *Blood Meridian*. Or this description of the sunset: "As if the darkness had a soul itself that was the sun's assassin hurrying to the west as once men did believe or they may believe again" (72–73), a line that predicts the collapsed and yet newly primordial world of *The Road*. Or the marvelous way that the wolf "looked bleakly at the ground that was not of her choosing" (73). Or the moment in which Billy begins to speak his heart, or at least his head, to the wolf, a great crossing in itself and yet so simply stated: "He began to talk to her" (76), a shift in relationship that is no less significant than when a man first addresses, honestly, a woman he adores. Or when the wolf's mouth is suddenly free to bite him and "He tried to move in a casual manner but he felt all his motives naked to her" (78), something I have felt on occasions of self-consciousness around some woman whose interest I seek. *All his motives naked to her. . .* What a line. Thirty pages on the smarts of the wolf would not say as much.

This evening I chanced upon "Travels With A She-Wolf," Robert Hass's front-page review of *The Crossing* in the *New York Times Book Review* of June 12, 1994. This review, illustrated with one of the worst drawings to appear in the *Book Review*, is unqualified praise for McCarthy. In the closest Hass comes to a qualification, "The language could easily seem affected," he writes, "but it rarely does; or, as with Faulkner, readers will find themselves yielding to the affectation and to the barren landscape it describes, and to the carnival of figures encountered on the road, who make a world that is at once unlike anything in American fiction and deeply familiar, since it is the site of one of the oldest stories, the one about having a task to perform in the world and learning what the world is from trying to perform it." I assume that he is correct in that Priola found himself yielding to the affectation, but he is wrong about Josyph—at least insofar as we are talking about *the rest*. It felt strange for me to read a review in which *the rest* is spoken about as if it's part of the same novel. But I am glad that Hass wrote that review, glad that *The Crossing* received it, for McCarthy deserved it. I only wish that I could buy that edition of *The Crossing* in which *the rest* is as good as *The Wolf Trapper*.

Best,

Peter

Dear Martster:

Treat this as a P.S. to my last, for what I meant to add is that I am not at all sure whether I understand what the hell the priest is talking about. For me he's a longwinded blowhard. It's partly to do with the fact that I was finished with God and the Godish late in my teens when, after reams of theology along with philosophy, even the theoretical side of religion ceased to interest me— excepting, perhaps, a few mad monk types, some of the deeds and sayings of the saints (my friend Kevin Larkin and I have a series of found-object assemblages called *Lives of the Saints*), or the rare, exquisitely rendered statement of belief in, or defense of, faith, such as the verses of Zen masters, or *Brideshead Revisited*. By now I am virulently anti-religion and have no patience for anything to do with it. I agree with Christopher Hitchens that it poisons (practically) everything—it certainly does for me, to a degree that when I have to attend a wedding or any ceremony, I am sorry to see a priest, a reverend, a rabbi presiding, despite that they are probably fine fellows. We've made a mistake in confusing religious toleration in law with religious toleration in intellect. When the French novelist Michel Houellebecq said that Islam is a stupid religion, the French authorities indicted him for inciting religious prejudice. Insanity. But I have a rule that, certain unpredictable exceptions aside, I won't discuss religion with a religious person, just as I won't discuss politics with someone on the Right. Nor will I discuss why I won't discuss them, for that would then become the discussion. So. . . I am partly reluctant to talk about the priest because I will probably disappoint you by refusing to engage in a religious conversation.

My guess, however, is that my fear is unfounded. You are far from a proselytizer. In all these years, you have never been obnoxious or even forward in the matter of your beliefs either political or religious, and that's rare. You and I have talked for hours and never gotten into one of those wasteful wornout scuffles about Right v. Left, G v. NG—for which I am grateful. You haven't even mentioned Bill Clinton—not once. But the Priest's Tale *is* a tale told by a priest, and it does have to do with one of my least favorite issues, really what has become the ultimate non-issue for me. Nor do I buy your explanation about the language of the priest, for I see that language generally in *the rest* of *The Crossing*, in McCarthy's own prose and in the speech of his characters, and for me very little of what I will call *the numinous* goes a very long way.

What does the Priest's Tale mean to you? Perhaps if I can see it as *yours* it will have a different feeling for me. This is stretching things, but I don't mind stretching. That's why we are having this discussion.

Best,

Peter

P.S. Where does McCarthy quote from C. S. Lewis?

Dear Peter,

The passage is where the priest says: "It was never that this man ceased to believe in God. No. It was rather that he came to believe terrible things of Him" (*Crossing*, 48). McCarthy's draft in San Marcos has a note next to that passage, something like: "After Lewis." So I went to Lewis, and found, in *A Grief Observed*, the journals that he kept following his wife's death from cancer, published before Lewis's death under a pseudonym. "Not that I am (I think) in much danger of ceasing to believe in God. The real danger is of coming to believe such dreadful things about Him. The conclusion I dread is not, 'So there's no God after all,' but, 'So this is what God's really like. Deceive yourself no longer'" (5).

—M

Hey M:

Here is McCarthy at his most powerful, about Billy when he goes to find the wolf: "He rode out the gate before his father was even up and he never saw him again" (*Crossing*, 53). The daring and immensity of that is breathtaking. Such scope in such simplicity. McCarthy is a terrorist of the sentence. You read that and you fear the next attack. Is there anything comparable in *the rest* of *The Crossing*?

I like what you say about the cats who have to listen to the priest not agreeing with him. The difference between me and the cats is that I'd have preferred running into the desert over one more day of that bloat. Poor Billy—for a plate of protein. If I were Mark Twain I would shoot the Priest's Tale with a revolver. If I were Fielding I would sentence it to life. If I were Cooper I would sue. If I were Poe I'd be drunk and insult its mustache. If I were Nabokov I'd mount it like a dead butterfly. If I were Freud I would chase it down the broad stone stair at Berggasse 19. If I were Hart Crane I'd take it with me into the Gulf of Mexico. Let me float a hypothesis: In *The Wolf Trapper*, dialogue brings people alive. In *the rest* of *The Crossing*, it obliterates them because they talk like McCarthy.

Why do I feel so bad about Heather? She has become real to me thanks to you and *The Crossing*, a book of which she is the opposite, even in her impossible name. Would she ever have imagined that she would be so remembered (or so reconfigured), and all way up here, by a Yank, in New York? If you were writing autobiographical fiction I would suggest altering the name of the girl and of the film and to change the shampoo to another scent—something less all-American than peach—in other words, I would ask you to de-cute four of the five sentences that you wrote initially, for despite that your description is accurate, I cringe a little whenever I read it again, as it's a little unbelievable. And yet if you had rendered her in any other fashion, would I have reacted the same way? Sentences are magic and they aren't retractable. As with the sight of a woman's face in the flesh, once we are sentenced and a spell has been cast, there is no going back: now I too have an ache and it's all your fault and McCarthy's. I also feel that I might have maligned a supermodel in referring to *Esquire* with "the model Vendela exposing her airbrushed thighs under a short white nightgown." How do *I* know whether her thighs are airbrushed? Thighs often are in the world of print fashion, but it's a bad thing to make a sentence sound smart when you're not really sure that a detail is true. Also, who *cares* whether a model is airbrushed—it's common knowledge now. Vendela—forgive me. I must have done it for the rhythm. Now I would change it to "exposing her thighs under a short nightgown." Decent honest writing's not easy, not even in correspondence. How does McCarthy do it so well?

Returning to the issue of writing *about* McCarthy: I was rereading one of the best books about an artist, *The Studio of Alberto Giacometti* by Jean Genet. I was in Heidelberg during my first exhibition there—at Galerie Signum Winfried Heid—when I found it in a little bookshop that I remember for several reasons. It was the first time I tried "Guten Morgen" on a German, the woman who ran the shop. And the place seemed so typically European, I would even say German (Germans don't like mega-bookstores), a shop you would use if you were filming Thomas Mann. But the Genet was not in German, it was in French—*L'atelier d'Alberto Giacometti*—in a thin paperback that I could never read because I have so little French. It is wonderfully illustrated with fine black and whites by a man named Ernst Scheidegger, and so during the years in which I lacked a translation I enjoyed the photographs. When I found a translation, by Richard Howard, in *The Selected Writings of Jean Genet*, I was able to quote from it in my book *Lost Worlds of September 11: Returning to Ground Zero*—that's the book on which I spent four years after completing the *Liberty Streets*, only to discover that no agent or editor would even look at it.

One passage in *L'Atelier* is relevant to writing about McCarthy. At first, Genet says: "If I want to tame a work of art, I frequently use a trick: I adopt, however artificially, a state of naïveté, I talk about it—and I also talk to it—in the most ordinary tone of voice; I even play dumb a little." By doing this, Genet finds that "the work loses some of its formality, its solemnity. By means of a familiar *reconnaissance*, I gradually approach its secret." But this does not work for Genet with Giacometti. "The work is already too far away. Impossible to fake a good-natured stupidity. Severe, it commands me to go back to that solitary point from which it must be regarded" (321).

This appears to be true for me and McCarthy. I always feel as if whatever I have written is a form of fakery, a strategy of avoidance, a Mississippi Shuffle, an act of vaudeville, a running of the scales, and that I need to return to the work in a truer mode, one in which I can really *see* what he has done and come to deeper terms with his art. And then, of course, to convey something of that. Was I tough on Kenneth Lincoln? He should hear me on me. Did I say that a bad book can make me feel better about my own *essaying*, my own attempts, with McCarthy? Perhaps for six seconds. After I have delivered a talk, published an article or a book—as when I have painted and hung a McCarthy-related exhibition—I couldn't be more ready to start over, to start thinking about the work and perhaps to say something that is truly worthwhile—and to say it powerfully. A work about McCarthy shouldn't be a Sinatra song, a Dowland pavane, the Apostle's Creed or the wind in the fucking willows—it should be the sound of a knife as the blade enters the wood of the table. Yeah, well—good luck to me.

Best,

Peter

Dear Peter,

Good luck indeed. One of my theories, long held but little expressed, is that literary criticism takes itself too seriously, and that critics flail about with their theories and adopt their professional argot to make them and their work seem more rarified than they are, or it is. It makes them a part of an exclusive and learned club. That provides job security, but it removes their writing from the level at which a layperson can understand it. This of course deprives the non-professional of the information the critic is allegedly seeking to impart, and it leads to a critical echo chamber in which the critic is talking to other critics. It's no surprise that postmodernism caught on. They don't have to illuminate a work, just keep talking amongst themselves. That's why I started the McCarthy site in the first place: because McCarthy's too good to be left to the professionals. They can kill anything. Malcolm Cowley might have made Faulkner's reputation, but precious few people read Faulkner nowadays and I have a problem with that. In a sense, then, I'm hoping the academics don't get McCarthy. They'll put their critical stranglehold on him, and that doesn't benefit anyone.

I had a discussion the other day with a friend. Nothing like the present discussion. But we agreed that we both despise the sentence, so common in today's world, "I'm spiritual, but not religious." The person who says that believes in the numinous, as you call it, but doesn't follow through. *There's a spiritual world out there, but it expects and demands nothing of me.* It'd be like Ed Tom in *No Country for Old Men* saying that a man would have to put his soul at hazard—then saying that *he* wouldn't. You're thinking of *Great Expectations*, I'm thinking of *Walden*. I can't imagine Thoreau refusing to engage with the woods. In the same way, I can't imagine Ahab not engaging with the whale. Now, those things are real, and you may believe that the numinous is not. But if it *is* real, refusing to engage it is weakness, impotence. About the Priest's Tale, part of what I like is the suggestion that some people go through a stage of refusal, then decide that God *demands* to be engaged. That makes sense to me. If God and the numinous are real, then refusing to deal with them is a kind of running away. But what the priest seems to suggest is that even running away is taking a stand. Maybe that's why I like it, but maybe it's even simpler. The cats and Billy (who is laconic throughout) and even the eggs all work against the priest in some way. There is combat there, and violence, same as in *The Wolf Trapper*. Some of it's in the priest's story, some of it's in *reaction to* the story. But McCarthy, as always, makes you work for it. He never says, "Billy thought that was one of the dumbest things he ever heard." And if I might advance a thesis of my own: *the rest of The Crossing is difficult and doesn't seem as good as The Wolf Trapper* not because everyone talks like McCarthy, but because McCarthy is telling the story over again, this time with Boyd in place of the wolf. And then, at last, it's all of the West. I'm embarrassed to say so, but when I first read *The Crossing* I didn't understand the event at the end. When I was at a conference and someone mentioned "the bomb," I thought, "What bomb? Where?" Then everything clicked for me about that whole book. The destruction of the wolf is the destruction of Boyd is the destruction of the West, mythically and for real. Killing the wolf leads, inexorably, to *the rest.* And the question the book asks is: are you going to be like Billy? Are you just going to stand there and watch? Maybe even more brutally: are you really going to chase away the dog?

I'm both Conservative and Christian, more or less. You know that. I had figured that things were much as you say they are with you, but this is the fullest explanation I've heard on these subjects, and no, your positions don't bother me. Unless you say that you are spiritual but not religious!
—M

My Dear M:
In conversing with Mark Morrow about the self-confidence of a writer or any artist, McCarthy said: "If you really do have it, you know—you *do* know— that absolute knowledge." And I think that is generally true for an artist in relation to any particular one of his or her works. You might be wrong about something being a masterpiece, but if it is in fact one, you will probably know it. It would be a lamentable error for an artist not to recognize his or her perfection. But art is a business of partial satisfactions, and I would wager that McCarthy knew, at the center of his talent, that with the last four sentences on page 127, *The Crossing* had ended as completely, profoundly, and finally as anything ever written. Why then did he write more? Everything about me resists reading on, as if by refusing to read *the rest* I can deny its existence. About Billy Parham, McCarthy has said: "That sort of boy is likely becoming something of an extinct species himself."[6] But look here: is that Billy again on page 129? For me, in the world of page 129 to page 426, the Billy of *The Wolf Trapper* is already extinct. And after the passing of that Billy, who dares to walk the world with his name? To whatever degree I say yes to pages 3 to 127, I tend to say no to page 129. The dubious but interesting rumor that an agent or

editor, perched in the silence of page 128, persuaded McCarthy to make a big-ger book, perhaps by calling *The Wolf Trapper* a novella—really an insulting word for a shorter novel—does not answer anything, for the mystery of how he could have written another word because someone suggested it would be as deep as the mystery of why else he would have done it.

I have heard that when Melville was up at Arrowhead in the throes of *Moby-Dick*, he read or reread *King Lear*, and under that powerful influence began to Shakespeareanize the novel. I associate this with its de-Ishmaelizing: the loss of that wonderful voice that is really only heard at the beginning, and the appearance of soliloquizing from Ahab to which no natural-born Ishmael could ever have been privy. Along with Melville's English publisher, who could charge more for a three-volume book than for a two and who I thus, in my foolish stubborn way, hold accountable for all the whaleological bonemeal added to fill its pages, I hold Shakespeare responsible for ruining *Moby-Dick* for me. There is Ishmael's first-person tale, with which I am enthralled—he is drunk on the English language, his drunkenness happens to be inspired, one can feel the motion of his life in every sentence—and then there is *the rest* of *Moby-Dick* with that bore Ahab, who has never interested me. I men-tion this because I'd be curious to know exactly what McCarthy was reading after he finished *The Wolf Trapper*. If I were a betting man, I would bet my financial portfolio (maybe a few hundred dollars in good times) that there is an author and a book or two to whom and to which we are, at least, partially beholden for the beast that is *the rest* of *The Crossing*. As this could be equally true of *Blood Meridian* or any of the best of McCarthy, let me dismount this particular high horse before I argue with myself on the same page, for in truth I am caution itself when it comes to speculating the act of composition. I have heard my share of wrongheadedness about my own work. When Carl Djerassi, a scientist who developed the birth control pill and who created the Djerassi Foundation in the Santa Cruz Mountains (on a cattle ranch adjacent Neil Young's Broken Arrow), listened to a reading of my play *The Last Colored Lightbulb in Louisiana*, I was told that it was rare for him to stay so long for a reading by a resident of the colony. Djerassi, a Viennese Jew who was born in 1923 and forced out of Vienna by the advance of the Third Reich, remained for another half hour to question me, refusing to accept that I had not had overt political intentions or references in mind. This full-length play for two men in which the one is held prisoner by the other had its origin in one interesting line—I don't recall it now, it might have been something like "You must pass on the horns of the goat—do it"—and, for that, an answer was necessary, after which the two men did not stop talking for three acts. Where they were, why they were there, where they went to at the end I haven't a clue, but in the cultural milieu from which Djerassi had come, and the world in which he lived to that day, it was inconceivable for me to have written such a play—a play that is set on the fringes of torture—without having some very clear conceptions in mind, let alone without having *anything* in mind other than finding out what these men would say to each other. For Djerassi, the play expressed something too well to have derived from a guy just jotting what was said, a guy who can chat about his work without reference to politics or social agendas. I wish you could have seen him trying to wring a confession from me—he was one step from tying me up and *making* me tell the truth. But I *was*. I also recall that at a major exhibition in which I was showing over seventy works of art—paintings, photographs, assemblages, etc.—I was confronted about one of them for over half an hour by a very smart man named Gerald G. Glass, founder of a reading technique known as Glass Analysis and director of the Reading and Learning Center at Adelphi University. For this show, called *Portrait of an American Town*, I had painted then Governor Mario Cuomo sitting at a table with then Mayor Dinkins, who happened to be there when I photographed Cuomo at the capital in Albany. On the table in this painting there were vehicles—trucks, I believe, and maybe a car or two. Dr. Glass, a really good guy for whom I had worked at one time, refused to accept that I had no *meaning* attaching to these vehicles, and, like Djerassi, he was convinced that I was holding out on him, belittling him, by refusing an intellectual explanation. "You can't tell me those vehicles don't stand for something," he'd say. "They do," I'd say, "they stand for trucks." As with Djerassi, the conversation went on forever. I was dying to walk around, talk to other people, perhaps sell a few pictures, and here I was trapped against the wall of my own painting by a man who was becoming more and more angry at what he *wasn't* hearing. Finally I said that I generally keep childlike stencils in the studio, and one day I tried a few to see how they might enliven the picture. That simple statement of craft settled his mind enough to understand that I was not talking down to him. He then admitted that he was terribly insecure around contemporary art and was overly defensive about what he perceived to be some kind of intellectual dodge on my part that was calculated to keep him at a loss in front of the painting. Hearing that these trucks were really not politics—not consciously so—but an impulsive experiment with a few vehicular shapes that happened to be at hand—that broke the deadlock. It's quite typical, though, for smart people to need a *conceptual* experience of art—visual art especially—when for me, equally as artist and as appreciator, the experience is more relaxedly *perceptual*. I suppose this would summarize what might distinguish my own adventures in reading Cormac McCarthy from those of another author. I generally don't read with *ideas*, or with all that much of a need for ideas. Before a performance of Brahms in which Glenn Gould was soloist, his conductor, Leonard Bernstein, used the word *sportive* for Gould's unorthodox approach. Sportive: that's a good word for my approach to McCarthy. Of course the fact that Gould had genius made it easier for Bernstein to disagree with Gould and yet want to work with him. It might say something about McCarthy that the House of McCarthy Criticism in which I am a misfit has welcomed my sportiveness with such toleration.

In *The Renaissance*, Walter Pater's view of art is that it strives "to be independent of mere intelligence, to become a matter of pure perception" (97). That's nicely stated. But after I expressed a similar view, in my own terms, amongst a group of painters at the artists' colony Yaddo, one of them told me that she had had to leave the room because it was too disturbing to think that her work might exceed her conceptual grasp. The worst thing for her was when I said that painting, for me, should be a dream from which I do *not* wake up in the same place. In other words, that I want to make art that *does not return me to me*. My ideal was her nightmare—and, alas, would be for the majority of painters I have met—writers, too. They need a kind of control that is worthless to me. I prefer to solve problems in ways that create further problems. I discuss this in connection with my series *Cormac McCarthy's House*, but it applies to most of what I do. Pater's phrase *mere intelligence* turns the sentence in which it appears into an act of bravery. What does Pater mean, *mere*? For Pater, as for Peter, the experience of art is often not accessible to reason, at least not at the point of impact, and being able to *speak* about it reasonably is not at all the same as creating it reasonably; or, when it is not yours, encountering it, face to face, with *mere intelligence*. In this age in which any real intelligence is rare, one hesitates to deride *mere intelligence*, but in matters of actual art—making it, perceiving it—we do, very much, need more, and less, than that. Art is not where people think it is. You cannot glide into a gallery or a museum and have a nice day looking at the art. It's not there. It's insane to think that you can sit down and read a book. To read a book properly you have to be destroyed. Same is true for writing one.

Tonight I reread the Priest's Tale, keeping in mind what you've said about it. The priest wants the world to be a great unsolvable mystery no matter what a man may think or feel or fear or love or experience in any other way, and he wants Billy to know that God is a great terrible something beyond understanding, and he wants Billy to tribute that. This is very McCarthy to me. McCarthy is often Ecclesiastesian: he strives to humble us, as does the Catholic Church and other religions. But I am not humbled by McCarthy or by religion, only by McCarthy's genius with the pen (really, the Olivetti). More importantly, I don't believe McCarthy could write this scene for the Billy who is in *The Wolf Trapper*—it would be pointless to do so, for by the end of *The Wolf Trapper* Billy is a boy who should never have to hear the Priest's Tale or anything like it from any man of religion. Tibetan proverb: *Where there is veneration, even a dog's tooth emits light.* Or a wolf's. Once Billy has felt that, no priest should speak to him: McCarthy has a duty to keep him clear of religion, not to use him as a prop on which to hang metaphysical flapdoodle. To write such a scene, McCarthy had to *un-Wolf Trapper* Billy. I refuse to go along with that betrayal, preferring to leave perfect enough alone. That's titsy of me, but I am such a sweetheart in the world of men and women that I am entitled to be a bastard in the world of sentences.

Best,

Peter

Peter, Old Man,

So... given all that you say, what do you think of the "Doomed enterprises" sentence that begins Part II? I rather like it, but every time I encounter it I think of Faulkner, who might have picked a better sentence out of the air with the start of Chapter 6, *Light in August*: "Memory believes before knowing remembers. Believes longer than recollects, longer than knowing even wonders" (487).

I don't know enough of the publishing history to have supposed that McCarthy added *the rest* because someone asked him to, and I rather doubt that he's that malleable.[7] You are right about *novella*, though: the term is a disgrace precisely because it's diminutive. But that groups it with *Heart of Darkness*, and I'm fine with *The Wolf Trapper* keeping that sort of company. But you can deny away, deny repeatedly: the whole book exists and demands that you deal with it. Nobody says you have to like it. Maybe we only learn that McCarthy should have quit while he was ahead, but I don't get that from the book. I gave you a good deal of commentary about the book in my last. You've done a nice sort of softshoe around it. I admire your nimbleness and grace, but we've not moved much beyond "but I don't LIKE *the rest*." You can say McCarthy's characters speak like McCarthy, but I need some specifics.

Let me flip your last metaphor on its head. Billy isn't *un*trapped, but continually *trapped* throughout the rest of the novel. Assuming that what you say about Billy makes sense—what he knows, nobody can take from him—the so-called flapdoodle is another trap Billy has to weasel himself out of so that he can continue his quest. Why does he have to keep questing? That's what men do. To stop is to lose something of oneself. Chaucer's pilgrims are on a journey, a spiritual one, but it is also a journey toward death. So too in McCarthy. McCarthy's pilgrim storytellers may be searching for the God that Chaucer's pilgrims would have assumed existed. The priest propounds a theory of story and narrative that attempts to encompass the entire universe. What results is a sort of metaphysics of story. The whole world is a tale, and all these stories, then, are really one story, whether from the pen of Chaucer or the pen of McCarthy. What you said of *Blood Meridian* may be applied as well to *The Crossing*:

> The novel is also a national epic, but an epic of that country called McCarthy, where there are two authentic heroes working together magnificently: the dreamer, the imaginist, the envisioner; and the teller, the one with the words, the one with the *epos*, the one with the music. Howsoever the great judge fiddles, we remember that he himself is being fiddled. . . all his power merely a song sung by another. (Josyph, *Adventures*, 180)

It is McCarthy's song we are hearing, after all, not Billy's nor the priest's nor the blind man's either. It's a song of great hardship, beauty, struggle, hope. The structure of *The Crossing*—story inside story, narrator inside narrator—reflects the multilayered, multifaceted complexity of the human drama.

Thinking about what you said in your last, I am reminded of a comment C. S. Lewis makes in *Mere Christianity*. A man came up to him after a talk and said, essentially, *I don't need your flapdoodle—I saw God in the desert.* Lewis, to his credit, didn't argue with the man or tell him his view was invalid. Consider, too, that it might *not* be flapdoodle. I had a professor in college, a tiny, ebullient woman who wore huge glasses on her small wrinkled face. She would get so excited that she would practically yell. "MAN—MAN is the measure of ALL THINGS!" Her eyes would dance. She looked a bit crazed. A few years later she was diagnosed with myasthenia gravis, the disease that killed her. She lost much of her eyesight. I went to her house to visit. I had heard that she couldn't read. She listened to books on tape. I had *The Crossing* with me. I brought it in, sat on her couch, and read the Priest's Tale to her. I would have read *The Wolf Trapper*, but it was too long. I finished, we talked for a while, she professed to loving that passage, and she talked about how she woke up one morning and one of her cats was kneading the blankets on her bed. She said that she was utterly amazed by the cat—by the complexity of the bones and muscles etc., and how, for lack of a better word, *perfect* that was. About a week later she sent me a lovely little note thanking me for reading to her and suggesting that McCarthy was, in that story, trying to "eff the ineffable." That might be the best single sentence I've read about McCarthy and *The Crossing*: it's an attempt at effing the ineffable. Whether he succeeds is another question, but as to his goals, I get the feeling that she was spot on.
—M
P.S. Why do you figure that *The Crossing* causes me to talk about people I've known who are dead?

My Dear M:
Doomed enterprises divide lives forever between the then and the now? I'm not so sure about that, but it's certainly true in books: that sentence is

the start of a doomed enterprise for McCarthy, dividing his book forever between *The Wolf Trapper* and... well, you know... which is why this morning I can't believe that you would need examples of how McCarthy's characters have started speaking like his prose. (I mean, after the divider between pages 127 and 129—the fateful p. 128: blank.) But I am in the giving vein today, so here is one for you from Señor Gillian, the ranching agent in Casas Grandes: "What remedy can there be? What remedy can there be for what is not? You see? And where is the remedy that has no unforeseen consequence? What act does not assume a future that is itself unknown?. . . . You do not know what things you set in motion. . . . No man can know. No prophet foresee. The consequences of an act are often quite different from what one would guess. You must be sure that the intention in your heart is large enough to contain all wrong turnings, all disappointments. Do you see? Not everything has such a value" (*Crossing*, 202). That's a *mild* example. Here is the Dueña Alfonsa: "'He claimed that the responsibility for a decision could never be abandoned to a blind agency but could only be relegated to human decisions more and more remote from their consequences'" (*Horses*, 230), and: "'He said that those who have endured some misfortune will always be kept apart but it is just that misfortune which is their gift and which is their strength and that they must make their way back into the common enterprise of man for without they do so it cannot go forward and they themselves will wither in bitterness'" (235). That is *not* human speech. Neither are Hemingway's bowdlerized translations of Spanish curses in *For Whom the Bell Tolls*—*I obscenity in the milk of thy ancestors* for *Fuck your mother*—but at least they are amusing. Happily, the primadonna from the opera company falls within the line of tolerance. I like her and her dragon fan, her stemmed opera glasses, her great arousing bundle of hair that she washes in the river and the well of Billy's desire, her contempt for gypsies and gypsy horsepainters, "dentists of horses," as if there were no worse insult (*Crossing*, 228). Speaking of Hemingway, there's a bit of Pilar in her. Her line about the road, that "every voyage upon it will be completed," sounds like typical McC flapdoodle but it's not, it's profound (230). She also says something that might appear to contradict that but it does not, and it reminds me of something in Paulo Faria's reaction when I asked for his opinion of *the rest* of *The Crossing* now that he is translating the novel into Portuguese. Paulo refers to McCarthy as "the Master" and he means it. He has vowed that only over his dead body will *some other* translator be assigned one of the novels before he has undertaken it, and Paulo has made many sacrifices to keep that promise. So you know how strongly he responds to the work and how seriously Paulo approaches the art of converting it into Portuguese. But about *The Crossing* he said: "The structure of the book, which repeats itself with successive trips into Mexico, becomes a kind of trap where McCarthy got caught. The characters that Billy and Boyd meet along the way, telling them stories with deep meanings, recall some of the characters in the *Odyssey*. Most of the telling is secondhand. You are listening to a story that is told by someone else to the hero or heroes and the narrator is, in turn, telling them to us. But McCarthy sometimes goes too far. One gets the uncomfortable feeling that maybe, at some points, he did not know what to do with the story." It is precisely the reserve and the deep compassion with which Paulo expresses that last thought that makes it so compelling for me. *Maybe, at some points, he did not know what to do with the story.* The novel contains many wonders, including some of the best writing of the century. It is 426 pages long. To me, that's a lot of book—a long journey for any author. When Billy explains his intention to seek the stolen horses until they are found, the primadonna says something that is not only true for Billy and Boyd but for the novel in which she says it: "Long voyages often lose themselves" (230). Eccentric though she is, this is a woman with a head on her shoulders. I would love to set her up on a blind date with Judge Holden—quite a pair.

I have four questions for you. This is not another Final Exam on McCarthy, so you won't be graded on your responses—and I'll give you more than 45 minutes.

1) Have you noticed that McCarthy loves to mythologize his characters? He does it in two ways at least: by saying it himself, and by having others look at them in wonder. This syndrome appears in *Blood Meridian, All the Pretty Horses, The Crossing, Suttree,* etc. He really is writing in the Superman/Superboy tradition. "He looked fourteen going on some age that never was. He looked as if he'd been sitting there and God had made the trees and rocks around him. He looked like his own reincarnation and then his own again" (*Crossing,* 177). For me, these attempts to underscore the wild, primordial, or mystical qualities in his men constitute a rare insecurity in McCarthy, who might be the most secure writer since Joyce. He can't just let them behave and

let one find them extraordinary or not; he has to *tell* you that they are and, in case you didn't get the message, he needs you to witness other characters—people on the roadside, inhabitants of a town—viewing them that way.

2) Do you see a relationship between what happens to Billy when he is away in Mexico, what happens to John Grady when he is in Mexico, what happens to Bobby McEvoy when he is away from Graniteville, what happens to the Kid during his years of wandering, and what happens to Suttree when he is in the mountains? What motivates McCarthy to drive his people to cultivate a scary, uncivilized wildness in which they are ready and willing to kill you or jump off a mountain or fall on a sword or burst into flames? Like Rimbaud in *A Season in Hell*, they "return with limbs of iron, dark skin and a furious eye" (13)—*noticeably*. McCarthy himself is not like that and, other than when he is writing, I would suspect that he has never been like that. (This is a trick question.)

3) Do you find it believable that Billy and Boyd talk so little about the murder of their parents and what went on for Boyd during the slaughter?

4) What was the dream in which Heather visited you? Was it after she died?

Halfway through this encounter with *The Crossing*, it is bothering me less than the last. The Priest's Tale has been the worst of it. The Hemingway *and*s are out of control and that can drive me to distraction. And McCarthy has lost his balance in presenting a detail that makes a scene believable and helps you to trust his authority, a virtue that has devolved into the habit of telling you that Peter cleared his throat and reached into the inside pocket of his coat, unclasped his cheap Staples ballpoint pen, depressed the thingamagig above the clasp (McCarthy would know the name), pressed the nib down into the face of the invoice at the line for his signature, moved it along in the form and structure of his name, lifted the pen, pressed the thingamagig again, returned the pen to his pocket, and folded the invoice by bending the top third down toward the center and folding the bottom third up toward the center, etc., when he should have said that Peter signed and mailed the invoice. Otherwise, I am moving along. Am I on the road to Damascus?

Best,

Peter

Dear Peter,

"This morning I can't believe that you would need examples of how McCarthy's characters have started speaking like his prose." Truth is, I don't—I just wanted you to quote me something! I admit that you are somewhat correct in your criticism, but that flaw doesn't lessen my enjoyment of *The Crossing*. Yes, the words of McCarthy's narrator and those of the priest are not always distinguishable. But this blurring of narrators illustrates the primacy of the storyteller in McCarthy's universe. And I suppose that if I wanted to be difficult, I would ask you whether there were any specific reason why the ranching agent couldn't speak that way, or wouldn't. I've known men like him: salt of the earth types, folks of the land, you know—not educated, well-bred gentlemen. You wouldn't expect them to speak in riddles, but sometimes they do. They are equally adept at saying *you ain't nothin*. It's not that they speak like McCarthy's narrator that bothers me, it's that they are sometimes self-important when they shouldn't or wouldn't be.

Your first question is intriguing. I agree with your supposition, but would add that of course McCarthy is writing in the Superman tradition, particularly when he is in the Western genre. That's one of the tricks of the genre. What are the great cowboy heroes if not Supermen? Even when he's ripping holes in the myths and stereotypes of the West, he is bound by that tradition insofar as that's what's expected of a storyteller. That tradition goes clear back to the *Iliad*, and in English it appears quite obviously in the kennings of *Beowulf*. In that sense it's partly a spinoff of the oral tradition. It lends weight, but it's just about all poetical weight. Those phrases don't necessarily tell you *about* the characters, they tell you how the narrator looks at them (and, by extension, how we should look at them). *The Crossing* is a novel concerned with the fate of Billy Parham, but it is also a protracted meditation on the function of the storyteller and his role in society (as well as his ironic removal from it), and with the constant conflict between the narrator and the hero. If there is no narrator, the accomplishments of the hero are meaningless. The storyteller, for McCarthy, is a person of great importance in society, despite the inherent non-reality of language and story. Can we trust this narrator of *The Crossing* (who is, after all, *not* McCarthy)? We give narrators a curious power. We trust them an awful lot. We shouldn't, perhaps, especially as the narrator in *The Crossing* expresses uncertainty about factual events. I recall an early passage where the narrator uses the word *perhaps*, a strange word for an omniscient narrator. Maybe the event didn't happen as it was described. Perhaps *something else* happened. A lot hangs on that little but vitally important word: *perhaps*. Given the force of McCarthy's prose, the reader must be wary of the seductive potency of the tale. In the passage after Billy and Boyd are surprised by the Indian, McCarthy's description is both precise and tentative:

> [Billy] booted the horse forward and they rode out through the trees. . .
> The indian watched them go. The younger boy rode with one arm around
> his brother's waist, his face red in the sun, his near-white hair pink in the
> sun. His brother must have told him not to look back because he didnt look
> back. (*Crossing*, 8)

The reader does not know, because the narrator himself is not certain, what, if anything, Billy said to Boyd as they rode. A few paragraphs later Billy looks back and sees the Indian following them. Boyd says, "How come you're lookin back?" Billy replies "I just am" (8). This confirms the narrator's hypothesis that Billy did indeed order his younger brother not to look. The narrator's suspicions are usually confirmed—but are they always?

About the Superman syndrome: if a character does a heroic deed, wouldn't you expect other characters to recognize it? About the scary, uncivilized manchild—or man, or child—I would guess that McCarthy believes we are all that way and we don't have to be driven to it. I don't think McCarthy is cultivating it in his characters; rather, I think he's suggesting that his characters already have that wildness in them. He's just putting them in situations where it shows up—and that makes for good stories. The darkness is already there; it's part of you and must be acknowledged. That's precariously close to a theological assertion, and maybe that is the trick in your question. (Because once acknowledged, what do we do about it?) Your question reminds me of one I asked you a while ago, before our present discussion: Why do we need multiple repetitions (to limit ourselves to the Border Trilogy) of what is essentially the same story of love, loss, and heartache? Is McCarthy beating us over the head with *Rightly heard, all stories are one*?

About Billy and Boyd not speaking about the murders, I can almost make myself believe anything. Billy doesn't seem to be the sort of character who would bring it up, as I think he's one of those suffer-in-silence Hemingway types. My theory is that he blames himself for his parents' death, and it goes *without* saying. I don't think Boyd would bring it up on account of his being there. I wonder whether Boyd knows that their parents' death was Billy's fault? I've always thought of him as too young to have pieced it all together.

Heather did come see me in a dream. She was in a room, everything was quiet, the room was empty, I was there too but I didn't speak. She was wearing a peach-colored shirt, and she looked the way she did the last time I saw her. Her eyes were all blue. She didn't say much, but she smiled and said that I was one of the people she wanted to talk with. She wanted me to know that she was all right. I had probably not thought about her in three or four years. When I woke from that dream, I had an email from a high school classmate. "Heather G died last night. Just thought you might like to know." I had not known she was ill. I had no idea about any of it. This unique experience probably explains my fascination with the epilogue of *Cities of the Plain.* Someone needs to write the definitive article on "Dreams in the Border Trilogy."[8]

Are you on the road to Damascus? I think you may be floored by the ending. I was. Still am. I'm angry with Billy over the dog. I haven't forgiven him for that. But the end, with the bomb at Trinity Site, and Billy sitting there in the road—I think it equals the end of *The Wolf Trapper,* and is a commentary on it and an amplification of it. To see Billy sitting there, utterly lost and alone like that—it's the perfect ending. You wonder how Billy ever recovered from it in time for *Cities of the Plain.*

—M

Dear Marty:
In *The Road,* "He could remember everything of her save her scent" (18). But you can remember Heather's scent. The man recalls the look of the theatre in which she held his hand in her lap. I wonder whether it's meant to be the Tennessee on Gay Street in Knoxville, or maybe the Bijou? "Gold scrollwork and sconces and the tall columnar folds of the drapes at either side of the stage"

(18–19). I've asked Wesley Morgan.[9] He has traced "the old frame house with chimneys and gables and a stone wall" (25) and yellow firebrick in the fireplace to the one that burned down on Martin Mill Pike outside of Knoxville. If Wesley can't decide on the Tennessee or the Bijou, *I'll* say that it's the Plaza in Memphis.

Best,

Peter

Well, Peter,

The Bookstar, which was formerly the Plaza, has itself closed since Christmas. The ticket booth and the outdoor theatre signage remain. The Plaza had black walls and maybe curtains, but it was nondescript except for the fact that it shone, beacon-like, in fog, and it predated the notion of the multiplex. In Memphis, for a theatre like the one in *The Road*, you'll need to go to the Orpheum. An old vaudeville house of a theatre, it sits at the southwest corner of Main and Beale. I saw Richard Harris on the farewell tour of *Camelot* there. Hal Holbrook played Mark Twain on that stage. Like many of those old vaudeville houses, it was hot for a while, then became a movie theatre. At some point it burned, but it was rebuilt. It's a grand old place, and it matches, more or less, McCarthy's description. It is, as you would imagine, haunted—by a little girl named Mary who was struck and killed by a horse and buggy. They keep a seat empty for Mary. That's one reason I love the South. Recently the Orpheum showed up in *Walk the Line*, the Johnny Cash biopic. It's where they have the big awards show, and I believe other parts of it appear doubling for hotel hallways and the like. Seeing a place that's familiar to you masquerading as another place in a movie is unsettling. One of its massive exterior brick walls shows up in the film and I think, "I've been there." That happens often in *Walk the Line* because it was shot here in Memphis. I am told, but cannot prove, that Johnny Cash lived next door to the house I live and am writing in now. I would expect Johnny Cash's ghost to be troubled, but I haven't seen him yet.

—M

Dear Old M:

So far, for me, the most satisfying description in *The Crossing*, once we've passed *The Wolf Trapper,* is McCarthy's evocation of the Tarahumara Indians. He is pitch-perfect there, much his old self. The whole thing *works.* So does the rescue of the girl: real old-fashioned boys' book stuff, but rendered for adults and literate. I love the hair of the sleeping girl falling on Boyd's shoulder as they ride. If that's not Robert Louis Stevenson, what is? One of the brothers *ought* to fall in love with her and die for her. Who better to die for? I love the fact—it's so McCarthy—that she wakes up and cooks for them. But then, one could get the impression that all of female Mexico is waking up to cook for them. In the lexicon of *The Crossing,* a female is a creature who brings tortillas to strange young men.

I don't seem to have had all that much of a problem with Part II—other than your sententious, narcissistic catman, that bloviator priest. Can't we arrange

another earthquake for him? While we're at it, let's toss in Senor Flapdoodle's twin: Senor Windbag, the blind man of Part III. Not since Anna Karenina threw herself under a train have I been so glad to rid myself of a character as when Billy departs from Senor Blindness on page 295. He reminds me of a limerick I wrote when I was a kid: "There once was a scholar of Zook/Who gave to the world his Great Book/But they found it so dense/That it made no sense/And a waste of the time that it took." He also reminds me of an old essay (1972) by Woody Allen called "My Philosophy," in which a section called "Eschatological Dialectics as a Means of Coping with Shingles" describes how the substance of the universe is called *atoms* by Democritus, *monads* by Leibnitz. "These 'particles' were set in motion by some cause or underlying principle," Allen says, "or perhaps something fell someplace" (29). That's my response to both the priest and the blind man. A pause, a thoughtful turn of the head like Brando's Kurtz in *Apocalypse Now*, then: "Or perhaps something fell someplace."

When I quoted the ranch agent, I suggested that he was *mildly* quagmiric. For less mild, listen to the blind man—although I shudder to say those words— "listen to the blind man"—for he is the definition of *stylistic quagmire*. "He will not know that while the order which the righteous seek is never righteousness itself but is only order, the disorder of evil is in fact the thing itself" (*Crossing*, 293). O brother Billy! Has ever a man so suffered for grub? The moral that I take from *The Crossing* is this: If you are ever in Mexico and someone offers you eggs—hardboiled *or* scrambled—better to risk death by starvation, for you will surely die of boredom. At the start of *The Tempest*, Miranda says to Prospero: *Your tale, sir, would cure deafness.* Well, here is blindness having its revenge, for its tale hath deafened me. Talk about stopping a story dead in its tracks—but yes, I know, that's McCarthy doing something special and we need to sound the secrets of the authorial mind to appreciate the fact that all of a sudden we are stuck with a clueless blowhard who should have been given a post in the regime against which he had rebelled, for if he had tortured dissidents the way that he tortures me he'd have proven himself a master of the profession. It's narrative mistakes like the blind man, the priest, Alfonsa's history lesson, that once led me to ask, during a conference, whether it might not be true that McCarthy, like Faulkner, is perhaps a better writer than novelist. With Faulkner I think of *Light In August*, in which the entire middle section is inferior to the rest, as if Faulkner didn't see that effectively *explaining* Joe Christmas, a character he had written so indelibly (and completely), was wholly unnecessary and, in the end, self-defeating, for he essentially explains him *away* because the writing is so prosaic. Concerning McCarthy and my question at the conference, I vividly recall the response from a young Stacey Peebles who, as we've seen, has become a fine writer and editor of the *Cormac McCarthy Journal*. She said that my question was "fraudulent" because there *weren't* any faults in McCarthy. Well, Stacey is older now, wiser and wider in view.

But often McCarthy enthusiasts who resist identifying his bad habits, his indulgences, his misfires, are like theologians who reach for a hazy concept to fudge a way around some logical inconsistency or rather obvious fact. For years a fine scholar who loves McCarthy unconditionally twisted herself into an intellectual pretzel to turn *The Stonemason* into a respectable offering by the Master. And if I hear one more word about McCarthy's deconstruction and reconstruction of the Cowboy Myth I'm going to bop somebody on the head. First, it's a bucket of eyewash. No novelist in his right mind—certainly not McCarthy—sits down to dull up his life by deconstructing the Myth of the Cowboy—it's just not how good stories are told, despite that it's how they get interpreted. Second, the cast of characters who stand and gape in wonder at his protagonists have often not seen them do a thing except to pass before their eyes. "The few cars that passed gave him all the berth that narrow road afforded and the people looked back at him through the rolling dust as if he were a thing wholly alien in that landscape. Something from an older time of which they'd only heard. Something of which they'd read" (*Crossing*, 334). McCarthy wants us to know that his men are such exceptions in their wildness, or in their dogged determination, or in their reverse socialization, that there is an observable aura about them. This is his insurance policy: in case he hasn't puffed them up enough to convince you, he shows you the numbers of awed wonderers in order to help you along to the same conclusion, which is: "Wow—scary wildass guys—big time." If there is nobody around, he'll say it to us himself.

Not that I mind it much, but it *is* a mannerism. Nor do I think that it's *darkness* necessarily that he wants you to recognize. What often happens to his people when they've been—what shall we call it?—*wilded*, is that they lose their capacity for certain kinds of tolerance, while, at the same time, increasing their capacity for others (notably for physical punishment), often with a kind of socio-psychic devolution—say, a reckless submission to impulse—a syndrome that can work either for or against their survival. In *The Gardener's Son*, when Bobby returns to Graniteville after his wanderings, it doesn't take much for him to follow an impulse and to plug a few bullets into his father's boss. For which he is hanged. I recall talking to Fred Murphy, the cinematographer (who went on to shoot John Huston's *The Dead* and win an Oscar for *Hoosiers*). "I actually liked the odd way of telling the story and making you fill in the blanks," Fred said. "The only thing I would say is that you weren't *entirely* sure what had happened to Brad Dourif [Bobby McEvoy] and why he came back and who he was when he came back. In a sense, he seemed like a terribly spoiled, self-indulgent character, even though he'd lost his leg."

By the way, you can find the Awed Wonderer Phenomenon even in *The Gardener's Son*. There it is nicely managed. It's when Bobby is playing a variant of what we called mumblypeg—stabbing his wooden leg with his knife—and on the same wagon a boy watches him. The boy just *knows*. And that's not a Western. You will find the same syndrome of Scary and/or Superior Person in *The Stonemason*—or is that, too, a restructuring of the Cowboy Myth? Am I allowed to quote myself?

> *The Stonemason* is literature that makes itself immensely unappealing when its author, despite the play's compassionate message, sends another message, equally plain, in the way that he cannot resist, through the autolithic Ben, looking down on the world of weakness, a curious strain that, although perceptible in *All the Pretty Horses* and *No Country* and, intentionally, the essence of *Blood Meridian*, seems here to have run out of control and to have wrecked his enterprise. This emerges most strangely when we are furnished with the detail that Ben's grandmother loved reading books. This is all we need to know, but that, in *The Stonemason*, could never be enough. She could recite, we are told, all hundred pages of *The Lady of the Lake*. So much the worse for her! As often as I have read this section of the play, my reaction is the same: *Come off of it, Ben—come off of it, McCarthy—can't you leave the old bird alone?* (Josyph, *Adventures*, 121)

And this about Ben:

At hewn stone he is, of course, an *obermensch*, laying seven hundred eighty-two at a time and, like John Grady in *All the Pretty Horses*, drawing galleries of adorers (as his grandmother must have done with *Lady of the Lake*)...
(123)

About the issue of wildness working against the interests of a character, even Billy admits that he didn't do a very good job of minding his brother. Billy's increased inability to check his impulses (in this case, those associated with a sense of injustice about the stolen horses—a theme that we have seen, of course, in *All the Pretty Horses*) gets Boyd shot and nearly killed. A character can do whatever he wants with his life—it's no skin off my nose if Billy and Boyd want to abuse their bodies—and their horses—for the sake of reclaiming other horses—but I cannot say that I am all that sympathetic. I do, however, like the fact that Billy seeks home in the war. There must be much written about the symbolism involved in being kept out of the war because of a murmur in the heart. I could see it being said that, as one definition of *murmur* is *a low continuous indistinct sound without the production of articulate speech*, it could be a definition of Billy's life, and we are the physicians who listen in to hear it—and so forth. It's a nice touch however you interpret it, and even if you don't.

Your dream of Heather is remarkable. Dreams are nearly always expressions—little dramatic reenactments—of moments of brief anxiety during the previous day, and not necessarily moments of highest import: dreams are equal opportunity expressants. It is also the case that whoever we see in a dream is generally an actor standing in for the person or subject involved in that anxiety. In other words, if you had had a normal dream about Heather, Heather would be standing in for someone or something else. But I have noticed an exception to this reliable rule: whenever my father visits me in a dream, or, better to say, whenever I dream my father, the dream does appear to be about *him*. Perhaps this impression is only because his presence in the dream is so powerful that I am unable to push past him in my interpretation. But this exception or seeming exception in my case leaves me open to accept that your Heather dream was really about Heather herself, and I can even believe that her spirit visited you to a degree that you were able to visualize her in your sleep—in other words, it wasn't *about* Heather, it *was* Heather. I know nothing of spirit, but if, in fact, spirit is not physical, then it is nonspatial and notions of distance and proximity don't apply. Heather visiting you is less a journey than a communication.

In reading Aristotle, I have found it the case that certain sentences, when extracted from the arguments in which they appear, are more compelling or evocative than the arguments themselves. Such a case is this from *De Somniis*: "Not every presentation which occurs in sleep is necessarily a dream" (625). Aristotle is talking about sense impressions, and Heather had to be that or you couldn't have "seen" her, but was it necessarily in a dream per se? That, to me, is the provocative idea. Might it not have been more of a visitation? You didn't prophesy in your sleep, for—as I understand it—it wasn't that Heather appeared to have died in your sleep and then she died in waking reality, it was that she died and then came to let you in on the secret before you awoke for conscious confirmation. I say "and then," but if she had, in fact, died, tempo-rality makes no sense to any entity that we could call Heather. It is not only our conscious thinking but our language itself that is bound to a sense of the temporal, making it nearly impossible to speak about these options *logically*—unless, of course, one is a New Age asshole, which, thankfully, we are not and neither is McCarthy. So let's return to him.

As I said in that essay about *The Stonemason*, McCarthy is disappointingly bad with dreams, for whether or not one likes the anecdotal content of the dreams in the Border Trilogy, and however well rendered they might be, it's a fact that McCarthy writes about them as if he hasn't the slightest notion of how dreams work. I don't know much about much but I do know dreams—it's my field, so to speak—and McCarthy's understanding is no understand-ing, however interesting the dreams might be. As I have also said, McCarthy seems not to have researched even his own dreams to see how they function. And so I am fairly turned off by McCarthy's use of dreams: they seem like writing devices, literary flights, by someone who doesn't know the dream world. It's like reading Don DeLillo, in that dreadful *Falling Man*, about the aftermath of September 11—or, really, reading DeLillo about anything: the *there* that is there is a fraudulent construct—fraudulent, that is, in com-parison to someone who can write. In McCarthy, the *there* is generally real enough that you know he has broken his ass to get it down. Not so with the world of dreams. If X dreams about Y then he's dreaming about Y. But that is nearly never the case. It's as unreal to me as if Billy mounted a horse and it flew through the air.

Best,

Peter

P.S. In verses 185 and 186 of *La Chanson de Roland,* the angel Gabriel comes to Charlemagne and gives him two distinctly cinematic dreams, each of which would take some fancy CGI. One is a fierce battle during a storm in which Charles's men are attacked not directly by the evil heathen Spanish but *by the storm itself,* then by animals, monsters, and devils. The dream ends, unresolved, with Charlemagne grappling with a lion. In the second dream, which is set in Aix (doubtless outside of what became Cézanne's house), a gang of bears appears out of the Ardennes to rescue one of their own, a bear whom Charles is holding in chains. "Sire, give him back to us!" the bears say (95). Their plaint is reasonable:

> "It isn't right for you to keep him here;
> We cannot choose but bring our kinsman help." (95)

One of the king's hunting dogs attacks one of the bears, and this too is left unresolved.

What is interesting here is that God has sent Gabriel to "guard the emperor" (94), and so he "stays close by his head all night" (94). But what, then, does he do for Charlemagne, who is "worn out by grief and toil" (94)? Fills his head with visions of strife—exactly what is needed in sleep between battles! Thanks, Gabe. But then, what can one expect of the angel who also inspired/dictated the Koran, the sourcebook of violence for all the Mohammedans against whom Charles has been fighting? All that blowhard Gabriel can do is to make big trouble. To paraphrase Thoreau, if I ever see an angel coming to me in sleep with the intention of doing me good, I shall run for my life in the other direction. And I am going to tell my friend Tim Hagans, the subversive jazz composer and musician to whom I dedicated my haiku novel *the way of the trumpet,* that if Gabriel approaches with an eye on his trumpet he should tell him to bugger off, for nothing good will come of it.

Let me hasten to add that none of the bears in the bearful scene of Aix that was written and directed by the angel Gabriel, and dreamed by Charlemagne, are any blood relation to the bears in *Blood Meridian.*

Dear Peter,

My first thought is to say, "But don't you see? McCarthy's laying it all out for us in these characters and their dialogues. You want to know what the man thinks about pretty much anything—as far as the big questions go, anyway? His thoughts are all there. He was right to refuse those interviews, teaching offers, and all that other claptrap because, as he has said, *it's all there in the books*, even if it's sometimes elliptical."

This view, however, presents problems. Reading everything any character says as representing McCarthy leads to madness. That McCarthy could believe both the Judge and Tobin seems irreconcilable. And if you hear McCarthy's voice and think, "Ah, that's McCarthy's opinion," you are suddenly not concerned with the character. Or the character is acting falsely. And I suspect that flummoxes you about these dialogues or monologues. I'm not bothered by them, but I find it difficult to articulate *why* I can let these folks speechify so vociferously without being annoyed by their chatter. Maybe I'm interested because (I think) McCarthy is interested. Maybe I'm lulled by the rhythms of the prose. Maybe (in some cases definitely) those characters *would* speak that way. Or maybe it's just the story. Even when I read him critically, I find myself sucked back into the narrative. Let's say I'm looking at dreams in the Border Trilogy. I can read that way for a while, but I have to keep reminding myself to think about the subject or else I am there on the road with Billy and Boyd again. In that way, I understand and agree with Stacey's remark. McCarthy's books have problems and faults, but one of their miracles is that *they are novels* and they refuse to be reduced—by any mode of thinking or method of analysis. I find it refreshing that a few of the conferences have had after-sessions, where folks sat around and read McCarthy aloud. There is always a music to it. A turn of phrase here, a funny little passage there. Something you missed. Something the book does that can't be taken from it. Or expanded upon by anybody.

You are, of course, right to point out problems. And I might even agree with almost every negative comment you've made about *The Crossing*. And yet. . .

Part II: better than you remembered it, eh? I'm waiting for you to reach the end of the novel. I want to know how it hits you this time.

About the dream of Heather, I've no "rational" explanation other than that she visited me. But that explanation suggests loose ends, that I meant something, missed something. Which of course I did. I can describe her, I can tell you about dimples or blonde hair or any other thing, I can tell you her eyes sparkled. She sometimes wore gold thin-rimmed glasses. She cried when Bambi's mother was shot. After the movie we walked into the bright sun and we were different people. Perhaps we held hands. I wish I had paid more attention, wish I could recall specific conversations, wish I could remember more of the sound of her voice. But maybe I don't need to. For me, Heather will always be an odd jumble of Beethoven and laughing and Gershwin and Bambi and popcorn and peach shampoo and bright sunlight and dense fog. The awkwardness of a teenage girl and the older, somber, but reassuring "I just wanted you to know that I'm all right." None of that, though, sums her up. Maybe that's what McCarthy doesn't understand about dreams. And what he does understand about memory and loss.

—M

My Dear Martster:
There is a revealing detail, what gamblers call a *tell*, in Billy's dream of brother Boyd coming to squat by the fire toward the end of the novel when Billy has been trying to bring the bones of his brother back to America. "In the dream he knew that Boyd was dead and that the subject of his being so must be approached with a certain caution for that which was circumspect in life must be doubly so in death and he'd no way to know what word or gesture might subtract him back again into that nothingness out of which he'd come" (*Crossing*, 400).

I have had countless dreams of, and dream conversations with, the dead, many of them famous, as recounted in a book that I wrote (while asleep) called *Morphic Memoirs*, in which Henry Miller, Picasso, Matisse, Blaise Cendrars, Churchill, Hemingway, Kipling, Gide, Camus, Sartre, and other world figures act out roles for which they were cast in the subconscious. During the time that I was focusing on chronicling *not* dreams as anecdotes or narratives (that's another volume) but dreams *as language*—for I often dream in interesting English, a kind of prose-poetry, at times extensively—I recorded these sometimes lengthy conversations with and between the great. In no case did the fact that they were dead enter the fabric of the dream: in these dreams and dream conversations they were completely alive. On the other hand, any time that I dream my father, he is dead or back from the dead (*undead*, which, oddly, is nearly the same in a dream, even though in life to be back from the dead would not be remotely the same thing), and I am acutely aware of the fact, and I wonder whether *he* is aware of it, and whether he'll be back to stay because, as Dylan Thomas says, *after the first death there is no other*, or whether he *will* be recalled and this is a temporary reprieve—and, most of all, *I wonder whether I can mention this to him.* As you have shared Heather with me, let me share my father in an example from *Morphic Memoirs*:

> Dad, returned from dead, looking trimmer than ever he did when he was alive. So good to see him that I can't keep from clapping his shoulders, thrumping his chest: "God Dad you look *great*," but what's behind it is that, knowing he's been dead, *he must be*, I figure, *in a precarious situation and could fall back to the Gloom in the blink of an eye.* It does not seem to matter that, having been dead for thirty years, he has had that eternal time to get in shape for living again, for dead is dead—who is given a second chance? And of course the rule is that I mustn't mention the fact that when he was gone, he wasn't just *gone*—like *gone to the store*, like *gone to Carolina*—no, he was *dead*. Whereas of course: "You were *dead*, damnit!" I want to say. "You don't *know* it? Where'd you *think* you were? How'd you fall back *here*? Will it *last*? What do you want to *do* in this condition?" Instead: "How do you feel?" "Fine," in that quiet way. "Fine. Yeah those dime ponies, they're on order. They may have started paying that soon if they reserved a ticket for me." "Well you *look* great, Dad, you look *terrific*," wanting to add: "And I don't mean for a dead man."

I suspect that McCarthy has had at least one such dream about a soul he has known, so I want to revise and amend my remark that he doesn't seem to have studied his own dreams. At least wtih regard to the circumspection with which the dreamer approaches the undead, McCarthy has got it right.

I have a Japanese friend, Masaki Katahira, whom I met on one of his tribuitve trips to Ground Zero on September 11. He was in full dress regalia as a Japanese firefighter; his little boy Shoto was dressed in the bright orange jumpsuit of a working firefighter; his petite young wife, Saito, dressed traditionally, was carrying flowers for the Ten-Ten Fire House on Liberty Street. I gave him a copy of *Liberty Street* as a kind of thank you, and as a result we started to correspond. At first his neighbor translated our letters, then it was done badly by internet providers. He told me that if the United States were ever attacked again he was ready to help. He sent me Japanese firefighter t-shirts with my name on them. He gave me his cap that said CALL 119. He sent me Japanese films. Knowing that I drink matcha tea, he sent me canisters from a friend who owned a matcha field. I made and painted a wooden firehouse for his son and sent FDNY figures along with firefighter patches from Manhattan. On one September 11 I met Masaki on Church Street opposite the site, walked him over the Brooklyn Bridge, showed him the Woolworth Building and the gaslights in City Hall Park. He brought homemade Japanese flags to present, with makeshift formality, to firehouses and places such as the old First Precinct, a stone fortress of a building (from which you see Popeye Doyle emerging in *The French Connection*) that is now the Police Museum. When we looked at the September 11 displays, Masaki was visibly disturbed, tapping his chest with his fist: "My heart. . . My heart." I don't know where he learned those two words of English. I know that he nearly died on the job in Sayama City and suffered severe post-traumatic stress—in a country in which you are better to die than disgrace yourself and your country by surviving a mishap or a catastrophe. There was no support system available to him. "My sickness is not understood." He was ostracized, reduced to mowing lawns around the firehouse. He had terrifying nightmares. His body was breaking down. Coming to Ground Zero was a way of assuaging his guilt for having lived. "I want to be useful for an embarrassed person of me." He was tributing those who did not make it through September 11—"I cannot write the book and make the picture like Peter"—and he volunteered for any municipality that would take him. He wanted to fly into Haiti from the U.S. after the earthquake. Before that it was Katrina. "I wanted to go to the typhoon of New Orleans." I was the only person to understand his distress. "Some time I think of if there is money, I jump out of Japan and want to work in a side of Peter." When we parted after his visit here a few years ago, he wept uncontrollably on my shoulder. His son had never seen such a display in Japan. I made gestures that he needed to stay strong and that I would help to remind him. I told him that he is a good man, a good father, a good firefighter. His wife left him and took his sweet Shoto with her, "because I had been completely absorbed as a volunteer." Masaki asked me to find out whether he could work in New York. "Now I am 53 years old and am I too old to work there or not?" Impossible, of course. I hesitated to tell him, feared that he would be driven to suicide. I had feared it all the time, now more. "My work is very dangerous as you know," he wrote. "If anything happens to me, please pray for me." Last week, a message from one of his friends: Masaki is dead. I am sure it was suicide. Masaki had asked him to thank me for all that I had done.

What had I done?

What's the point of being a friend if you cannot save a life?

"There might be a place where meaning is not transmitted," Masaki wrote about our software translations, but I blew my chance to hear a clearer call, address a deeper need. I keep seeing him in his white shirt and tie standing on the Brooklyn Bridge as if he were waiting for me to take him off, as if I never came, as if he were forced to jump. *I jump out of Japan. . .* The morning after I heard the news, I awoke (but was not really awake) and, seeing him alone on the bridge, I realized that I should call him, speak to him, let him hear the sound of my voice—despite that he doesn't comprehend English. The voice of Peter-san alone would reassure him. Then I realized no, I can't call Masaki on the bridge or anywhere because Masaki is dead. If I did call him, there would be the discomfiture of wondering whether he knows that he is dead—same as I've felt about my father—and what might happen if I were to mention it? If I ever have another visitation from the dead (or, in the dream, the undead), and if it is not my father, it will be Masaki.

If I could be standing with him again on the Brooklyn Bridge, *really* there, what could I do to save his life that I did not do before?

What could Billy have done for Boyd that he had not done before?

What could Billy have done for John Grady?

What could John Grady have done for Blevins?

What could Black do for White that would ensure a long life for him out of the subway tracks?

Black feels that he has failed in his mission. Billy feels that he failed to take proper care of his brother. I feel exactly the same way about Masaki. But what is *proper care*—and does it even have a meaning in this life when someone is that disturbed, that out of place in his own universe?

Best,

Peter

Dear Peter,

My recollection of Heather's visit is that I never said a word. Of course when I had the dream I didn't know she had died that evening. But your point is a good one. If I had spoken back to her, something would have broken. My purpose in that scene was to witness it. And maybe, years later, to recall it and tell of it. Your story about Masaki seems similar. There's a fatalistic tone, an inevitability, with which you write about his death. Even *before* he appears, he is doomed. And the loss is tragic: for you, for his family, for the people he helped, for *us*. You ask what you could have done to help. "What's the point of being a friend if you cannot save a life?" I just watched *The Sunset Limited* on HBO, and that's the essence of Black's crisis at the end.

But I think McCarthy might say, and I might agree, that it's not about saving, it's about *seeing*, witnessing. Heather is dead, Masaki would have died, you'll die, so will I. But you saw him on the Brooklyn Bridge and you have reported it. He was no more forced to jump than you or I would be. But your scant report makes him matter. Because he *was* on the bridge, because he *did* help others, because you held him while he cried. Maybe that's not enough— for him, for you—but maybe it's all he needed to go on a bit longer. What do you figure is the worth of even a single day in a man's life?

I've also been pondering how Masaki relates to Heather and vice versa. Which is worse, the loss of a family man who was trying to expiate his demons by doing good, or the loss of a young woman, childless, in her early twenties with her "whole life" before her? As it happens, her life was whole, complete, finished—I think too early. Masaki's too, I'd guess. The question "Which is worse?" is nearly a nonsensical question but we ask it anyway. We don't have control over when people we love are taken from us, or how. Billy is trying to deal with that too, and he clearly thinks he could have taken better care of Boyd. And I of Heather, Black of White, you of Masaki. We are given or we make moments with people. And then they are gone. What we do with those moments, how we interpolate them into our own lives, is a tribute to them. In that sense, I think McCarthy's priest in *The Crossing* is right: that bearded heretic berating God for his suffering affected the priest. And the priest told his story. Billy listened. The priest couldn't save the man nor any other, but I don't believe lives are futile, and I don't believe stories are either. Maybe, in the long light of things, the story is enough.

—M

P.S. Masaki "out of place?" Not for you, no, I don't think he was. The life you save may be your own, but the life you live may not be *for* you alone.

Dear Marty:
What did you think of the HBO *Sunset*?
Best,
Peter

Dear Peter:
I thought it was very effective. I enjoyed it more than the Chicago produc-tion.[10] Samuel L. Jackson was particularly fine. And the blocking change for the jailhouse story was especially effective. I liked the final shot in which the camera tilts up and out the window into a kind of sunrise. It gave more clo-sure to the piece. I am struck, again, by the way the play moves. Throughout, Black seems to be getting the better of White—until the end, when White decides that he has no alternative but to tell Black what he really thinks. It's not so much that Black loses the argument. White is written differently. We get less background, he's less fully formed as a character, and his speech is less colorful. All of this seems correct, as White—given his condition—is more

or less incapable of joy and enthusiasm. To play White properly is to under-play him, and I think Jones got that right. But it's *really* difficult to like White. For me, Black's case is more persuasive. But then I like Black as a character more. White is aloof, removed (again, as he has to be). What's interesting to me about White's case is that he doesn't so much make an argument as state a fact, a fact for which Black has no rebuttal. I would like to see Al Pacino play White. Jackson was about as good as I can imagine Black being played. Is it worth seeing? Yes. And I have a feeling there's a lot of subtlety there that will show itself on repeated viewings.

—M

Dear Marty:

The Jones *Sunset* is beautifully rendered, with many fine touches. Jones is a good director, and he and Samuel Jackson are topnotch in this. I like LENNOX AVE. INDUSTRIES scripted over the pocket of Black's janitorial shirt, despite that it's not how you spell Lenox Ave, which is named for a philanthropist and bibliophile, James Lenox, who did a lot for New York. I like the crucifix hanging on the wall under the roll of paper towels in the kitchen over the two-bowled porcelain sink with rust on its unglazed underbelly. I like White's chapped lower lip, and his three shifts of the chair closer to Black while proposing not to make another attempt—a delicious piece of business that might seem trivial but plays a role in bringing the screenplay to life. Yes, it is a momentary detail, but in art there is never a just *only* for details, and as you know, I agree with the primadonna in *The Crossing* (can I play her in the film?) when she says: "I think it is better to make a study of smaller things" (239). I like Jones's first pronunciation of *Jeee-zus*. I love the way that he says *Hap-peeee*! I like the soli-tary orange on the counter, one of the few spots of bright color in Merideth Boswell's superb production design, *superb* being an adjective you mightn't expect to hear about the set of a rundown Harlem apartment. I like "2 × 7 × 52" on the page of Black's marbled notebook, what could easily be the measure of the door he wants to replace. I like Black finger-spraying his hanging plants. I like the double lamp—an old one with a new one clamped under it—by the big old blue easy chair. I like the amber glow on the perimeter of the windows. In fact all of the lighting and cinematography is firstrate—the DP, Paul Elliott, who won a prize for the TV film *Truman*, deserves much credit for this movie.

I much appreciate the beautiful closeup "stills" of the apartment during the credits at the start, the sort of thing I did in *Liberty Street* (I called them, for shorthand, Kubricks), and I especially like the overhead insert of White's coffee cup, unusual angle and isolation of object, especially interesting because *the coffee has nothing to say* and constitutes a pause, a silence, a rest, despite that we hear a dog barking in that silence. One could write a second act—perhaps a monologue—from the perspective of that cup. I like the amusing suggestion of Freudian therapy with White stretched out on the torn couch and Black in a chair behind his head, an especially evocative bit because White, known to Black as Professor, is talking about his father to Black, who is standing in for Freud, generally called Professor by his patients. I like the Foley work (everyday sounds added to the audio track): the sound of someone learning to play trumpet downstairs; the sound of a woman calling someone an asshole, then spelling it incorrectly. I am glad for all the little cuts to the text because, as you know, I am not the greatest fan of the play. And I am fascinated by the daring of Jones's choice to place White *outside* of the duet and thus to render him impervious to any strength of argument.

The two live stagings of the play that I have seen supported my presumption that White was never going to try to kill himself again, at least not in the near future. One feels that Jones's White could say, like John Grady Cole when Rawlins asks him whether he would leave for Mexico without him: "I'm already gone" (*Horses*, 27). Jones's choice makes Black's—and Jackson's—task a hell of a lot harder because he is, in effect, striving to convert to Christianity a man who is already dead to the world, a ghost to himself: the undead. The man in *The Road* says: "If only my heart were stone" (11), but White doesn't need to wish for that: it is already. Jones's choice creates a seeming paradox: it is precisely because White knows that Black can have no effect on saving his life—because his life is already over—that he can linger and accept Black's ministry as possibly the last that he hears from a human being. The last thing he hears could be anything at all—what does it matter?—he's not taking it with him any more than he'd be taking the sound of the subway. But it is apt, in a way, that it should be Black's pitch for Jesus and the Bible, for it represents exactly the kind of drivel White has sought to escape and, in fact, *has* escaped.

Jackson and Jones play so nicely together that I wanted the script to be more of a comedy, more a disquisitional *Odd Couple* with Oscar (White) becoming more and more frustrated by Felix (Black). That's as far out a critique of *The Sunset Limited* as you are likely to hear, but there were several bits in the beginning of the film that made me think of it as a missed opportunity. Even the jailhouse story put me in mind of this, for when Black acts it out, as if to a child, one could easily believe that he is making it all up. It is sacrilege to say that nothing would have been lost had it been written as less of a drama, more of an entertainment, but one of the first rules that I learned as a man of the theatre is that if you make an audience laugh, you can take them anywhere.

As a performer, Jackson is naturally in a position to garner more attention. This is partly, as you suggest, in the nature of his role as compared to that of White; partly in his charisma and skill; and partly due to Jones's choice to render White as a kind of post-holocaustic ghost, a distant nephew to Rod Steiger's pawnbroker—distant because his frustration with Black is amusing at times. But there is a singular virtue in Jones's performance that is equally visible in *No Country for Old Men*. This is the quality of *doing nothing more*, generally a virtue in older performers who no longer have a thing to prove and who, instead of relying on a bankable bag of tricks (actors too have their trick bags), allow all of the old song and dance to fall away and perform with a kind of lyrical purity. I first noticed this phenomenon, consciously, with Henry Fonda's performance as Clarence Earl Gideon in *Gideon's Trumpet*, a Hallmark Hall of Fame film for TV based on a book by Anthony Lewis. As you know from the Gideon v. Wainwright ruling that assistance of counsel *must* be considered essential for fair trial, Gideon was charged with a burglary in Panama City, Florida and, after being *denied* court-appointed representation, managed his own case and was sentenced to five years. Appealing from prison, he claimed that he was denied his 6th and 14th Amendment rights. In time, Abe Fortas (played by José Ferrer in the film) was appointed to plead the case before the United States Supreme Court that led to the landmark decision. In the movie, I was struck by the fact that Fonda, an actor who, like Spencer Tracy, was known for his down-to-earth simplicity—who was ever simpler, more free of *effects*, than Henry Fonda?—had managed to cut his performance even closer to the bone. There was nothing at all there and so everything was there. Similarly, in *No Country* and in *Sunset*, Jones is all sinew, muscle, bone. There's no fat anywhere. During the days when *The Orchard Keeper* was prepping for publication, McCarthy wrote to his editor, Albert Erskine: "As a general rule, when in doubt, do not punctuate, do not hyphenate."[11] This is what you see in Jones: *he is not punctuating.* Of course a part has to lend itself to that approach, but the actor must have the courage of that simplicity, for in art it is always a bold thing to do less in order to make more. Dylan showed that he was aiming for this when, around the release of *Modern Times*, he said that at last he was working with musicians who know *how not to play.* Toulouse Lautrec understood it when he said that at last he no longer knew how to draw. In Zen, it is the point where the arrow shoots you, not you the arrow. As an actor I have felt only once the sensation of working with such apparent lack of effort that it was no longer me, not quite, on the stage. In a one-man play, *An Hour at Walden*, one night Thoreau played me and *I was a little elsewhere*, not quite even in my own body, for it was moving, correctly, without me. The character I had created out of more than a year's work was behaving on his own, and the experience was exhilarating *and* unsettling, for it is no small thing to surrender the kind of artistic control on which you have come to rely for consistency. Now, *you are inspired*: not just breathing but *being* breathed. Marvelous—and scary. In the Zen aphorism *Nothing holding you, nothing to hold onto—you are free*, what is most striking and wise is the *nothing to hold onto*. Artist or civilian, we all want something to hold us safely on the earth, but of course one cannot be free *and* safe at the same time—one of the cardinal tenets of *Suttree*.

It would be nice to have Fonda around to be acting McCarthy. He was alive during *The Gardener's Son*. It was shot in 1976, six years before Fonda died, but I doubt that Michael Hausman, the line producer, could have worked him into a budget of $200,000. Too bad, because it might have rescued Fonda from *Tentacoli*, an Italian thriller about a killer octopus.

I saw Al Pacino's Shylock at the Delacorte Theatre in Central Park this summer before it came to the Broadhurst on 44th Street. He owned the stage. With Al you get your money's worth. It is always a privilege to share a space with him, in this case that plot of ground in Central Park. I've also seen him in *American Buffalo*, in *Richard III*, and on West End Avenue filming *Sea of Love*, on which I did stunt work (long story) and wound up walking into a scene with him— *that's* sharing space. A few days prior to seeing *The Merchant*, I had handed in to Pacino, through a security guard, my *Rue Picasso* screenplay, for which Al would be perfect in the part of Picasso. And you are correct: he would make a

compelling, original White, equally as tortured, but differently. I'd love to play
Black to his White. I'd love to play *the coffee cup* to his White. Pacino's film of
Ira Lewis's *Chinese Coffee* is also, essentially, a two-man play between Pacino
and Jerry Orbach, also set—with cinematic openings out—in a single room
of a small Manhattan apartment. The film is in a boxed set along with *Looking
for Richard* and *The Local Stigmatic*, which is another essentially two-character
play that Pacino had wanted to film for years. The play and the screenplay were
written by an Englishman, Heathcote Williams. Williams is also an actor who
gives an astounding performance reading Dante's *Commedia* on Naxos Audio.
Dante himself is enjoying it with Beatrice in Heaven, teasing her that it was
worth falling in love with her, and writing his love for her, in order to hear Williams reading his *Commedia*.

I thought of *The Crossing* and what you've said about it when I heard this from
White: "The Bible is full of cautionary tales. All of literature, for that matter.
Telling us to be careful. Careful of what? Taking a wrong turn. A wrong path.
How many wrong paths are there? Their number is legion. How many right
paths? Only one" (*Sunset*, 31–32). This perspective very much suits *The Crossing*. Then it occurred to me that White has a "last" meal with Black—Black's
gumbo stew—and that *The Sunset Limited* is, in a sense, one more case of
a McCarthy character paying a high rhetorical price for a meal: an hour of
Black. I must admit, though, that as rough as I find Black's salvationism, he is
easy to listen to compared to the Mexican flapdoodlers in *The Crossing*, or Ben
in *The Stonemason*, or the Dueña Alfonsa in *All the Pretty Horses*. When I hear
them I think: "Black—come back!" Also, in moments when I am only half a
Frankenstein, what you've said about Heather, Masaki, and Boyd makes me
wonder whether White's Last Supper isn't perhaps all the life he ever needs:
a bowl of good gumbo, a cup of black coffee. One can see the amazing leap
as a way of knocking on Black's (not Heaven's) door and of passing through
that array of dropbolts and latches to take a seat at Black's table, a table he had
avoided all of his life.

Did you notice that in the shorter HBO promo for the film, McCarthy's
brown boots are so well polished, so richly toned, that they look almost red?[12]
There is also this line from McCarthy during the brief snatch of rehearsal with
Jackson and Jones: "See, that's the question. But it's not a question—it's an

accusation." I suspect that this is White's line: "Do you really think that Jesus is in this room?" (8) (It is there that we hear Jones's *Jee-zus*.) For someone teaching the play, that would be a sweet little assignment: *Find the question that is really an accusation.* I liked, too, the shot of McCarthy wearing headphones. Brings him a little further into civilization, a feel of the contemporary. Strange, though, that despite establishing shots of the 155th Street/8th Avenue station with its rows of yellow I-beam columns at every few yards, they kept the line about the absence of posts in the subway, along with the line about Bellevue Hospital being *up* when it's 120 blocks *down*town. They also kept references to the subway as a commuter train, which—as every New Yorker will tell you—it is not, and to a train with a name, the Sunset Limited, as if New York subways are named. And no one refers to the subway as a train station—it's a subway, a stop, a station, never *a train station*, despite that a subway *is* a train—that's just how it is in Manhattan. Genet said: "If we maintain that life and the stage are opposites, it is because we strongly suspect that the stage is a site closely akin to death, a place where all liberties are possible" (*Letters*, 12). Yes, but not quite all. New York must not be forced, or even allowed, to stop New Yorking.

I'll be watching again tomorrow night.

Best,

Peter

P.S. Boy that's some patch of real estate for someone on a limited income. In Manhattan one cannot afford a place to piss.

P.P.S. The National Gallery has a Picasso *Cup of Coffee* (1912) in which the cup and the saucer are two pieces of paper, one dark brown with white chalk, one off-white with charcoal. Before Picasso glued them the pieces were pinned, probably to a wall, and if one sees it live one can see the pinpricks. There is other imagery in this stunning masterwork (it made me cry when I first saw it)—a table, a guitar—and there are interesting effects wherever you look— e.g. two boldly chosen patches of wallpaper bleeding off the edge of the picture plane; a stark rectangle of blue alongside the guitar (or a part of the guitar)—but for all that, the brown and white cup of coffee retains its compelling existential power, *without saying anything at all,* not even *I am a cup of coffee.* In other words, it asserts itself without announcing itself. Strong coffee, but one is not to taste it, one is only to know its existence. The insert of the coffee in *The Sunset Limited* reminds me of the Picasso, and the Picasso reminds me of the insert. If, some day, you get to see the Picasso in the flesh—more precisely, *the coffee* in the Picasso—you will be seeing White in Black's terminal apartment.[13]

Dear Peter,

It's not really proper to call Black's stew a gumbo, and I've been curious as to its origins. Although, as they say, you can put anything in a gumbo, it's not like any gumbo I've ever heard of. Mango? Was there pineapple or coconut, too? Sounds to me suspiciously like a Caribbean dish, which wouldn't have been prevalent down here during Black's Southern sojourn. Cajun (the word is a corruption of *Acadian* or *Acadienne*) cuisine is derived from French Creole cuisine. As far as I can tell, the difference between Cajun and Creole food is that Cajon is country and rustic, Creole is more refined and citified. A gumbo, to my mind, is a soup-like dish whose thickening and principle flavor components arise from cooking equal parts flour and fat (which varies by gumbo type) together in cast iron, slowly and for a long time. The mixture darkens, sometimes even blackens, then you add what Cajuns call the trinity: onion, celery, bell pepper, usually green (like a French *mirepoix* of carrot, celery, and onion). Typically, gumbos are seasoned with salt, cayenne, and not much else—maybe a little thyme, a little bay leaf. Always garlic. Black's stew would be shockingly sweet, which might work well with the black coffee but it's not like any Southern food I've ever had—or Cajun or Creole either.

I never saw it that Black had saved White. Perhaps quite the contrary. Black's God is a Protestant one, and so he expects that He will help Black. Being a non-Catholic, that whole notion of an active God working in the world, etc., seems to me a decidedly non-Catholic way of looking at things. A Catholic wouldn't expect God to be that close. Nor would he expect to hear God talking to him. Black's failure to detain White represents a crisis of faith for him because God has let him down. My father was raised Catholic. He doesn't attend Mass—never has—but he maintains a Catholic understanding of the world. One of the most revelatory things he has said about religion was that he intensely disliked the English-language Mass. "I liked it better in Latin. I don't think God ought to be that close." This sentiment might be anathema to Christian doctrine as a whole, but it says a lot about the difference between a Catholic's and a Protestant's conception of God. Catholics never get to approach God directly. Not so Protestants. And I think that's Black's problem. He is presented, at the end of the film, with a God in whom he believes but who has not—as far as he sees it—helped.

—M

P.S. What do you make of the sunrise at the very end of the film? That brought to my mind *Blood Meridian* and a whole host of other McCarthy references.

Dear M:

When I said that in the two previous stagings of *Sunset* I never felt that White would make another attempt, I didn't mean as a result of Black's mission, I meant that in White's decision to remain (or inability to leave), and in the way that White participates with Black, Black's mission is, in a sense, already accomplished, at least insofar as saving White's life, if not his soul. In those stagings it made no sense to think that White was really in danger of killing himself in the near future. With Jones's choice for the part, I felt the opposite: that Black might've been talking to a wall.

Watching the film again tonight, I realized that although I have spent the last several years trying to think of what to say to my dear friend Masaki that would keep him alive, and have come to see that I said nothing at all to him and was totally ill-equipped for the task that was entrusted to me, I do not identify with either Black or White. Unlike White, I am not depressed from disappointment in the things in which I believe; and about Black's Jesus, I feel as White does: I don't think in those terms, I don't believe in those things. I find the idea of salvation offensive. But I *can* relate to Black's enjoyment of life and to his enthusiasm. I am, as you know, a secular enthusiast, especially in my art. Also, I too am a bit of a blowhard; I like to coddle stews (of food and of prose); I own less than anybody I know; I believe in the word (if not the Word); I like John Coltrane; I have worked, as an adult, at the lower end of the scale—taxi driver, stock "boy," sales clerk, security guard, packer on an assembly line, etc. *And* I have failed to save a life. So Black and I have that much in common. By the way: Black's stew has molasses, bananas, mangos, rutabagas, and Black makes a point of explaining that he learned it in New York, *not* in Louisiana, so you are probably right that it's not a Southern thing.[14] I still find it extraordinary that no one volunteered to McCarthy the New York fundamentals, or that, if someone did, McCarthy rejected them. Beyond the blunders I have mentioned, you don't—really, cannot—*leap* into the tracks of Manhattan subways, you simply step off the platform and there you are—it's a drop of a few yards, and if Black were to catch White during his amazing leap "off the edge of the platform" (14), Black would have to have been down in the tracks already, presumably enacting his own suicide. And, as I have said, subways are named in letters, so the notion that a subway called the Sunset Limited is a kind of poetry doesn't wash. If I set a play in Santa Fe between two types who ride their horses to Taos and hitch them to lampposts (as some men still do), it would be taken as typical East Coast arrogance/ignorance to have them refer to riding their horses on the Expressway, and my calling that poetry wouldn't cut it. 155th Street/8th Avenue is served by the IND Concourse line, and its trains are the D and the B. In fact you see a D roaring through the stop at the beginning of the film. Disappointing, too, is Black's satiric reference to a train schedule (there is no such thing for subways), and seeing "when that next uptown express is due" (*Sunset*, 17). We assume that the Sunset Limited is, in the world of the script, an "uptown" express. If Black were on the same platform as White, he would have to have been waiting for an "uptown" train, for the southbound platform is on the other side of the tracks. But Lenox Avenue runs from 110th Street to 147th Street. The avenue stops there because the Harlem River is in the way. At 155th, Black is already above the termination of Lenox Avenue (now co-named Malcolm X Boulevard). Why would Black be taking a subway farther "uptown" if he is working at Lenox Avenue Industries? Could the business have moved and kept the name? Not likely. What business that was not on Lenox Avenue would want to be associated with Lenox Avenue? And, anyway, the next stop on the IND Concourse is *not* uptown. On the surface above the 155th Street station was the famous Polo Grounds, where I saw the New York Giants before they moved to San Francisco. Next stop: 161st Street, the Bronx—Yankee Stadium. That is *not* uptown—that is out of Manhattan entirely. Was Black secretly on his way to a ballgame? Well, no—not that early, and not in the rain. What we *can* say is that the costume designer gave everybody an out, for Black's shirt says **Lennox Ave.** and thus refers to a street that doesn't exist in Harlem. As for White leaping in front of an "uptown" express, if we correct that to being a northbound express, even that doesn't fit the facts of the subway, for the D that roars through the station without stopping during the morning rush "hour"—which is more like two hours and forty-five minutes, from 6:15 a.m. to 9:00 a.m.—is the *south*bound

D in what is known as "peak" direction. In a career of such immensity none of this matters much, other than to verify that Cormac McCarthy, one of fiction's most fine-tooled research machines, dropped the ball here, either because he was writing about New York, or because he was writing a play—or, perhaps, for both of those reasons. A play set in Manhattan doesn't matter as much to him as a novel of the South or the Southwest.[15]

When I spoke with Tom Cornford about the play, I mentioned that Black was not very smart in his choice of topic. If he had had even the most elemental understanding of human psychology, he would have made White comfortable, chatted with him, taken his mind off himself, drank a few cups of mud, and established a friendship such that he could, perhaps, meet with White again—*if he lived*. The notion that he would save White's life by converting him to Christianity in the course of a single sitting is almost insane. After this viewing, my friend Joan, a therapist, made an interesting point about Jones's performance. For her, White was too exhausted to leave at the start, and the very thing that Black was trying to do with White—talk him into Jesus—fired him up, gave him the energy to leave, the will to accomplish his task. Whether or not this was on McCarthy's mind or a part of his discussions with Jackson and Jones, the film lends itself to that interpretation.

Thinking about the way life develops for Black after the rescue of White reminds me of a line in James Baldwin's *The Fire Next Time*. It's in the brief beautiful letter to his nephew, called "My Dungeon Shook," that opens the book. "To act is to be committed," Baldwin says, "and to be committed is to be in danger" (20). The backstory to *Sunset* is that White placed his own life in mortal jeopardy. The story as we know it concludes with Black's life in jeopardy. One could even stretch it and say that in saving White's life and committing himself to do more for him, Black unknowingly inflicted a kind of soul suicide on himself. But on stage and in the film, the ending is just too hokey and stagey for me, too much a Dramatic Moment before the lights go down— or, in the case of the film, up, for after the tilt out the window to what you interpret as a kind of sunrise, it fades *up* to a whiteout. I am also puzzled about the choice of music there, a composition layered over an old field recording made by Alan Lomax of what is described as "8 Kirby Industrial School Girls." Nothing wrong with any of these touches—I just don't find them effective.

They are the sorts of things that one tries out, then removes. "Forget it—we'll go to black after Sam and we'll listen to the neighborhood underneath the credits." Also, to be a nitpicking son of a bitch for a moment, Jackson's reaction to White's final statement of despair and his longing for death is a little forced, as is the entire orchestration of that sequence as written and directed. It reminds me of Lee J. Cobb's conversion at the conclusion of Sidney Lumet's *Twelve Angry Men*: there's just not enough screen time for Cobb to unravel convincingly, and Cobb as an actor wasn't up to the nearly impossible task on that day. Neither, quite, was Jackson with *his* nearly impossible task—but this is just the cineaste in me (you would say the director) who sees that a moment doesn't work as well as it should and wants to know why. Black's "I'll be there in the mornin'" (59) is too melodramatic for me. In Coventry the actor who played Black, Wale Ojo, struck the most beautiful pose after he finished his lines, and that was more eloquent, and believable, than any of his lines after White leaves the room. I'll show you a photo of it. I wasn't impressed with, or engaged by, the suggestion of sunrise before the credits. It was too much of a pointer for me—pointing where I didn't know and didn't care. Overall, though, Jones did an extraordinary job with less than stellar material. And both men are a joy to watch.

Best,

Peter

P.S. Would you like to see a second act?

Dear Peter,

The play itself seems finished, but if I could have a second act I think I'd take it. I'd like to know what White's apparently inevitable suicide does to Black. And I'd like to see Black out in the world instead of cloistered away in his apartment. How you make that work, after the confinement of the "first act," I don't know.

Your comments about the New York City subway system aside, what time of day or night do you figure it is when the play starts? The amazing leap is said to have occurred in the morning. Black says that he was on his way to work. White says that nobody was around. That fact suggests *early* morning. But the noises in the film all seem to be nighttime noises, even though I suspect that New York never sleeps. I'm wondering if perhaps the scene is meant to take place hours after the rescue. Are we in the afternoon of the same day? Morning of the next? These men wouldn't, believably, have that sort of discussion as pure strangers. One might also assume that there would have been police and city officials and ambulances and hospitals, and that would take time. White is clearly a danger to himself or to others, so he could have been locked up if he had seen a judge or even a doctor. I need to fix the time of day or night in my head.

—M

Dear Marty:

Trust me: with *The Sunset Limited*, it won't help to inquire too far beyond what we call the *given circumstances*. Leave that to those of us who have to play the thing. Lend no more circumstantial credence to the fact that White claims that no one was around when he leaped than to the fact that there were no posts in this magical subway station, which is more on C. S. Lewis's Perelandra than the Earth. Make it morning and the station was sparse, and now it is still morning, albeit raining and dark under the clouds. It makes no sense that any authority/institution was ever involved with these men between the rescue and the debate, which is really a second rescue—or second attempt at one. Nothing suggests that: not their description of the event, not from the rest of their dialogue, not the sense that we get from their personalities, not from how things work in McCarthy or McCarthy's Manhattan, perhaps not even from the way they work in mine. You would be forcing the issue, and denying one of the most important hints as to where we are at the start of the play. When White first rises to leave, Black too rises to go home with him. Clearly this is the first time this has happened. If they had been together a while this would not have been a first for that sort of business. Interesting that in the film (not the play) it is raining fairly hard and consistently, but when Black rises to leave with White he puts on a sport jacket, which no one would do unless they had a raincoat as well—but we see no sign of that, and having only a sport coat makes no sense to Black's practicality: it's a flaw in the conception. Jones & Co. might have decided that since Black knows that White will not take him home with him, he's not going out into the rain anyway, but I could then argue that Black is not doing a great job of convincing White that he is determined to leave. In any case, the play begins fairly soon after the two of them sit, having walked together directly from the subway. It's in the dialogue that the scene is not at night: White says so distinctly. Instead of justifying this peculiar dialogue by extrapolating more time for them to know each other, better to realize this is a whole 'nother world, and in the world of *The Sunset Limited*—where subways have names and platforms have no columns to support them and janitors improvise imaginary newspaper articles—strangers will argue religion for ninety minutes in between two attempts at suicide.

After driving through Times Square a few nights ago, I was crawling eastward on 42nd Street when I saw a huge billboard advertising *The Sunset Limited* on HBO. In the backseat was Ingela Ögren Weinmar, a Swedish curator who helped me to hang *Cormac McCarthy's House* at the Kulturens Hus in Luleå, a prosperous seaside town in northern Sweden. She knew about McCarthy from me and my work, but think of what she was seeing in Norrbotten: a small simple house on Coffin Avenue in the old Texas town of El Paso—that was her association. Now she was seeing rather hugely tangible signs of McCarthy's work in Times Square. The billboard features closeups of Jones on the left, Jackson on the right. I returned to the scene to take pictures. It was around seven degrees and I shot for an hour and a half. The result is a cold that is taking my voice away—and some very nice shots of McCarthy's imaginary world lit large in a sea of insanity. I'll enclose a few. McCarthy has indeed entered the modern world.

Best,

Peter

P.S. Toward the end of my least favorite scene in one of my least favorite McCarthys, the wife in *The Road* expresses a sentiment remarkably close to White: ". . .my only hope is for eternal nothingness and I hope it with all my heart" (*Road*, 57). That could easily have been a line for White. It practically is. When White is at the door at the end, he says: "Now there is only the hope of nothingness. I cling to that hope" (*Sunset*, 59). Both the thought and the expression are practically the same. And of course both characters are on their way out of a dwelling to kill themselves. What do you make of the fact that a woman who is certain that her husband and her son will be raped, murdered, and eaten, feels much the same about ending her life as a guy who has taught in a New York City college?

Dear Peter,
I guess being a professor is harder than I thought, especially in New York City!
—*M*

Dear Marty:
That's what *I* was thinking: McCarthy's got some dismal view of New York academics!
Peter

Dear Peter,
About Black putting on his sportcoat (never heard the term "sport jacket" down heah): McCarthy and I are from roughly the same part of the country, though it gets a bit colder in Knoxville than in Memphis. Down here it's common for folks to wear sportcoats without raincoats—even when it's raining. If you had a raincoat you'd wear it, I suppose, but it usually doesn't get cold enough to make the two necessary. Add to that that *we don't walk anywhere.* Driving is how one gets around, so we're not as much in the elements as a commuter in Manhattan. I might not, even if it were raining, grab a raincoat to go with my sportcoat because I'm walking a few yards to my car, driving to where I'm going, and walking a few yards to the door when I arrive. The issue of a raincoat never occurred to me until you mentioned it. Black may not own one, or if he did, it could have been stolen by one of the junkies. He makes a point of not needing things, and I can see his clothing pared down to (almost literally) the clothes on his back.
—*M*

Dear M:
Interesting what you say about the use of sportcoats in the South. It could easily be the cause of the mistake. In Manhattan no one would put one on to go out in the pouring rain, and Black would have to have rain gear in Manhattan, even if only a zipup jacket or parka for colder weather that would serve in the rain. One can buy old coats around the city. Black would know where to go. As an older man, he would know how to take care of himself and his clothing.

The multiple locks tell you that. Southern guys *driving* everywhere—it's an amusing spin on McCarthy's approach to Manhattan. It reminds me of when Woody Allen referred to Mia Farrow driving him places and him getting *off*. No one gets *off* a car, you get *out*. As it is raining only in the film, not the play, the rain might have been a Jones addition—but then, Jones is not exactly a New Yorker himself.

Incidentally, when Michigan State was publishing *What One Man Said to Another: Talks With Richard Selzer*, I cast about for an image that would suit a book of congenial conversations. A nice image of a couple of guys chatting—that's all that I wanted, where exactly—in a café, a rowboat, some ancient arched corridor—I didn't much care. I discovered something: *Men don't talk to each other in Western art*. I finally found something locally, *The Conquest of the Air* by Roger de la Fresnaye, a 1913 oil on canvas in the Museum of Modern Art. It worked well for the dustjacket and the wrap on the CD that I recorded with Raymond Todd for Blackstone Audio. But I can tell you, beyond that the pickins is mighty slim—and I looked everywhere. What does it mean?

Apropos two men talking, I have noticed a major difference between the North or the Nor'east and the South and the Southwest. Here on Long Island, for example, you will never see two mature men driving together. I know that it happens, but rarely enough that if you glance into almost any car you will never see two men above the age of 50 riding alone together in the front, and if you are looking for a pair of men above the age of 60, you can forget it entirely: *it simply doesn't happen*. But a couple of old codgers driving along in an old (or a new) pickup is a common enough sight in the South. I suppose this says something about human relations in the two hemispheres, exactly what I don't know. One approach to writing an Act Two for *Sunset* would be to justify the image of Black and White riding in a pickup together, the way that we see Robert Duvall and James Earle Jones driving together in *A Family Thing*—which, incidentally, was directed by Richard Pearce, who directed *The Gardener's Son*; photographed by Fred Murphy who, as I've said, shot *The Gardener's Son* and who directed second unit on *All the Pretty Horses*; and it was co-written by Billy Bob Thornton who, as you know, directed *All the Pretty Horses*. And Duvall is the blindish old man in *The Road*. So there are a lot of McCarthy connections in that film. With Black and White, don't assume a happy ending. They could be doing a *Thelma and Louise*—sunsetlimiting together—over a cliff. . . and Act Two would be what exactly gets them into the truck.

A different Act Two would be the conversation between the Judge and the Kid in *Blood Meridian*. In both encounters do we have a kind of certainty and religious—or, in the Judge's case, near-religious—zeal facing off against obdurate resistance. In both cases does the one express the need to escape from the other but is hindered by something either within his own psyche or the force of the other man. White's refrain is repeated with little variation throughout the conversation: *I should go, I need to go, I'd better go*, virtually the same as we hear from the Kid: "I got to go" (*Blood Meridian*, 327). It is also the case that both White and the Kid are now being badgered, rhetorically, by a man who presents as a kind of advisor/protector, and both Black and the Judge carry a leatherbound book—Black's Bible and the Judge's ledgerbook—to which each adds his own marginalia, the Judge literally, Black in other ways. Over the years I have contemplated a kind of anthology film consisting of separate dialogues extracted from Shakespeare. One could do the same with McCarthy. Many of them can more or less stand on their own without the necessity of context. Much would be lost, but they would still be powerful—and amusing. They could even be done in contemporary dress. Such a film would be more interesting than 99% of the crap at the multiplex. Of course it would cost a fortune in rights.

One more thing about two men talking that might be another difference between the North and the South, one that works, in this instance, to McCarthy's benefit and that enables me to more or less contradict myself. Despite the accelerated pace of New York as compared to, say, Memphis—or, perhaps, because of it—it's not that improbable for strangers to plunge into a serious conversation and thus to become *unstrange* perhaps more swiftly than their Southern counterparts. And don't forget that when you've interjected yourself between a man and eternity, you have established a bond such as he'll have with no other.

At the start of *Suttree*, during Suttree's first visit to the ragman—not the second visit, in which the ragman begs Suttree to burn his body with gasoline—the ragman says: "They say death comes like a thief in the night, where is he? I'll hug his neck" (*Suttree*, 12). White chooses a different part of the body, but the sentiment's the same: "I rush to nuzzle his bony cheek" (*Sunset*, 59). Love of God, longing for death—these are not small issues. When Nicole Laporte, reporting for *Newsweek*, asked Tommy Lee Jones what *The Sunset Limited* was about, Jones said: "I don't think there is a message. The idea, it seems, is to make the biggest ideas in the history of the world entertaining and immediate. It would seem, therefore, that the questions become far more intriguing than the answers." I am not so sure that suicidal depression's a great idea, but it is certainly a force. I would easily say the same about the notion of God.

Interesting that the sunrise at the end of *Sunset* reminds you of *Blood Meridian*. What about "after a while the right and godmade sun did rise, once again, for all and without distinction" (*Crossing*, 425)? Is there not this theme through-out McCarthy, that the logos of things carries on without regard for the sound and the fury of this man or that, and we can achieve wonders, die, even kill ourselves today but still that morning sun will shine? About that "right and godmade," do you take it as anything more than *inevitable*? Could it be inter-preted as a kind of theism? Do you, as a rightmade Christian, attach special meaning to the lack of initial cap for *God*—or, to put it another way, does it generate tensions within what it means to you and/or to what you think that it means, or would like it to mean, to McCarthy? For me it reverberates the close of *The Orchard Keeper*: "Over the land sun and wind still move to burn and sway the trees, the grasses. No avatar, no scion, no vestige of that people remains. On the lips of the strange race that now dwells there their names are myth, legend, dust" (146).

Interesting, too, that the word *reverberate* does not, as one might think, refer to the repetition of a word: re-verb. It derives from the Latin *reverbare*: to repel. When something is re-sounded repeatedly, it is being thrown away from its source again and again. Remarkable how that meaning developed, no? In Oxford, *our* meaning—those of us on this earth, rather than those who make the Oxford—is only the 3rd meaning. Before that, it is to strike back, repel (meaning 1), or to dazzle (meaning 2). In all those respects, McCarthy reverberates.

Best,

Peter

Peter, Old Man,

Perhaps because I presume that the sun is [G]odmade, I've always read that passage with particular emphasis on *right*, or with some special power given to *and*, as in "right *and* godmade sun." McCarthy is obviously contrasting that sun with the other, false sun in the form of the bomb, so I am not so much reminded of *The Orchard Keeper*, as I believe McCarthy is talking about that specific sun on that specific morning and it doesn't have, for me, that same sort of elegiac tone. I have, however, always thought that passage was echoing the Sermon on The Mount: "But I say unto you, Love your enemies, bless them that curse you, do good to them that hate you, and pray for them which despitefully use you, and persecute you; That ye may be the children of your Father which is in heaven: for he maketh his sun to rise on the evil and on the good, and sendeth rain on the just and on the unjust" (Matthew 5:44–45, KJV). Just before the passage above, there is this: "Give to him that asketh thee, and from him that would borrow of thee turn not thou away" (v. 42), which is especially interesting in light of the fact that the whole of Billy and Boyd's misfortune arises from feeding the Indians. McCarthy doesn't seem to be consciously writing a theological tract, nor do I believe his sense of irony is that savage. But these sorts of thoughts reverberate inside my head when I get to thinking about *The Crossing*. And yes, *to repel* is a fascinating way to think about reverberation. The sound emanates from your mouth at the edge of the canyon, strikes the canyon wall, and is repelled. Which brings up another question involving the Priest's Tale and the nature of God that it posits as able to "create everything save that which would say him no" (*Crossing*, 154). I think the God of that tale is not different from the God who made McCarthy's right and godmade sun. The Priest's Tale seems dedicated to saying what God in fact *isn't*. God's act of Creation in Genesis is an act of *speaking into being*, like Werner Herzog's assertion, the other day on the radio, that McCarthy creates worlds *by dint of declaration*.[16] Did God's words reverberate? If I read Genesis correctly, they couldn't have. McCarthy's do, at least for me.

The questions raised in *The Sunset Limited* are indeed big ones, but they aren't asked, they're asserted, held up to scrutiny, turned about, reflected upon. In short, treated seriously. As in any debate, evidence is brought and the witness is left to decide. Of course *The Sunset Limited* admits of personality, which converts it from a rational exercise into something higher. The story is two men struggling with themselves and with each other. The conflict *is* the story. Dialogue is a very old form of examination. In the West it's as old as Plato, but beginning with the Renaissance, dialogue seems to have become less fashionable. Does it have something to do with individualism as a philosophical notion? Or is the artist, working alone, an exalted seeker of truth? Ask the same about the critic. Sad, too, because dialogue gets at the nub of things in a way that nothing else can.

I wouldn't characterize Black's position as love of God. He's after *faith*, faith in the Divine Nature, belief not only in the existence of a godlike being but also in His goodness. About longing for death, you have to include some notion of lust or desire, not longing merely. Also, in White's case, pride. White might know that his decision is foolish, but he is so certain about his view of things—in the same way that a fundamentalist is certain—that he cannot admit it. Such an admission would destroy him. Here, the questions aren't more interesting than the answers, they *are* the answers. The truth of the thing inheres in complex portraits of these two men, their beliefs, their struggles, and their own internal debates. Herzog's phrase, *by dint of declaration*, is perhaps more complex than Herzog knows. He means *by dint of* in the sense of *by means of*. But *dint* has an archaic meaning: a blow or a mark made by a blow. That's similar to another word: *inspiration*, which is much like Genesis 2:7: "And the Lord God formed man of the dust of the ground, and breathed into his nostrils the breath of life; and man became a living soul."
—M

Dear Old M:
As an artist one is, indeed, inspired by the breath of the gods, but they can be busy elsewhere—presiding over the slaughter of the American Indian, pushing couples out of the top floors of the North Tower, etc.—so it helps to be self-reliant on a lot of hard work. In a very bad film of Kerouac's *The Subterraneans*, Leslie Caron takes a drag on a cigarette and gently blows it into George Peppard's ear. O George! I am not a smoker, but I could become one—that's the breath of a lifetime. If Kerouac could have survived that far into the film

he'd have adored it as well, and viewed it as a moment of both literal and artistic inspiration.

Interesting that John's *In the beginning was the Word* is fraught with ambiguity, as Logos is not only *the word* but THE WORD, meaning THE LAW OF THE UNIVERSE and thus meaning God, so that if the Word is with God then it's really not saying much. Interesting too that King James admits this in the next phrase: *and the Word was God.* So that John begins with a kind of ecstatic babbling, translatable as: "Wow! Son of a bitch! Life! Universe! Holy Guacamole!"
Best,
Peter

Peter, Old Man,
Though not in John so much, the New Testament and Christian dogma taken together suggest that God Himself has personality, and that would seem to me to separate him from the Law of the Universe. God can't violate laws He enunciated, but that also suggests that they are separate from Him. Those observations, however, are fraught with peril, because we are moving into the Doctrine of the Trinity. The Word was "with God" and simultaneously "was God." That's not much different from saying Jesus is God but is *not* God the Father, who is in Heaven. When you start saying there's one thing with three personalities that is/are both unified and separate, well, you're in an area that language really can't do much with.
—M

Dear Marty:
As I said about the priest in *The Crossing*, God is a dead issue for me. And the discussion in *Sunset* seems terribly elemental, really old hat, far from McCarthy at his best—far, even, from art. But the film, while it doesn't attain the level of high art—it would need a better script for that—is indeed a work of art in its own right, and that, of course, derives from everything McCarthy has written and has meant to the artists involved. It also derives from their dedication, talent—and inspiration. Once again McCarthy has had cinematic luck, and one can also say that he has earned it. What's interesting is that, as I suggested

about your friend Heather and *The Crossing*, discussing *The Sunset Limited* with you has changed my relation to the work without necessarily changing my view of it. More than a good film of a weak play that was written by the best prose writer of his day, *The Sunset Limited* is something about which I've had a good discussion with Marty Priola. All of this is just a way of reading Cormac McCarthy, of taking him into the world; and reading McCarthy like this is a way of living a life.

In Robert Drew's 1969 documentary for NBC called *On the Road with Duke Ellington*, the Duke, smoking in his hotel room, says this: "If a man *were* given the power and the privilege of *seeing* God, he still wouldn't have the power to show God to somebody else. Beyond that, it's that much more impossible to show God to an unbeliever. If you don't believe, you can't see him." I wonder how Black would have reacted to that if White had said that to him, or if the Duke had run into him in Harlem and they had got to talking. The humility involved in that first simple statement—"If a man *were* given the power and the privilege of *seeing* God, he still wouldn't have the power to show God to someone else"—seems quite religiously wise to me, and yet so far from Black's conversional enterprise.

Best,

Peter

Well now, Peter,

That's an interesting quote. I've always thought Ellington wise, but this quote suggests he was wiser than I knew.

Living in Memphis, it's not uncommon to be asked, on the street, about your personal relationship with Jesus by someone who is a total stranger to you. I once had a dental hygienist quiz me about that subject while she was cleaning my teeth. Difficult to respond, and more that a little funny. I've never been comfortable with the conversion enterprise myself. Talking about Christianity seems to put a nonbeliever on the defensive almost immediately. I think it's best to simply live your life and do what you do. The Christian *ought to be* different enough from the nonbeliever that the nonbeliever notices the difference and wants to understand it, at which point he'll initiate the conversation.

Black's conversion attempt is clumsy at times, but put yourself in his shoes for a moment. If you had risked your life to save a man who didn't want to be saved—even literally, much less metaphorically—wouldn't you pull out everything in the "trick bag"? Theologically speaking, the problem is that Black's sin is the same as White's: pride. Black is waiting for God to speak to him. But God is silent. Expecting Him to speak to you is an act of supreme hubris.
—M

Dear M:
There has been a play in a small theatre on the Upper Westside off Central Park West called *Freud's Last Session*. Written by Mark St. Germain, it's what the British call a twohander: Freud during his last days in London, and a visitor, C. S. Lewis, who appears during the blitz to talk about religion.[17] Very conventional mainstream theatre is not my thing, but this production is so good at what it does—in the writing, staging, performances—that I recommend it to you, especially as I gather you are interested in Lewis—and, of course, approaches to the concept of God. It has been extended several times and appears to be running forever. I respect it the way that I might prefer a straight-on painting of a tea kettle, or of sailboats in the harbor, over the usual run of amateur expressionist dumpster art. It makes a fascinating contrast with *The Sunset Limited*, for they are both two men with opposing views of religion for which the script provides a room and a situation in which to engage. Someone could write a fine piece about the two. You should take a short trip into Manhattan and have a look. It's inexpensive and brief. The theatre's a little jewelbox. I'll meet you for coffee and discussion and I won't have leaped or even stepped into the subway tracks.

In a collection of Russian proverbs, I read this morning: "With God you may cross the sea; without him, do not cross the doorstep" (38). As you know, it has been my complaint that Black makes the mistake of trying to save White's life *and* his soul in the very same hour of sanctifying grace, and that he might have done better for White's body *and* his soul if he had simply made him feel more at home, without that array of conversion strategies. Clearly the temptation was too much for Black to resist. But that proverb helped me to clarify something: for Black, *it's the temptation of a lifetime.* My friend Tom Sheridan, an Irish Catholic whom I've known from high school, used to love to interpret the look on my face as what he called "blasted." Despite my remaining in a productive state of mind throughout nearly every hardship, he would decide that I was down, then he would love to argue that I could never be *that* down if only I were Catholicized. And of course there was the deliberate conflation, so common amongst proselytizers, of hard luck with faithlessness, of good luck with God, one of the most absurd of religious inanities. Another way of looking at Black's bad timing (in thinking that the timing was perfect for a conversion) is that McCarthy couldn't resist the temptation to place a religious man opposite a man who is so entirely not that he is ready to end it all.

But as an actor playing Black, this reflection won't help me on stage. I need to decide what it is that Black is doing, what *exactly*. It's easy to say that I would like to have White accept Jesus as his personal savior and I will see him at church the following Sunday. But realistically speaking, what is the immediate goal with which I am hoping, as you say, that my God will assist? If I knew that by converting White to Christianity (by convincing him that his life is an empty one because it is empty of belief), White would at least walk out the door with Jesus walking with him, *would that be enough for me*, even if it were no guarantee that White will not step in front of another train? Or do I imagine that no believer will ever kill himself, and that Jesus is the surest way—perhaps the only way—of keeping White alive? As a performer inhabiting Black's psyche, I need to know what it would look like if I got what I wanted, know it realistically moment by moment. Do I honestly expect the Professor to say: "You know, man, you're right—I never saw it that way—let's get down and pray"? Or: "Maybe you've got something there. In all my life of thought I've never heard such things. Can we get together tomorrow for Bible study?" What is the picture that I, Black, want to paint of reality an hour from now in this room, at this table?

You would like to see Al Pacino as White. I would like to see me as White, and in fact Tom Cornford has agreed to direct me in *The Sunset Limited* if we can arrange a venue. But I would also be interested in seeing McCarthy himself playing the part of White. Having sat with him around a breakfast table, my imagination is spurred, now, to see him at the kitchen table with Black. In that case, I would have to be the director. Neat notion—directing Cormac

McCarthy in his own play, the sort of thing one would dream. "Had this odd-ass dream last night in which I was directing *The Sunset Limited,* and somehow McCarthy was both there as the author but also *in* the play—in fact I think he was playing White. . ."

Best,

Peter

Dear Peter,

Your Russian proverb reminds me of a comment William F. Buckley, Jr. once made in a debate. The moderator asked Buckley whether being a Christian made him a better person. The question was something like, "When you wake up in the morning and look in the mirror, is there something about being a Christian that makes you different?" Buckley's response was, "Imagine if I weren't." The audience and the debaters all laughed and they moved on. But Buckley was making a serious theological point. Christianity should change a person. After Black has seen the light, there is no other way. For Black, saving the life and saving the soul are the same exercise. I do agree, however, that Black probably moves in too quickly, much as your friend Tom Sheridan did. I also agree that one can't conflate hard luck with faithlessness, or good luck with God. Witness: Job. As to Black's motive—the WHAT he's doing and why—I would argue that he believes his preaching is not an option but a Christian duty, and I suspect that he doesn't know the outcome or ideal solution—short of some vague notion that White will realize that all is not hopeless. Remember, Black believes in an active God who, in the person of the Holy Spirit, intervenes in situations like these and *helps.* So the outcome isn't all up to him. He has to stir the pot. God's supposed to pitch in. That's the rationale behind my saying that the play ends with Black in crisis. It's not an easy thing for a God-fearing Christian to feel abandoned by God. The slick doctrinaire response is that God takes the long view, that what we want or need or desire may not, in the long run, be the best outcome. That's not helpful, however, when it's your own child lying there dying of cancer. But something allows the Christian to accept it, to deal with it, to move on—and to maintain faith.

I'm not trying to dodge your question. Black hopes for divine assistance, and he hopes that White will see the light. But I'm not sure he knows what that

entails. Church on Sunday? Bible study tomorrow? Black's smart enough to realize that those successes are down the road. If it were me, I'd want White to admit that something is valuable about life and living it. As you have suggested, Black gets closest to receiving this admission when they share that meal, and maybe that's enough. "This is good" (*Sunset*, 42) is not a statement I imagine White making lightly. If the food is good, other things might be good. From there, you can work. But White's a hard case. For Black, though, God is a fact, and God loves White regardless of White's opinion, so Black has a duty *to witness*, this time in the religious sense of the word. What White does with it, what God does with it, is out of Black's control—and that's Black's crisis at the end.

I can see you playing White, inasmuch as I can see myself playing Black. I like Black, I sympathize with his position and his argument. He speaks like people I know, although most of them don't discuss these things as directly—unless prodded. I can see McCarthy playing either or both. But I don't read McCarthy as being as hopeless as White about the present and future of humanity, nor as confident as Black about the Ways of God and Man. McCarthy is right there in the middle of that discussion. Remember *All the Pretty Horses*: "Between the wish and the thing the world lies waiting" (238). One of the questions *The*

Sunset Limited raises is: which is the wish and which is the thing? For me, it suggests that you need both to make the world.
—M

Martheimer:

Look at you, using the Dueña Alfonsa to bolster an argument—and it's a line from her storystopper discourse. But I shouldn't complain about her too much: if she hadn't existed, I wouldn't have met Miriam Colon, who plays her in Billy Bob's film—or what would have been his film if the studios had not deputed his editor, Sally Menke, to cut off a pound of its flesh. Miriam is also in *Lone Star*, a very bad movie that Rick, inexplicably, adores, and in *One Eyed Jacks* with Marlon Brando, about whom she spoke to me glowingly. It's one more favor for which I have to thank McCarthy: being able to sit in Miriam's New York apartment and talk about Brando, John Grady Cole, Billy Bob Thornton. I loved how, in talking about Alfonsa and John Grady, she voiced what we can call the *conscientious ambivalence* of a woman in that touchy situation while, at the same time, revealing how the actor cannot be lost in his or her own personal preparation:

> When I am doing a scene with Matt, I cannot be thinking of an imaginary person who is an American coming into our territory and suddenly he is giving eyes to my niece. *I have to use Matt Damon.* And therefore, no matter what you have established here, intellectually, about who this guy is or what he might do, you have to play with the actor you have in front of yourself. And in my observation as the character, you cannot help but say: "My God, he's very young. He's *very* young." And thoughts crossing: "Could there be cruelty in this young man that comes here to try to make friends with *my* niece? Is he. . . is he okay? Would he make her sad? Would he betray her? Would he betray *us*?" But you have to work with *that* face, *that* sensitivity, and what he is giving you. And of course he gives so much. He was so right for that role. But many things occur to you, even with all your preparation. Observations. He is so young and. . . he looks okay, but. . . mmm. . . I shouldn't be so sure. No, I'd better. . . I'd better not let him in. He's a stranger. What does he want here? Could he be a nice person—maybe?

Miriam Colon—what a doll. Best was when she said: "Mostly, I want to find out exactly what his intentions are, and what is he doing in my *estancia*, my property. After all, he takes care of horses, no?" Wonderful. It was like the primadonna of *The Crossing* calling him a dentist of horses. I also liked it when, in discussing the drastic cuts being made to the film, she said: "Why should everything be in a hurry? Why should one scene go rapidly after the other, moving the action and more action and let's move it, let's move it, okay, let's get it moving! Why should everything be this rush rush rush to the end, rush to the climax, let's get out as soon as possible?" I can picture her saying that to Harvey Weinstein.[18]

Thinking further about dreams in the Border Trilogy: John Grady's dream of horses is rather purple, no? Oddly romance-novelistic for a man of McCarthy's tough texture. Alejandra has a dream when they are together in Zacatecas: that John Grady is carried dead through the streets of a strange town with children praying for him. And there is the moment, not necessarily a dream but dreamlike, in which John Grady senses, correctly, that his father has died. Or did I make that up? In *The Road*, we hear this about the man: "He said the right dreams for a man in peril were dreams of peril and all else was the call of languor and death" (18). But a man is always in peril. Study September 11, who was safe, who was not, proof that, as Thoreau said, *a man sits as many risks as he runs.*
Best,
Peter

Dear Peter,
No, you are not imagining that passage. It's just after Grady watches the doe he's shot die. He sleeps and wakes and: "When he woke he realized that he knew his father was dead" (*Horses*, 282). But the dream he had, if any, is not recounted.

The Border Trilogy has been criticized for being overly romantic, but that's part of its charm, and I believe it works. You forget that the characters here are 15, 16. McCarthy *should* be purple when recounting their dreams, because that's how John Grady would see it. Add to that the whole notion of the Border Trilogy—in some ways a meditation on the end of the cowboy, the end of the West—and that kind of elegiac prose is pretty much what's called for. Alejandra, of course, has that dream because it prefigures, exactly, what *does* happen to John Grady. I remember being shocked when I encountered it on my first reading of *Cities of the Plain*.[19]

While I was looking for the passage you mentioned above, I realized how much *All the Pretty Horses* is about fathers. There's a scene, the last time John Grady sees his dad, where they ride out together. "So thin and frail, lost in his clothes. Looking over the country with those sunken eyes as if the world had been altered or made suspect by what he'd seen of it elsewhere. As if he might never see it right again. Or worse did see it right at last. See it as it had always been, would forever be" (23). I'm finding the novel a good deal more languid and poetic than I remember, and I'm vaguely shocked that you've not unleashed upon it a similar vitriol, which you reserve almost exclusively for *The Crossing*. Although your recent remarks do seem less vitriolic than I remember from before. Am I correct in detecting this change in tone?
—M

Dear M:
Look at this face and read how impressed I am with your defense of the purple horse dream in *All the Pretty Horses*. McCarthy is enough of a genius that he doesn't need us to defend even the worst of his lapses, and this is far from that, it's just a paragraph that came too easily to do proper justice to the story. A better dream in a lesser novel is the boy's dream of the unwound mechanical penguin that (or who) moves inexplicably in *The Road*. There's a credible and a creditable dream. I wouldn't be surprised if McCarthy himself, or his son John, dreamed it. This dream is not the most dramatic in McCarthy—it's not dramatic at all—nor as engaging intellectually as are some of his other dreams (e.g. the Kid's dream about coining in *Blood Meridian*). However—this will sound condescending but I can't think of another way to express it—this dream made me proud of McCarthy for having improved his understanding of dreamery, or what Freud calls the dreamwork.

As for Alejandra's dream of a dead John Grady, he is of course dead to her life now, and of course McCarthy has already written the screenplay for *Cities of the Plain,* so McCarthy knows the fate of his character. He knows it anyway if he counts John Grady among mortals (which is sometimes questionable for this Texas Superboy). One could also see the deathdream as perfectly suitable because John Grady doesn't go to Mexico to ranch, to get away from oil, to find a new father and/or home: he goes to Mexico to get himself killed. For me he fails in that goal, for I agree with Peter Josyph in *Adventures* that the quality of writing in *Cities of the Plain* is so inferior to *All the Pretty Horses* that John Grady Cole isn't the same character; ergo, he lives forever between his grandfather's wake and his ride out to the world ahead—which is, of course, death—but not quite yet.

Best,

Peter

Peter, You Know,

I recall your telling me that Billy Bob Thornton's *All the Pretty Horses* was supposed to begin with a voiceover during that purple horse dream. It would have been a better film if it had begun that way, but the way that film was released, it didn't have time for poetry. The penguin dream does work in *The Road,* although I don't have a clue as to what it means. Ditto the man's dream at the beginning of the book. Their inscrutability may be *why* they work, and I gather that's something of your point about dreams.

Defending McCarthy puts one in a precarious position. He doesn't defend himself, and I don't suppose he's required to anyway, but it only seems fair that someone speak up when he's attacked, especially by the likes of that halfwit B. R. Myers.[20] Your assaults are more effective than Myers' because they come from a ground of admiration. One senses that Myers doesn't recognize the genius of McCarthy; he runs it all down as pseudo-intellectual hogwash. *The Crossing* is a great book. The Border Trilogy is magnificent, even though *Cities of the Plain* is not up to par. The Trilogy is essential, important, and big. The last thing I want to do is discourage people from reading McCarthy, any McCarthy. Even the bad stuff is good—better than most—and deserving of some kind of respect.

I was hoping to get up there for Pacino's *Merchant of Venice. Freud's Last Case* is intriguing. I've been interested in Lewis for a long time, and for several reasons, not least of which is the lucidity of his prose. I believe the radio broadcasts that became *Mere Christianity* are available. It would be fascinating to hear the man himself reading. Lewis's non-apologetics are as good as his apologetics, e.g. his book about Medieval literature, *The Discarded Image*.

Ah that three-legged scrawny dog who approaches Billy and Billy throws stones at, chases away and yells at. For me, the problem with the dog is that it didn't do anything—it just suffers—and yet Billy chases it away. He's rather mean to it. I suppose that it bookends nicely with the wolf, but the incident makes me think less of Billy. He's so alone that he can't even accept solace from a wounded dog. I get that too, but it distresses me. The dog is an innocent, it seeks companionship and is met with cruelty. Which suggests, of course, that Billy has learned nothing. Or that he's forgotten what he knew at the start of the novel. My problem with *Cities of the Plain* is probably similar to yours. The Billy of *The Crossing* is not the kind of guy who will let anybody get close enough to him to develop the sort of relationship he does with John Grady. Unless, of course, Nell Sullivan is right and Billy is really a girl. In which case, all bets are off.

—M

Dear M:
Many years ago I read *The Allegory of Love*, also by C. S. Lewis on Medieval literature. *Out of the Silent Planet* I read when I was 14, along with *Perelandra* and *That Hideous Strength*. Even at that age, and a very strong advocate for *Out of the Silent Planet*, I knew that the trilogy weakened as it progressed (does that remind you of another trilogy?), then went off the deep end with *That Hideous Strength* (does that remind you of another trilogy?). Nothing wrong with bringing the Devil to Oxford, it's just that it didn't work—it was way overdrawn. Years later I read *The Abolition of Man* and *The Screwtape Letters*, then Lewis's own letters, which are always better, for me, when he steers away from religion. As you know, I am anti-religion. I am, at least, pro-hacker, although I shouldn't say that to the webmaster for cormacmccarthy.com. Of course I don't mean Russian mafioso who spread internet viruses, I mean guys who locate, study, and shall we say *inflect* (= tamper and fuck around with) technology as a hobby, and who only make trouble for entities that make trouble for us.

Here is my problem with *Cities of the Plain*: it is not well written. Neither is the screenplay. I remember Mike Hausman—who line-produced *The Gardener's Son*—telling me how they tried to get backing to film *Cities* and nobody would touch it. Ironically, whoever said No helped develop the Border Trilogy. But let's leave *Cities* and get to the dog at the end of *The Crossing*.

I *like* the fact that Billy chases and abuses that poor benighted creature, pelting him with mud and rocks, threatening to pipe him upside the head. For me it's the finest choice in the latter part of the book, really the best and the smartest from a novelist's point of view. There's a toughness about it that appeals to me precisely because it makes Billy unattractive. Billy doesn't want to see himself in the mirror: a fuckedout, beatup cripple of a homeless cur, "Repository of ten thousand indignities and the harbinger of God knew what" (*Crossing*, 424). He also doesn't need *yet another* charge: the dog is, of course, Boyd as well as Billy. Enough responsibility! Enough caring! Enough love! Enough guilt! Enough my brother's sister's horse's dog's keeper—bugger off!

I am sure that you can see the analogy with the thief in *The Road* after the man makes him strip and leaves him to his own crippled karma, naked and without one possession. The novel needed that. So did I. When he returns with the boy to render him mercy—"They went up the road calling out in the empty dusk, their voices lost over the darkening shorelands. . . . hallooing mindlessly into the waste. . . ." (*Road*, 260)—the calling of the man and his son is an echo of Billy when he calls for the dog: "Standing in that inexplicable darkness. Where there was no sound anywhere save only the wind" (*Crossing*, 426).

To be human is to go too far because you have been driven to it. It is also to see that you've been driven too far and to try to take at least a half step back. I like this in both novels, but I prefer the toofarness over the retreat. I recently went a little too far myself in an exchange with someone about the boy in *The Road* as a hopeful kind of vitality and conscience. I said: "In *The Road* I tend to side with the thieves and cannibals. What's the point of the world going all to hell if you still have to behave yourself?" If *The Crossing* had ended with the cur on the run, I might have liked it better. I would have liked both the man and *The Road* a little better if he had *not* shown the thief some quality of mercy, however strained, however enforced by the boy, when they try to return the thief's clothing. I am not being contrary. I wish that *I* were better at chasing the dog away, at stripping the thief down to his barest in the road.

Best,

Peter

P.S. And if, at the end of *Outer Dark*, Culla had cautioned the blind man (another) against walking into the swamp, I might have choked up over Culla's evolution into something resembling humanity. . . but I have seen enough of that when Culla sees his son in the hands of the homicidal triune—"That chap. We could find her and she'd take him" (236)—really the moral climax of the book—and *Outer Dark* is a far better novel for its fierceness, its refusal to appeal, appease, acquiesce, a refusal that follows from a note McCarthy penciled on a manuscript page that is in the archive. Paulo Faria first read it to me when we sat beside each other with the stages of *Outer Dark* composition. It's in Box 8, Folder 1, a page marked "73 April 23rd." It reads: "THEME: the triune kill all that Holme wants to kill—ending w/child." Half an inch away from that a question mark that was *probably* added later—we don't know— makes the note even more interesting. In any case, I rejoice in that gesture of letting the blind man pass toward the swamp without warning. When, at the last conference, a smart scholar explored various biblical connotations of Culla's transgression—I would not call it that—I suggested that he send me the piece so that I could counter his argument. He agreed, but he never followed through, perhaps out of forgetting, perhaps out of fear. That's understandable, but there is a bittersweet pleasure in being opposed—although it is more often the case that literary opposition attaches to some misrepresentation rather than to what you really meant. At least I would have reminded him (and the reader) that the blind man himself invites it of Culla, for when Culla says: "Still I believe you'd like to see your way" (*Outer Dark*, 241), the blind man responds: "What needs a man to see his way when he's sent there anyhow?" (241) This presages the flapdoodlers of *The Crossing*, for it's a question that only has meaning if bumping into a wall or stepping into quicksand or walking in front of a train is of no concern to you—in other words, it brackets civilized behavior for the sake of making a claim for the Ways of the Lord. Go ahead—make your claim, but if you can't finish your thought because the muck is closing over your eyes, don't complain to me.

I celebrate this passage in *Outer Dark* the way that I celebrate the scene in *Tropic of Cancer* in which Miller beds a whore—a twitchity, crybaby of a whore—in her apartment on the Boulevard de Clichy. Restlessly he awaits her return while she attends—*allegedly* attends—her ailing mother. Miller decides to beat it, and during his escape he rummages her purse and retrieves his hundred francs, then he takes the rest of her money—a little tip, you might say, for his troubles. "I pocketed the hundred francs and all the loose change besides" (*Cancer*, 218). I am never not thrilled to read that sentence. "Then, closing the door silently, I tiptoed down the stairs and once I had hit the street I walked just as fast as my legs would carry me" (218). He throws a meal into himself in the Café Boudon, trying to recall whether he really saw the words *first-class* on this irritating (and, in bed, exciting) whore's diploma. It is one of the more exhilarating scenes in literature. My heart leaps up each time that it happens. He robs her and he beats it—thank God! And thank you, Culla, for letting the blind man sink or not sink like a stone into the marsh. Fuck *her*—and fuck *him*!

Does this sound like cruelty? It doesn't feel like it, it feels like jubilation over a job well done by Culla, HVM, McCarthy, and Miller. This is all by way of saying that if I wish to chase away the dog, and strip the thief and leave him in the road, I also wish to take my hundred francs back from that nutcase of a whore and shake the loose change out of her purse in the bargain.

P.P.S. What's all this about a bomb at the end?

Peter,

Your anti-religious stance is somewhat troubling. For me, that's like being anti-literature or anti-science or anti-philosophy. Of course what I'm railing against, more precisely, is that you're anti-theology. Which you may or may not be. One can be pro-theology and anti-religion, I suppose. Theology is an area of study with a specialized body of knowledge that has evolved, like the other disciplines, over many centuries. It provides another way of looking at the world. And it's experiential. It's not in conflict with science any more than mathematics is in conflict with history. The other arts and sciences are as much based on faith as theology could be said to be. We are all limited by how our perception affects the objects we look at to determine what reality is. That's not to say theologians have it right any more than critics or scientists, it's only to argue that writing off the whole discipline seems a bit rash.

Which brings me to the bomb that ends *The Crossing*. We know, because

McCarthy tells us, that the book ends in July of 1945. ". . .in July of that year he drifted south again to Silver City and took the old road east past the Santa Rita mines and on through San Lorenzo and the Black Range" (422). To get to 1945 requires some math from the date on Boyd's tombstone. Walking distance via roads from San Lorenzo to the White Sands proving grounds is about 205 miles. San Lorenzo is almost directly north of the site. Wikipedia reports that the 4:00 a.m. detonation planned for July 16 was postponed due to rain and lightning. On page 425, McCarthy makes a point of saying (twice) that "It had ceased raining in the night." This would fit weather conditions on the morning of July 16. The countdown began at 5:10 a.m. Wikipedia quotes General Farrell, writing in an official report, "The lighting effects beggared description. The whole country was lighted by a searing light with the intensity many times that of the midday sun. It was golden, purple, violet, gray, and blue. It lighted every peak, crevasse and ridge of the nearby mountain range with a clarity and beauty that cannot be described but must be seen to be imagined. . ." Wikipedia also says, "News reports quoted a forest ranger 150 miles west of the site as saying he saw 'a flash of fire followed by an explosion and black smoke.' A New Mexican 150 miles north said, 'The explosion lighted up the sky like the sun.' Other reports remarked that windows were rattled and the sound of the explosion could be heard up to 200 miles away." Now look again at the last page and a half of *The Crossing*: "He woke in the white light of the desert noon and sat up in the ranksmelling blankets. The shadow of the bare wood window sash stenciled onto the opposite wall began to pale and fade as he watched. As if a cloud were passing over the sun" (425).

Note that McCarthy is precise here: he doesn't say a cloud is *in fact* passing over the sun. "The road was a pale gray in the light and the light was drawing away along the edges of the world" (25). There is no sunrise, because "he looked again at the road which lay as before yet more dark and darkening still where it ran on to the east and where there was no sun and there was no dawn and when he looked again toward the north the light was drawing away faster and that noon in which he'd woke was now become an alien dusk and now an alien dark. . . ." (425)

So here's how I read it. The sound of the explosion at Trinity Site wakes Billy and he sees the shadow receding on the wall, the light source moving, starting

to fade. He goes outside. Several times, he looks to the north and sees the light "drawing away faster and faster"—the light from the south, from Trinity Site. That reading also makes sense of the last sentence: "He sat there for a long time and after a while the east did gray and after a while the right and godmade sun did rise, once again, for all and without distinction" (426). Billy calls for the dog and sits in the road and cries. And what, really, is the alternative—realizing what he had just seen? Only a few pages before, Billy is told: "This world will never be the same." Billy replies: "I know it. It aint now" (420).
—M

Dear Old M:
I have a feeling that you might be dealing with at least two Peter Josyphs: the one who is writing to you, and another who is a kind of strawdog and is, perhaps, easier for you to answer when it comes to politics or religion. That's understandable, but I need to separate my Peter from yours. I have read more theology than most of the people I've met, despite that I'm the son of a nightclub dancer and a bookie from Little Italy and was not exactly raised in pursuit of the intellect (which is why I can only show you how to *flunk* the final exam). Who is exactly a theologian and who is not is, of course, debatable, but I've read the two different Pauls, plus Aquinas, Augustine, Anselm, Avicenna, Ambrose, Abelard, Duns Scotus, William of Ockham, Clement of Alexandria (a very big Gnostic!), Boethius, Boehme, Bruno, Bonaventura, Boniface, Theresa of Avila, John of the Cross, Gregory the Great, Ignatius of Loyola, Anthony of Egypt, Francis of Assisi, St. Jerome, the Desert Fathers, Meister Eckhart, Moses Maimonides, Vico, Luther, Erasmus, John Chrysostom, Catherine of Siena, Merton, Lewis, de Chardin, Buber, Watts, Weil, tons of mystics, Eastern theologians and God-fearing philosophers—Descartes, Pascal, Spinoza—who straddle the border between philosophy and theology because of the way that they combine in their thinking, or writers such as Dante who, in the little-read and little-liked *Paradiso*—my favorite of the *Commedia*—presents an astonishing picture of religious adoration, attainment, and deficiency that is more profound, complex, and compelling than many a dry bundle of simplistic theology. This is all by way of saying that if I were, in fact, dismissing theology, you wouldn't be right to say that I was down on what I wasn't up on. How do you feel about astrology? Astrologers

make exactly the same case for taking astrology seriously as you have made for theology.

Thanks for that excellent explication of the bomb at the end of *The Crossing*. I had heard that too, I believe from Rick Wallach. What you say about it in relation to Billy Parham is unclear. You say: "Meanwhile, Billy, who has recanted, calls for the dog and sits in the road and cries. And what, really, is the alternative—realizing what he had just seen. Only a few pages before, Billy is told: 'This world will never be the same' (420). Billy replies: 'I know it. It aint now' (420)." What do you mean when you say that Billy has recanted? Do you mean that he regrets his treatment of the dog? Are you making an analogy between Billy being sorry that he chased away the cur, and scientists of the Manhattan Project feeling a pang of guilt about blowing up the world? Also, "realizing what he had just seen" suggests, in your phrasing, that Billy himself realizes something. Realizes what? Are you suggesting that Billy, who didn't even know that there was a war on, knows about the bomb and it makes him cry? Or knows that something is not right with the world and *that* makes him cry? If that's the case, have we left the issue of the dog in the dust? Lastly, have you quoted the end of the conversation between Billy and the rider—"This world will never be the same," "I know it. It aint now" —as if they are talking about the bomb and know about it? Or as if they are talking about the bomb and *don't* know? Or as if they are chatting together about the world at large (in Billy's case, perhaps, the fact that his brother is dead, as are his parents), and happened to have struck on something that is more profound (because the bomb is about to go off) than they quite realize?

Let's talk, for a moment, about *The Gardener's Son*. You will recall the scene in which Gregg offers Bobby a coin to get the hell out of his office. This spurs something in Bobby, and it carries the hint that Bobby knows about Gregg having tried to seduce Bobby's sister, Martha (as he has done with other employees); but later in the script it is clear that Martha never discussed this with Bobby, and in fact she overtly denies it. It is also evident that this is not why Bobby shoots Gregg. And yet there it is in the film and in the screenplay, complicating the moment for the viewer, as if McCarthy and Richard Pearce wanted more ambiguity than is fair to the viewer's knowledge of given circumstances—or as if they didn't properly make up their minds. I spoke with the cast about this, and with Fred Murphy, the Director of Photography.

"It's not about his sister," Fred told me. "That's an interesting red herring that's thrown in there. The sister even *thinks* it's about her at a certain point. Obviously Gregg used his power to do things to other girls in the mill, but that's a Cormac red herring, a kind of twist. The reason Bobby kills Gregg is vaguely accidental. Bobby didn't walk into his office to kill him. I'm sure he didn't entirely know *why* he was in his office. But that's what the story's about: the forces that are driving Bobby are something that he doesn't have control over. There's his own personal psyche and all of that, but there are cultural forces that put him in that place."

Anne O'Sullivan, who plays Martha, said: "I had always remembered that he shoots him because Gregg had tried to seduce me, or had made seductive moves. Then, when I saw it again, I thought: 'O. Huh. That's a totally wrong memory, because Bobby doesn't *know* when he comes into the office. This is never broached.' Then she tells Gregg's mother: 'He didn't know nothin about it.' I don't know what to say about that. I really don't think Martha *would* have told him. She seems too reserved. She would not start the trouble. She's too private in that way. So I can't figure that out. I think it should have been made more clear. It would have made Bobby's motivation stronger. He had the gun, but I don't think he went in with the intention to kill Gregg. I think if that had come out in the argument in the office, it would have upped the stakes a lot."

Fred said: "In a sense, they are both hotheads, so that's also part of it."

I raised the issue with film critic Andrew Sarris.

"Yes," he said, "they don't establish his motivation. It seems to be almost two people with bad tempers who happen to collide. It felt like an afterthought."

Brad Dourif, who plays Bobby, agreed.

"Unclarified, yes," he said. "That was very much intentional. But sad, in a way, because I don't think that's what they were really trying to say about him. I think he had a bigger problem that goes back to how he valued the kind of life and dignity he had at the old place that was lost. It's a mistake. I don't think it was ultimately handled well. It was because of how he valued them. It was: 'What do you mean *our* kind.' That's where the anger came from, and that's why he could not back down when he needed to. Gregg pushed this guy, and this was not the guy to push."

Jerry Hardin, who plays Bobby's father, said: "My feeling was that this was

a boy troubled by circumstances, unwilling to face the realities of our situation, that we came to work in this factory, because it was a financial necessity,
that we had to put up with the circumstances, because that was the only way
we could live and prosper on some level, and he was unwilling to accept that.
He feels crippled. His associates, let's say, are more like the guys that are in the
Ned Beatty scene. They drink a little whiskey, they do a little gambling—that's
the kind of society he's a part of. And, being young and crippled, he has the
gun. My grandfather carried a gun. This was not so extraordinary. What was
extraordinary was that Bobby pulled it on someone in a position of authority.
My feeling about the boy is that he's a rebel, and that he will learn, and that he
was never the kind of person who was just a murderer, so that there must have
been something that set him off."

What, exactly?

Kevin Conway, who plays James Gregg, said: "It could also be that I don't
want this guy going around telling people that I'm molesting his sister. Is he
spreading tales about me? That coin—he's telling them that I buy young girls?
The coin triggers a definite response in Bobby, but it's a response that Gregg
doesn't expect. I didn't know whether there had been a scene where Bobby
saw in Martha that something had happened. Gregg didn't touch her, at least
as far as we know. But the coin does trigger a memory in Bobby. Gregg is also
fascinated by Brad's character. This guy who seems to follow no rules, McEvoy.
He takes off, comes back, does this—doesn't have any responsibility. I wonder
whether James has ever been out of that town, whereas McEvoy at least has.
Gregg says a lot about work hard, they don't work hard enough, they don't
like *the water* so they left their jobs to go back. But *he* didn't have to work hard
either—he inherited it, and I don't think that escapes him. So I'm not saying
that his death was brought on by himself, but to reach for a gun while another
guy is pointing a gun at you is not a very smart thing to do. And there's a certain cloud that seems to hang over him, that when he sees McEvoy, it brings
out almost primeval kinds of feelings about McEvoy, and Gregg does something irrational. Goes to get his gun when McEvoy is right there. If I had said:
'Get out!' and Bobby turned and got out, I would have won the confrontation,
even though he was not respectful by coming into my office in the first place.
But when he stays, I've got to at least best him with the difference between
us, which is that he is nothing, he's a failure, a terrible human being, a wastrel,
and I am who I am. He doesn't give me that pleasure. He doesn't give me the

victory. But I think Bobby was threatened, he knew Gregg was going for a gun, and he said: 'Don't go for it.' And the lifestyle that he became a part of had made him ready to do that, and the general rage that he had against what was being perpetrated against his family and against his friends and *his kind*, if you will, fed into that."

In *Adventures*, there is my talk with Robert Morgan in which he says: "The story is about moral ambiguity to a great extent. You don't know, finally, why he is so angry. It may have been almost an accident" (148–149).

That *almost* is important. Brad said: "My feeling about that is, they perceived a mystery in the *reality*, in their going over the material, their research. *What really did happen?* And they kind of liked it and they wanted to preserve an ambiguity about what happened. I thought it was clear. They got into an argument, Gregg went for the gun, McEvoy said 'Don't do it,' Gregg did it anyway, McEvoy shot him, left the office, Gregg followed him out, shot at him with a derringer—incidentally, it was very very hard in those days to hit anything with a pistol—he missed McEvoy completely, and McEvoy turned around and shot him again and he died."

Overall, Brad was disappointed in the last part of the script.

"Cormac's sense of dialogue was great, the way that it worked in the first two acts," Brad told me. "But what he chose to do with the third act didn't work—it didn't add up. I thought that the film asked a question of what's wrong with Bobby. In the first act, when they're sitting around the diningroom table, the father says: 'He just has a troubled heart.' So: why does Robert McEvoy have a troubled heart? What's *really* bothering him? That's the question the film asks. It doesn't answer it. I think the attempt to answer the question is in the scene between him and his sister before he's hung. They have a meeting in the street. She has an agenda, which is about money she was offered by Gregg. Bobby has another agenda, and so they don't really communicate with one another. It's not believable that someone in that position, before they are going to be hung, would be able to communicate what he communicates to her, so the scene doesn't work and we aren't really satisfied with his answer."

Brad hadn't watched the film in a long time.

"What struck me this time," he said, "because I've played a lot of crazy people in my life, is how sane McEvoy is. He's arrogant, he's confrontational, but he is very sane in the way that he looks at people, and he really is unafraid to look at them as they are. You know, the South was built on the English system of class—it was people running away from Cromwell, that's how it was made—and McEvoy cannot stomach it.

"I hope if Cormac looks at it again," Brad said, "he will understand what happened in the third act, because his first two acts were very good and workable. If he had had a really good resolving third act, he'd've had a movie. It was close."[21]

Well: that's a hell of a lot of discussion, a lot of uncertainty, around an issue that is central to the film: the shooting of James Gregg by young Bobby McEvoy.

I've mentioned this partly because I've been meaning to share with you some of the wonderful conversations I had with these people. Of course you recall the roundtable discussion that I filmed with you, Bill Spencer, and Chip Arnold in my room at the Menger Hotel in San Antonio one night in which you all spoke brilliantly about *The Gardener's Son*, an event that I have labeled (literally, on the digital tapes) the Lone Star Session because of the liquid refreshment at hand. That night we discussed this very issue, the possible piling on of *too much* meaning or ambiguity, a tendency that Andrew Sarris told me he felt was more typical of a younger director—which Pearce certainly was—because of the fear of being too obvious. But apropos our discussion of *The Crossing*, I wonder whether this syndrome isn't, perhaps, at work in the conclusion of *The Crossing*. I don't mind it that Billy's upset over the dog. I wouldn't mind it if Billy were upset over the bomb. But I find that hard to believe—unless you feel that McCarthy is suggesting that Billy, birdlike, senses that the world has been tipped on its axis. In which case the dog is a confusion of the issue, not a ramification of it. A dog and dog-remorse is quite ending enough for me. Having the bomb as an unknowable strangeness in the background is also fine with me. But I cannot see Billy crying about *both*. It makes no psychological/circumstantial sense.
Best,
Peter

Peter, Old Man,
The ambiguity you speak of is definitely part of *The Gardener's Son,* and your conversations prove the point. I would add only that that sort of ambiguity of motivation seems to be present throughout much of McCarthy. You get so

little inner life that you're forced to disconnect motive from action. There's no reason for the Glanton gang to act the way that they act in *Blood Meridian*. There's no reason the Judge is a child-molester with the ability of teleportation. They just *are* that way. They are not provoked to it. The same is true, I think, of John Grady and Billy. The most motive John Grady has is losing the ranch. Billy has some motivation viz. his family's death and the wolf. But those factors, powerful as they are, do not figure into their ultimate destinies. Nothing about losing the ranch forces John Grady into the relationships he has with women (although maybe—contra what I'm arguing here—his relationship with his mother figures into the process). And Billy—well, Billy's lot in life is that he carries and buries dead things: the wolf, his brother, John Grady. But this arises as much from who he is as from any concrete motivation he might have, such as aiding and defending the helpless.

I do think Billy is crying and has recanted about the dog specifically. Billy is aware of the war, but I don't picture him sneaking into a theatre to catch the latest Movietone News, and I have a hard time imagining him reading the newspaper. What exactly Billy realizes when he sees that remnant of the explosion is open to question. Descriptions of it as brighter than the midday sun suggest that Billy would have been horrified by what he saw, even if he didn't understand it. Seeing that sort of thing with no warning—especially when you're tied, as Billy seems to be, to the natural rhythms of day and night—would probably confuse, frighten, and distress him. McCarthy makes the point that What Billy Saw disturbed the natural order by including the movements, shadows, and calls of the animals as though it were morning. I think Billy cries about that disruption, and the possibility for the destruction it represents. And he cries for Boyd and for the wolf. In *All the Pretty Horses* McCarthy says that John Grady stood like a man come to the end of something. Billy has *literally* witnessed the end of things: Boyd, the wolf, the cur, the pre-nuclear world. He has come to the end of this novel in quite the apocalyptic moment. And all of it—the weight, the enormity, the fear and trembling of it—finds him inadequate. Billy cries over all of these things.

If McCarthy's priest is to be believed, then all these separate stories are one anyhow. So the story of Billy and the wolf is the story of Billy and the cur is the story of Billy and Boyd is the story of Billy and the bomb. Each of them ends with searing, soul-rending loss. And it's Billy who is both its witness and its. . . enactor. . . maybe even its intercessor, though I haven't yet thought that notion through. I like best your last explanation for the exchange between Billy and the rider: Billy is speaking of his brother (and sister) and parents, but the import of the bomb changes how we approach that passage later. It mightn't have been all that profound for them, but I believe it's supposed to be for us.

Finally, you say: "A dog and dog-remorse is quite enough ending for me." I've read that sentence several times and I continually find myself *mis*reading you, thinking you said that "a dog and dog-remorse is *a quiet* enough ending for me." *That's* an interesting concept: Billy, quiet but for the sobbing, sitting there in the vast and silent desert watching the sun rise after witnessing a calamitous event about whose import he can only speculate. Quiet seems the best ending there. The sun rises and things are the same, even though they are unalterably changed. It's a completely different book if someone drives by in a car, sees Billy desperate on the road, and offers him a lift. It's a completely different book if he turns on a radio and hears about the bomb. As it is, we and Billy are left to that great shining sun. Nothing speaks to anybody. No birds chirp with the real dawn. That's a quiet enough ending for me. There's an oddly reverential tone, as though McCarthy's whole point with all this talking and all these stories and all this movement is *Hush! Just listen. . .*
—M
P.S. I'm a damned liberal. I think I may have just argued that *The Crossing* isn't even about what it's about. Or at least, not in the way it *seems* it's about it. I might have a future in criticism after all—or is it politics? Or law?

Dear Old Marty:
To have a future in criticism you need to have a present in criticism. Hopefully our exchanges have helped pry out your pen from wherever you've been hiding it for too many years and has fired you to use it more on McCarthy. This was my secret purpose in asking you to attack me. If, along the way, I have turned you into a "damned liberal," even for the course of a single tongue-in-cheek sentence in which you are really taking a poke at liberals, I'll consider

myself even more successful than I had hoped. It also helps me to keep you out of politics. I'll save that sentence for blackmailing purposes: run for this or that and I'll get Karl Rove to buy ads with that sentence in the middle of the screen. . .

Best,

Peter

P.S. Weeping again today. I miss my dear friend Masaki—horribly. *I want him back.* I want him off the Brooklyn Bridge. Poor Black, working at Lennox Avenue Industries, perhaps with a mop in his hands, picturing White on the platform again. If he reads it in the paper. . .

PART TWO

THE AUTHOR AS VISUAL MOTIF

Cormac McCarthy's House

A MEMOIR

Nobody knows the other side of my house.

KEROUAC

I am working at my wooden table, seated on my wooden chair

with my wooden penholder in my hand, but this does not prevent me

from being in some degree responsible for the course of the stars.

COCTEAU

CHAPTER ONE

Resolution 158

1.

In paintings, as in dreams, all houses are self-portraits. One reason to paint a house—any house—is to find out what a house looks like.[1] On the street there is too much light. In the studio, under the glare of the bright floods, a painter can close his eyes, let a house build him.

Houses are part of the natural history of a landscape, remnants of a remote civilization of which I have only the sparest clues: its dwellings, its people, its bones, its business. Spare because they betoken so little that means anything to me. The house of a hardworking writer signifies something I understand. A great poet's house is something to celebrate. But a motif—which is only an impulse for dreaming in paint, an organizing principle for visual improvisation—does not derive out of admiration, likes or dislikes. It is hardly a choice at all. Nor is it an intellectual process. Walking across Paris, looking to find the house in rue de Villa Seurat in which *Tropic of Cancer* begins, I was walking toward a new series: *Henry Miller's House*. In my apartment at number 6 bis rue Ravignon, diagonally across the cobbled stone from where, in the shipwreck known as the Bateau-Lavoir, Picasso painted the inaccrochable Gertrude Stein and the razorous, death-dealing harlots of Avignon, there was handmade paper from Moulin de Larroque—thick, coarse, impossible to violate—like working on a slice of tree—the finest in the world. Not that I needed to prove *a Paris painter*—it was enough to be writing novels there, assuming the identities of the city and of my narrator-adventurer Matisse, for whom I devoured the streets greedily in eighteen-hour days. On the other hand, why *not* do in Paris what I do back home—breathe in and out between painting and writing—and why *not* Henry Miller? For that, all I needed was a sketch in brown ink or a couple of snapshots.

But Henry Miller's house, number 18 in a cobbled cul-de-sac named after Georges Seurat, ranked among the dullest of any dwellings in the city. Located a few blocks south of rue d'Alésia in the 14th arrondissement, this *maison* belonged in a suburb of Buffalo or Cincinnati—anywhere but Paris. This was anti-Paris, a Paris mistake by which the trustful alliance of the city was taken from me, with the consequence that I was alone—a feeling that is almost impossible in Paris. I took a few perfunctory pictures the way that one mechanically completes a self-assignment, knowing I'd be bringing back the image of a failed day. On another of these excursions I tracked down a location that was less than disappointing or uninteresting, even less than *not there any more*, for along with the building the block itself had been demolished. In Manhattan there is always a block starting up again, but this was not rebuilding: there wasn't a scrap of explanation nor an engine of reconstruction anywhere, and in Paris you can lose an entire street that way, for some of them are barely a block long. But even that rue of nothingness had more of an impact than what was left of the house, or had been done to the house, in which *Tropic of Cancer* begins so powerfully. Even the Villa Seurat of my dreams, in which Miller would talk like this: "Hard to believe there was a time when Miro lived directly across the square, hmm? And everyone else, don't you know, that we knew in Paris, lived across the square too, hmm. . . Yes. . . For approximately four twats they traded in four sighs and a radio. It's all right—I got a whole half a hang from a new neighbor with bless-me-too's. What do you make of that, hmm? Yes. . . I should say so"—even that subterraneous Villa Seurat was somehow closer in spirit to *Tropic of Cancer*. It didn't help to know that Miller wrote parts of *Tropic of Capricorn* and *Black Spring* here. . . or that Salvador Dali and Lawrence Durrell had lived here too. . . or that, in a studio in the back at the top—formerly occupied by Antonin Artaud—Anaïs Nin had kept house here with Miller around the time that she conceived—and aborted—a child by Miller, borrowed 5,000 francs for the printing of *Tropic of Cancer* by the Obelisk Press, and collaborated with Miller on the preface. . . didn't matter that Soutine and Derain had lived on this street. . . didn't matter that this was the door at which Blaise Cendrars—that mythological creature I have tried, in my work, to mythologize further—came knocking (with his only hand) to introduce himself, congratulate Miller on his roundhouse punch of a book, and toss down a few in celebration. . . no, it didn't matter from what perspective I examined that mournful building, trying to conjure up some intimation of magic. The logs wouldn't kindle. *Dead end* was right: this was not a place where *anything* could begin. Henry Miller's house was contraceptive! Intellectually, temperamentally, the idea was perfect. But painting is more an issue of the hand than of the mind—or of the feet.

How was I to know? I had had an idea, but ideas are a dime a dozen—I winds 'em up, spins 'em round—then what? McCarthy's house, too, might have been a dead duck. A house that is more architecturally interesting is not necessarily more of a motif. I am not *Brideshead*'s Charles Ryder. The look of what Poe, in "The Fall of the House of Usher," calls *the mere house* has to at least say, however quietly, even esoterically, the name of the author or his book.

This is all by way of saying that an image arrives and assigns itself to the brush. When that happens it is not for you to argue. When it does not—forget images: paint a picture about paint.

2.

One of McCarthy's namesakes, King Cormac MacAirt (third century CE), recommends a cheerful face and a warm welcome to poets who visit the alehouse—as well as silence during their poems. As a respecter of the counsels of Cormac, I applied that advice to the visit of this poet, through the medium of his house, to my Long Island studio. As for the silence—no; but I wonder whether a third-century alehouse, with or without a king, would have followed that part of the rule either.

Cormac McCarthy's house—I didn't ask for it. I, who have never owned a house, not even in my sleep, have now got a hundred of these houses in my name. Why so many? I would ask that. Having a sandwich in the studio or tweaking a manuscript, I would look up at the walls thinking: *All these fucking houses!* But I might have an answer, at least the beginnings of one.

Returning to the same motif—relentlessly, drunkenly, somnambulistically—helps me to inhibit imagination. Imagination is essential to me as a writer but destructive to me as a painter. So is cleverness, facility, polish, anecdote, *respect for one's materials*. Without contempt for one's materials one is lost to professionalism.[2] In my approach to painting truth is elemental. Elusive, too. Fortunately one can lie to a picture a thousand ways but it will never lie back. Thus painting can be a path to a kind of virtue.

3.

It was my Florida friend Rick Wallach who asked me to make a poster for the second El Paso conference of the Cormac McCarthy Society. He was in the midst of a gladhandle—"I'll see if I can throw some money in your direction" (Gladhandle #6)—when I interrupted him. "*This* is what I want," I said. "I'm going to do a series of variations. A lot of them. I want walls. I want a show." I would choose the best image after painting the exhibition, then hand-letter the poster directly on the piece.

Thanks to an imaginative administrator, Florence Schwein, an exhibition was arranged for the Centennial Museum, which is part of the University of Texas at El Paso. The fact that the Centennial, a three-story building with an 1857 Breese & Kneeland locomotive and tender in front of it, was not an art museum but dedicated itself to the history—natural and cultural—of the Chihuahuan Desert region, did not bother me. Walls—lots of walls there—and I could have some. I went to El Paso, stood on the street with a Nikon instamatic, and took a few shots of McCarthy's small white house on Coffin Avenue in a well-kept, popular neighborhood known as Kern Place, the city's first suburb, an area that bordered on the desert when it went up during World War I. There are parks and a busy strip for college nightlife, but Coffin Avenue—less than two-fifths of a mile—shows no hint of that. On one side of the house were a pickup and two cars, including McCarthy's old purple Barracuda. When a red and white pickup on the street in front of the house started up and drove away, I averted my gaze out of respect for her privacy, I took a few more shots and I disappeared. I had not come for anecdote, had not come to rummage. When I was introduced to McCarthy's sisters at the Manhattan premiere of Billy Bob Thornton's *All the Pretty Horses* (what McCarthy referred to as "his little project," about which I was making a documentary), one of the sisters said: "You're not the guy who goes through his garbage, are you?"[3] "That's someone else," I said. I have spent enough of my life sorting through my own garbage.

4.

The Coffin house is about a dozen blocks from the Centennial, and it is closer to the Village Inn, a kind of luncheonette where, in January 1992, Dale Walker, then director of Texas Western Press (which published Rick Wallach and Wade Hall's *Sacred Violence: A Reader's Companion to Cormac McCarthy*), encountered McCarthy proofing the galleys of *All the Pretty Horses*. I had dinner with Dale one night in El Paso but I don't remember a thing that he said about McCarthy, a lapse that leads me to wonder whether we talked about him at all. But in the *Rocky Mountain News* of April 1992, Dale gave a description of his encounter that is a glimpse into McCarthy's public life in El Paso:

> He was alone, working, bent over his task in his booth, and I went over to say hello, as I've done many times before—in restaurants, bookstores, outside movie theatres. He has a squarish welterweight prizefighter's face which lights up in a broad and good smile, is casually dressed in open-collared cotton shirt and chino trousers. We traded some friendly words and I left him alone, which is what I always do. Leaving McCarthy alone, in fact, is a sort of unspoken conspiracy of El Paso writers and his local admirers. He is not a recluse or inaccessible or unfriendly; he is simply a very private writer who perhaps came to El Paso for privacy (it is a good place to get it).

One afternoon, in a Barnes & Noble on Sunland Park Drive in El Paso, I shared in this leave-alone conspiracy, although *conspiracy* is too strong a word: *confraternity* or *cooperative* might be better. McCarthy passed a foot in front of me, returned an automotive magazine to the rack, and left the store unencountered. Yes, that's him—work well. In fact it was Rick Wallach, who was next to me reading, obliviously, about model airplanes, who shifted into gear as soon as I said: "That was McCarthy."

"Who?"

"The guy who was just here."

"Just now?"

"A minute ago. McCarthy. He was three feet from you."

"Where'd he go?"

"He went out to the parkinglot. Someone picked him up."

After a moment of disbelief, this mountain of indifference to the Cult of

Personality, this professor of Urtext and the primacy of The Written Word, Papa Poststructuralist, moved as fast as I've ever seen him in a Jackie Gleason shuffle out the door. "*What* kind of car? What *color* was it? *Which direction* did he go?" I began to fear a chase such as you see in *The French Connection*. But this endearing display only hardened my belief that the Sanctity of Text In and Of Itself is to be taken with a grain of salt, even—perhaps especially—among its most strident and vocal adherents.

On another field trip to Kern Place, by which time McCarthy had moved, or was moving, to a house on Franklin Mountain by the Coronado Country Club overlooking the border and, across the Rio Grande, the hellforsaken town of Juárez, I returned to the Coffin house after the cars and the pickups had departed with McCarthy, and I took better shots with a Konica SLR, shots I can tell that I never used because there isn't a smudge of paint on any of them. This time, as I recounted in my essay "Older Professions," I walked the grounds a little. There was not much to look at. Two-step stoop at the street with a private lamppost. Weedy hay-colored lawn lost to dirt. Cast-iron fence on the stoop in front of the door. Bars on the windows. A few rugged cacti at the entrance to the drive leading up where the fleet had been parked, an area that is hard to distinguish from the "lawn," making it look as if you could drive clear around to the front stoop. But in the essay I thanked McCarthy's play *The Stonemason*

> for helping me to nose my way, with no map and no working knowledge of El Paso, to the house of which I have painted a hundred pictures, and to nudge me across the front yard, abandoned now to political handbills and soda bottles, to crouch under a low tree and to kneel in front of a few yards of freestone wall, a modest little wall that I had not noticed before, a wall with a rusty pipe and an open bag of trash behind it, a wall such as a man might make in his spare time just to keep his hand in, a wall McCarthy built while constructing one of the sturdiest reputations in America. . . and to put down my pen, my glasses and my paper and to lean my brow against it, not to tribute the man, the work, the wall, or this play that has led me to it, but to ask myself what the hell do I do now that I'm here. . . and to answer that by easing myself down from the pressures of life and to feel myself kneeling on McCarthy's old land and to realize *this is the point of reading*, to

be brought to a place you wouldn't have thought mattered, to touch something you never expected to find, to kneel in dirt you are happy to have
beneath you, to follow an indefensible impulse as if your life depended on
it, to dream the world back that insists on dreaming you, to make an ass
of yourself and to get yourself arrested or chased off or shot in the head or
healed for being a trespasser on property not your own. (Josyph, *Adventures*, 135–136)

Yes. . . but with regard to these houses, that visit made no definitive imprint.
McCarthy's house? This is it—now what? Paint. Good paper. Fresh floods
for the dead spots. Audiobooks to keep my head away from the brush. Those
good metallic pushpins to tack up the work. The novels, the novels or reverberations of them in the underground precincts of mind. That was enough.

5.

When I hung the exhibition during the summer of 1998, a swell spunky
reporter named Betty Ligon, who used to see McCarthy around town and
chat with him cordially but never was able to wrangle an interview ("Sorry,
Betty—I just can't do it"), wrote a very nice plug for the show in a local paper.
"If Cormac McCarthy doesn't go by the Centennial Museum at UTEP to
see Peter Josyph's stunning exhibit of paintings based on the writer's former home on Coffin Avenue," she began, "then he deserves to be called a
misanthrope. It's one thing to keep an indifferent attitude about worship-
ful devotees who hang on his every written word, or about the phalanxes
of journalists panting for interviews, but this is something he, of all people,
should appreciate." Had McCarthy read Betty's headline promotion—"Even
McCarthy Should Appear at This Show"—the author could not have wanted
to rush on over. The reason is obvious. And if he has any taste, he would
have expected the show to be bad—most exhibitions are. Still, when anyone
would ask me—as if I should know—whether McCarthy were going to view
the exhibition, I would say: "I wouldn't expect it, but it's hard to imagine a
guy, *any* guy, would not be at least a little curious to go see sixty-odd depic-
tions of a house in which he has lived and done some of his best work—especially when it's right down the street." I wouldn't have called it misanthropic

(Betty was being sweet), although you could say that it was different—or indifferent. Generally speaking, no one has his house painted at all, never mind a hundred times.

When I was working on my film about the making of *The Gardener's Son*, I wrote to McCarthy asking a few factual questions, and one afternoon he called me at home. During the conversation, McCarthy said that they faced an important choice in making *The Gardener's Son*: to shoot it in 16 millimeter color, or in 35 millimeter black-and-white. Seen in retrospect, the choice of the former was, he said, perhaps the one big mistake they had made. To compliment the fact that, despite an inferior film grade, *The Gardener's Son* exhibits a high level of integrity—I used the word *austere* to describe it—I told him that whenever James Cagney played a bad guy, he liked to invent a way of "dropping the goodies" as he called it—a gesture, a shrug, a little something to soften the character, make him more sympathetic, memorable. This, I said, is something *The Gardener's Son* as a movie never does: it *never* drops the goodies. On hearing the Cagney quote, McCarthy chuckled. To the degree that I pictured McCarthy at the Centennial, taking a few minutes to walk those gallery walls that were strung with his former dwelling and studio, I liked to think that they might, at least, have raised a similar chuckle: brief, quiet, avuncular. But whether he came or whether he didn't, McCarthy, a brilliant man, would have known that this was another McCarthy's house. If these houses are my own artifacts, my own El Paso, then the man of the title has to be my own McCarthy.

6.

For the July 1998 *Texas Monthly*—in which the cover story jauntily asks the question "President Bush?" ("The latest polls show him beating Al Gore," the cover reads under the juvenescent face from *Mad* magazine on a campaign pin, "and he isn't even running—yet. Can George W. Bush win the White House?")—Michael Hall wrote "Desperately Seeking Cormac," a better piece than its title, in which he quotes me as saying about McCarthy: "His house became an image for how I feel about him, his work, the West, and writing in general. Ultimately, it's about any writer who takes his work as seriously as he does" (111). If I were Hall I might have said: "Well, Peter, that about covers the field. Is there anything the houses *aren't* about?"

Facing each other on pages 78 and 79 of the magazine are two illustrations. One of them is a black-and-white photograph by Robert Ardovino of McCarthy squatting in the disembodied cab of an unnamed vehicle (another kind of house) that has been lifted into the bed of a pickup; the other is a house that became the postcard for the exhibition, a house that is now in McCarthy's house in Santa Fe. It is hard to see the man who posed for Ardovino's camera on page 78 as the owner of the house on page 79. . . but then, it is hard for me to see myself behind the quotation attributed to Josyph, as I don't recall being in the article at all, and I can, perhaps, see myself better in the face of George W. Bush, whose 9/11 administration dominated my life and my work for a decade. . . and I can at least recognize the house as a thing that I had a hand in—the modest dwelling of this Rhode Island Shakespeare, as much a Maison Pierre as a Maison de Le Mot, a portrait of the man or the painter I used to be, someone who had not yet gone to Ground Zero but who *would* go there—or somewhere equally impossible—when it was time.

Even so. . . these houses, painted in New York. . . formed out of the madness of my life there. . . inspired by seemingly uninspiring snapshots. . . taking the light from color made in Switzerland, Japan, Germany, France. . . carved, clawed, scroddled, scraped. . . stabbed, scrubbed, blotched, brushed. . . draggled, flung, teased, glued, and pounded into very expensive paper molded by dark hands in a small Mexican town that I've never known because the New York supplier kept it a secret from me (in the same way that no French retailer would tell me the whereabouts of Moulin de Larroque, as if I would travel across France and hike a mountain forest in order to knock on the door of the paper mill, or drive to Mexico, to avoid the markup). . . these houses, while they mightn't have been McCarthy enough to lure him into a gallery, are, after all, reverberations of his achievement, and so too are they, in their own small way, part of the history of Texas.

7.

In the Texas Senate on February 7, 2001, the good senator Eliot Shapleigh offered, and won approval for, a resolution to welcome out-of-towners to El Paso Day. In that resolution he tributed Cormac McCarthy.

In 2006, Shapleigh, a dedicated Democrat descended from the first residents of El Paso, defeated a challenge for the 29th Senatorial District of Texas by a Republican named Dee Margo, about whom the less said the better. . . except that Margo—a friend of the Bushes—followed Karl Rove's advice and hired a protégé and former colleague of Rove, Kevin Shuvalov—of Olsen & Shuvalov, formerly Karl Rove's consulting firm, with which Shuvalov helped elect Bush in 2000—to advise his campaign under Rovean principles—or lack thereof. . . and it was in the gallery of Margo's wife, Adair Margo—who used to live in Kern Place—that I had wanted to exhibit these houses after they left the Centennial. Florence Schwein had tipped me to the Margo Gallery as the best place in town, and Ms. Margo had promised to keep me in mind for her clientele. But as a Bush devotee, she then went to work for Bush 2000 in El Paso, becoming a Bush Pioneer (pledged to raise $100,000), and in 2001 she became chairman of the President's Committee on the Arts and the Humanities. This worked out well for the houses, which were spared the destiny of contributing, by however slight a commission, to the business, the life, and the Republican politics of a woman who supported the criminal conspiracy that, to my surprise, became the next house—the 9/11 White House—to shape and to shadow the principle motifs in my art. In fact my return to these houses to write this reminiscence was, I had hoped, the beginning of a return to my former life as an artist—until I turned up this issue of *Texas Monthly* with Bush's face on the cover and I remembered Ms. Margo and my correspondence with her, which led me to her husband and to further investigation into the Rovean cloacae with which I had hoped not to toxify my worklife again. . . and I see that my intuition, which I had hoped was incorrect, was in fact on the money: House of Bush, House of Saud (as the title of Craig Unger's book aptly phrased it)—those are two disintegrant houses from which I shall never escape, and neither will any of us for a long time to come.

What was I to do, then, but to speak to Senator Shapleigh about the Margo-Shuvalov campaign against him? I knew that the senator was one of the Texas Eleven, a group of Democratic senators who, in 2003, had protested Representative Tom DeLay's redistricting scam by taking off to New Mexico for a month and a half. I also knew that, according to an eleven-vote block rule, Shapleigh's seat—the eleventh for Democrats—was important for the balance of power, for without it the Democratic minority would have no power. Margo lost, Shapleigh won—but what was the battle?

It tells you something about El Paso politics—how small is the city, how high are the stakes—that in the course of nearly an hour's conversation, Shapleigh gave me only a few carefully crafted sentences to use on the record. With Roveans at your heels running slanderous push polls and using whisper campaigns to plant gossip in courthouses, mass mailings, coffee shops and beauty parlors (known as "hair mail"), the rules of discourse cannot be left to goodwill, to a sense of camaraderie and trust. One cannot be too careful. But I had already scouted out most of the details, for which the literature was plentiful. The Roveans practiced every one of the black arts—what the Watergate hustlers called ratfucking—and enlisted even the precincts of art—Adair Margo's gallery—to offer Margo's candidacy as if a senatorial seat were a gift he deserved rather than something to be earned. *It's not what you know*, Margo said openly, *it's who you know.* The campaign tried to prove this by bringing the First Lady, Laura Bush, to appear for him in El Paso. His wife, Adair, was intimately involved, at one point debating Shapleigh in place of her husband, who was no better at his task—and no better suited for office—than the president. Prototypically Republican and fundamentally Rovean, the Margo campaign perfected innuendo that attributed to Shapleigh the interests and favoritism of which Margo himself was guilty, and it demonized segments of society to which Margo was intimately attached, making it sound as if all that were Shapleigh territory—as when push polls asked whether you'd like to have a trial lawyer as your senator, or when they tried to brand Shapleigh as a man who was slandering the University of Texas at El Paso, when in fact it was Shapleigh, not Margo, who was fighting to increase the funding, and raise the standards, for a campus where the graduation rate was an astonishing 3.8 percent. To gain access to one of the most popular men in El Paso, Coach Don (The Bear) Haskins of UTEP basketball, the Bushes invited his team, the Miners, to the White House, and Ms. Margo gave the revered coach a solo exhibition of his juvenile art and posed the coach with her husband for a picture that they then used for campaign purposes ("Miners for Margo") on stationery stamped with the UTEP logo—without, of course, permission from Haskins, who had never endorsed a candidate, was appalled to have been used so poorly, and eventually exacted an apology from Margo.

"Here's a guy who stole a photo of Don Haskins and promoted himself at Coach's expense for narrow political gains," Shapleigh told me. "That gives you a flavor of the Karl Rove era in Texas. And it's exactly the way they think about art. Art's in service of a political end. And that's how Adair Margo became Bush's commissioner of art."

But of course Republican politics are more radioactive than that and, as always, have mortal consequences for the citizenry. One of Dee Margo's donors, ASARCO—the American Smelting and Refining Co.—owned an El Paso copper smelter that contributed to the thousands of tons of lead, cadmium, and arsenic that was deposited in its air, in its soil, and in the blood of its children every year (a business that was finally shut down by the EPA of the Obama administration). A Rovean campaign entails saturating television with ads for which the high cost is met by appealing to, and placating, industries that don't mind pollution in your house or in your lungs just as long as it doesn't enter the political discourse, for they have left what Shapleigh called "a trail of tears" for which they refuse to be held accountable.

"Here is a standard Rovean technique," Shapleigh told me. "Attack and decoy, distract and anger. So on the issue of a hundred-year lead smelter, they would ask: 'How many of you want Superfund?' Naturally, people said no. But when the question was asked: 'How many of you want children with lead in their blood?' that issue resonated in our community."

"I found a quote from you," I told the senator. "'Democracy is best when it is open, transparent, and vigorous.' So you must be a very frustrated man watching what's been happening over the last eight years."

"Our last eight years have been the darkest in American history," Shapleigh said. "Our core values have been threatened. Threatened, abused, annihilated."

I assured the senator that his work in El Paso is appreciated even in New York.

8.

Reading, in *Texas Monthly*, that I had made a sketch of McCarthy's house when I went to Coffin Avenue, I thought: "That's strange, because *I've* never seen it," and I thumbed through the small black Alwych notebooks in which I jot my travels. One of them begins with notations on a Degas exhibition in Miami and shards of conversation from Robert Antoni, author of *Divina Trace*, about which I recorded a talk with Antoni as a favor to Rick Wallach, who introduced me to the novel the way that he had introduced me to *Blood Meridian*:

he ordered me to read it. . .[4] then there is a Freudian slip of the tongue from Robert Bly in a reading at the Walt Whitman House. . . an unsourced line from Louis Kahn ("The sun never knew how wonderful it was until it fell on the wall of a building"). . . gems overheard at a highbrow expo of works on paper in the drill hall of the Seventh Regiment Armory in Manhattan ("He was so arrogant, I should have said: 'I don't sell paintings to anyone who doesn't have better legs than you'"). . . lines from Richard Selzer that I might have wanted to use in *Letters to a Best Friend*, an edition of his letters to me ("They're my *unbaptised* writings"), and—because the Selzer house is on St. Ronan Terrace—a note that Ronan was summoned on charges that he was a werewolf who had eaten a child. . . a reminder to get a biography of Dante, which I neglected to do until yesterday. . . a sketch of Matisse's *Pink Shrimp* (1920) and a prod to start a new Matisse story with that in mind (instead, I wrote a novel about his adventures with Gertrude and Alice during the Great War). . . sketches of musicians at the Café Florian, Piazza San Marco, for another series I didn't do (I painted Venetian pile drivers instead). . . a note that my Uncle Joe arrived in the U.S., sailing from Naples on the *Saturnia*, in 1934. . . a list of cigars for another Matisse novel. . . a description of a Picasso *Glass of Absinthe* that I spent some quality time with, alone, unframed, and from which I could have plucked an olive and taken a green sip (not of the glass, which wasn't green, but of the background, which was). . . and, along with the names of contacts, books, and literary magazines, none of which were ever pursued, there is a brown ink sketch on the muted yellow Alwych paper: Cormac McCarthy's house with at least one pickup beside it. The sketch is execrable and would have served me well if I had remembered it. On the facing page there is a note: *Adair Margo & Dee*. . .

O boy. . . how little did I know at the time, and how little does that little black Alwych notebook know to this day. . .

9.

But to pretend, for a moment, that Texas counterfeiters, big-oil brats and snake oil salesmen are not in the picture: Senator Shapleigh's Resolution 159 for the Texas Senate contains thirteen **WHEREAS**s and two final **RESOLVED**s. Here is the fifth **WHEREAS**:

WHEREAS, One of the most famous authors in the country today is an El Paso citizen, Cormac McCarthy; a writer who was not truly discovered until recently...[5]

...and so, **WHEREAS** McCarthy contributed to a Senate **RESOLVED**... if that was Resolution 159, then my McCarthy houses are Resolution 158... for it is a proud thing indeed to have the author of *Suttree*... *Child of God*... *All the Pretty Horses*... making his home in the town of El Paso... in Texas, in the USA, where there are few such houses because there are few such poets. In writing about *Blood Meridian* and *All the Pretty Horses*, Harold Bloom has said: "I speak of McCarthy as visionary novelist, and not as a citizen of El Paso, Texas" (*Novelists and Novels*, 539), and Bloom does so nobly. Pictures, though, can speak of him as both in one breath. That is at least the ideal—and to reveal about the house that, as Kerouac would say, "it's been there a million years and it doesn't want me clashing darkness with it" (*Big Sur*, 12).

Since the days when these houses and the poster were produced, McCarthy has moved several times, and for years he has lived in Santa Fe. But as a result of these vignettes—decorations, really, which is what all paintings are—McCarthy can move to the ends of the earth: this is his house forever.

CHAPTER TWO

Finding the Where

1.

Standing before McCarthy's house, it struck me that if an enthusiast, setting out with no information—no address, no description—were to walk the streets of El Paso with the intention of finding it, he or she could point to it and say, with certainty: "There it is." When I first found the house on my own with spotty directions and no map, I did not so much look for it as smell for it, or listen. I was impressed, but not with any skill on my part. The house had marinated, with the right amount of grit, the right amount of seed, in Thoreauvian simplicity. The house quoted King Cormac:

I was one who listened to the woods
I was one who watched the stars...

That sounds like poetic puffing up but it's not. The house also said:

I was one fated for
the paper from Mexico...

At one time the neighborhood of Kern Place was introduced and advertised by ornamental arches spanning North Kansas Street. Commissioned by its enterprising developer, Peter Kern, the gate was full of esoteric symbols reflecting Kern's interest in matters mystical—symbols that surely *Blood Meridian*'s Judge Holden could explicate around the campfire—and it was lit by more than four hundred bulbs, a touch that made it even harder to miss and reminded the world that this new neighborhood had been electrified. Now, with the gate gone, the glow in Kern Place was from McCarthy's house, in which the neighborhood has been electrified by placing one word, the right word, in front of another.

At the time McCarthy was there, Kerners might not have agreed about *the glow*, and a friend of McCarthy's neighbor told me that the property was considered an eyesore during his tenure. Artists and students live in Kern Place but it isn't a poor neighborhood: it is higher educated than the rest of El Paso; one of the city's mayors lived here; the president of the university lives here now; and on the streets around McCarthy the houses are generally well manicured. In other words, like most American neighborhoods it looks like Squaresville. And so... if you wish to argue that a way to have found the house was to look for the one that was *the least* manicured, I will agree to drop this issue of *the glow* if you will agree that there is more to McCarthy's house than a frumpy front yard. There is a similar syndrome with Hawthorne's place, the Old Manse, on the Concord River; or Samuel Johnson's in Gough Square; or Delacroix's *maison* in rue Furstenberg; or Poe's little whitewashed morgue of a lovenest in that shitheap the Bronx. Feel it, you'll find it. This is not lyricism, this is more like birdtalk: *homing,* sort of the way old uncle Bill Burroughs could radar his way through a world of hygienic façades to score the nearest piece of H or larcenous old croaker who could write him a ticket to the mainline. It is by homing that out of hundreds of streets and thousands of dwellings in the large Long Island town of Great Neck, I found the one house designed by Frank Lloyd Wright, found it without a map or any references at all—I just closed my eyes, drove around, and there it was—the best, really the *only* house on Long Island and one of the few real houses in New York. And McCarthy's is really the best house in El Paso, not because it is funky—there is plenty of that elsewhere in town—but because of *the quality of the funk,* a funk that was made more perfect and oddly beautiful because of its inhabitant.

One more word about the frumpy front yard on Coffin Avenue. Gardening has its own fateful turns, as McCarthy suggested in *The Gardener's Son* in which, as you know, the son of the title, Bobby McEvoy, kills his and his father's boss in heated cold blood and is hanged for it. There have been gardener-authors, even some, such as my friend Richard Selzer, who have written about their gardens, but in McCarthy's case you have to choose which of the two you want of him—a nice yard or a novel, in the same way that you have to choose interviews or a novel, a memoir or a novel, photographs of him at New York parties or a novel, speeches at award ceremonies or a novel, attendance at your conference or your grandson's bar mitzvah or anything else or a novel. This might be heresy in England, where gardening even appears on the radio, but given a choice between the garden or *The Gardener's Son*, I'll take the screenplay and the film—fuck the flowers. The landscaping on which he broke his back in *Blood Meridian* compensates for the lack of it on Coffin Avenue. Rimbaud: "The hand that guides the pen is worth the hand that guides the plow" (7). Still, along with the people in their fiction, novelists open another portfolio, one that is less in their control and, in some cases, less in their favor; a cast of secondary characters, some sentient, some not—the houses in which they live and work, the two-inch pictures on their dustjackets, their wives, their lovers, their stimulants of choice, the films that are made from their books and so forth—any of whom or which might be scrutinized with a level of attention that could seem out of proportion, and beyond any meaningful connection, to the work on the page. Don't be stupid about it: *it can't be stopped.* Did you imagine you could wrap it all neatly in a book? When you write that well you end up writing with everything you are, everything you do, everyone you know, everywhere you go, everywhere you don't, everything you say, everything you won't.

Although I walked over the property on Coffin Avenue, I never cared to see the inside of McCarthy's house. Anyway, I knew what was there: cotton fiber. . . gesso. . . oil pastel. I am not being clever. To know the inside of a house you would need to know the inside of the inside, and who knows that? Once we have determined how McCarthy's house is furnished, how do we determine how McCarthy's brain is furnished? Easy enough to see McCarthy moving in through that unadorned doorway. No need to imagine what poured out of it: one can read that. But there are no elevations, no blueprints—neither before nor after—for the profoundly pandemonian assembly that is the artist's life. Can you say what happens, truly, to a ship as it crosses the ocean, even in the calmest of seas, let alone a *Bounty*, a *Bismarck*, a *Lusitania*? When a McCarthy enthusiast came to a *House* exhibition in Berea, Kentucky, he was probing my interest—or seeming lack of interest—in the interior of the house, then he volunteered this: "How about an automobile engine in the livingroom?" Fine—I'll take it. Thinking about the mechanics of those narratives, their volatile combustion, nothing would surprise me, least of all a heavy old lump of a dead thing out of a car. Grease on the carpet? Oil in the floorboards? Sparkplugs stuffed in tchotchkes over the fireplace? Coffins are at the start and the close of *Moby-Dick*—one of them is Peter—and without both of them we wouldn't have heard from Ishmael. Who is to say how much the house on Coffin Avenue, along with whatever might be in it, had or hadn't to do with McCarthy's workday—or, to put it another way, while McCarthy was writing *All the Pretty Horses*, do we know to what degree the house on Coffin Avenue was writing McCarthy? At least one can say that they bore that fruit together. And that every architectural façade has its own tale to tell. In some instances everything is facial: exterior is all—or all for now. In *The Fall*, Camus' protagonist says that after the age of forty every man is responsible for his own face. If it is true of a man, it must be true of his house, and of my version of his house, which is really a version of me, for by these houses I have painted another face, perhaps a truer face than is standing in front of the art. But I do insist that a picture is as much a part of the landscape of a town or a country as a tree or a river. All right, then—go ahead: walk in it.

To the ugliness of Chartwell, Churchill responded with the view *from* Chartwell, which he regarded as one of the best in England. But during the rise of the Third Reich the view from Chartwell, aided by documents smuggled from the Foreign Office, included a view of Germany—and of the future—that few Englishmen could, or would, share with Churchill. We can all see it now, as we can all see the view from Coffin Avenue of what, in those days, McCarthy called "my 'western,'" that little patch of pulp that became *Blood Meridian*.[1]

2.

Mentioning the sea puts me in mind of William Langewiesche, who wrote an exceptional book called *The Outlaw Sea* and who went to Ground Zero and made that his study for over seven months before writing *American Ground: Unbuilding the World Trade Center*, about which we have a conversation in my book *Liberty Street*. We talk there for twenty pages but I have no illusions, for no one can know what it was like for him to work in such a place. Look at that site in the prime of its life, then imagine a man *under* it, writing. If that was where he lived, if that was where he worked, then it really was Langewiesche's study at the time—certainly more than the nondescript hotel to which he walked up from the site and where he showered off the dust and slept for a few hours. When we wrapped up the session I was grateful for a memorably engrossing conversation but as for comprehending the task, I could only look at the man and marvel.

3.

One day I walked into one of Picasso's houses. It was number 7 rue des Grands-Augustins in Paris, where Picasso lived and worked under the Nazi Occupation. . . a house that Dora Marr found for him. . . a house where, prior to Picasso, actor-director Jean-Louis Barrault had started a theatre called Le Grenier des Augustins. My friend Tony Rudolf, an English author who had translated a Balzac story, *Le Chef-d'oeuvre inconnu* (*The Unknown Masterpiece*), a tale that is said to have been set in this building, told me that when he, with his fluent French, tried to explain to the concierge what he was there for— "Monsieur Picasso, Madame"—he was told to fuck off and was shoo'd out of the building. I managed to slip in by walking beside a member of a motorcycle club that was meeting on the ground floor of the premises. I stood alone in one of the rooms upstairs, twenty-six feet by forty-six feet, where Picasso had worked through the war. I was glad to be there, I made a sketch or two, but it was an empty room, empty in every corner. What did I find there? Me. There was more of Picasso's place in a play—*Rue Picasso*—that I had set there a decade earlier, and more of Picasso's place in a film that I wrote, another *Rue Picasso* (the one that I gave to Pacino), a decade later. Now, if you were to ask me how to get to Picasso's, or how to get into it, I would have to tell you to see the film.

In Thomas Merton's *The Wisdom of the Desert*, a mellifluous transcription of stories about the Desert Fathers—hermits of the fourth century CE who left crowded cities for lives of contemplation in the deserts of the Near East— there is a striking anecdote about Abbot Macarius, who one night sleeps in a pyramid and, without thinking twice, uses a mummy as a pillow. "The devils, seeing his boldness, flew into a rage and decided to scare him" (57). These devils ventriloquize a lascivious conversation between another mummy and the one on which Macarius is resting his head, as if Macarius were sleeping on a woman who is now being called to the baths. But Macarius, unspooked and unphased, beats it (or her). "Get up and go swimming if you are able," he says. Merton rounds off the story in this way: "Hearing this the demons cried: You win! And they fled in confusion" (57).

I mention this anecdote for anyone who wants to know more about the inside of Cormac McCarthy's house during the time that he was there.

4.

Let's be honest: at this moment I am sitting on a bench in Belle's Park on Centre Street in Jamaica Plain, a subset of Boston. . . and, at the same time, I am sitting on a dock of the bay in Mantoloking, New Jersey, reading aloud from *Visions of Cody*, in which, as you would expect, Kerouac's Sixth Avenue and his metropolitan subway hold their own against this nature all around me (nature—with its delusions of grandeur). . . and, to be strict, I would have to say that I have never been to El Paso, for I have yet to walk it in the rain. But. . . is there rain in one of the pictures? Then I can walk it there.

While I was painting the first hundred of these houses, I wrote my fictions about Matisse and I painted pictures of Paris. I did not paint Henry Miller's house. I did not paint the Bronx-type neighborhood to which I was taken by my friend Laurent Danchin, who published the mad letters of Antonin Artaud (who lived, as I said, in rue de Villa Seurat) and who was eager to introduce me to an American expatriate, a sculptor with a studio in a drugged-out street where a young Arab boy had just been shot in the head.[2] I did not paint the Corsican *patron* who played guitar in his own restaurant in the shadow of Sacré-Coeur. I did not paint the plainsong and harpstrings of the nuns in that church who are up in the rain at dawn to personify mercy for a straggle of congregants—and *for me*, who wanted them to sing my aunt into the heaven in which she believed all her life, and *for me*, who wanted to die in the arms of the music, music that must have known, for it kept repeating the name Josyph (or maybe it was Joseph). I did not paint the lazy transvestite hustlers I passed every night in rue des Martyrs, one of whom was laid back enough to be walking his dog on the job and who, when he saw me biting into a baguette, said, in a voice that was half her business and half just a neighborly walk-of-the-dog:

"*Bon appétit!*" I did not paint the unlabeled bottles of what I called Resistance wine, throat-throttlers that I bought on the street from a crone at the bottom of rue Mouffetard. I did not paint what was once the center of French cinema, the Pathé Studios, burning to the ground in the middle of the night so that the roaring was visible from rue du Mont-Cenis and I could see people in danger on their balconies conversing, with astonishing presence of mind, with the *pompiers* below as to whether the flames were going to reach them. I did not paint the gypsy beggar bent so low, her head half a foot from the ground, that you believed, in spite of yourself, that her affliction was legit until you saw another gypsy beggar three blocks away in precisely the same posture, so that you marveled at the audacity of the deception and wondered whether there was much of a difference between the real and the ruse, given that they spent impossible days in that position, memorizing the sidewalks of Paris too closely. I did not paint the showstopping window display of Messieurs the Aurouzes, a family of ratcatchers from before the Great War who hang stuffed samples of their prey for advertising and who chatted with me genially amidst the pesticides and the traps. I did not paint the window upstairs at 54 rue Lepic, behind which van Gogh wrote to his buddy Émile Bernard that "you will come to realize that in the studios one not only does not learn much about painting, but not even much in the way of a technique of life: so one is obliged to learn how to live, as well as how to paint, without having recourse to the old tricks and optical illusions." (*Letters to Émile Bernard*, ed. Lord, 19). I did not paint the Cité Pigalle, the short cobbled dead-end street just south of Place Pigalle where, at number 8, brother Theo was living with his wife and infant son when, in July 1890, Vincent came to visit on his last trip to Paris, less than two months before his suicide. I did not paint the husky grocer in rue Caulaincourt who used to cut my gray-crusted mite-cratered *mimolette* with a two-handled knife into which he worked his muscle, inching downward into the chewy-hard block of salty orange—orange that comes not from cows that are orange but from the seeds of annatto, which make achiote—and who agreed that this *fromage* is really the tops and who liked it, in a working sort of way, when I told him it was that son of a bitch de Gaulle's favorite cheese, only I didn't call him that, for I wanted my mimolette. I did not paint the tiny little Chinese woman back of the tiny little counter in the art supply shop where I bought my little jar of mineral spirits, walking back up the other side of the mountain with my wedge of mimolette and a few fair sentences, wondering whether, when I lived there forever and had earned the use of a cane, I'd be called Monsieur Pierre. I did not paint Renoir's house. I did not paint the first pair of Paris legs, long and slender, crossed on a shortskirted beauty on the Pont Neuf, huddling with her lover and remembered as if she were five minutes ago; remembered, perhaps, better by me than by her longlost lover. I did not paint the morning adulterers in Saint-Julien-le-Pauvre who, believing they were alone and that the wall of paraphernalia on the chairs in front of them obscured their liaison, loved each other dearly with her head in his hungry lap, redefining religious ecstasy. I did not paint the *glace* that I sauced in a dish with a dark shot of rum when I ducked out of the snow beside Saint-Séverin, or the waiter who was willing to give me a refill, gratis, because he was on my side, like a waiter in Hemingway, and it made the work night a little nicer for him. I did not paint the home of Gertrude and Alice in the street of flowers, 27 rue de Fleurus, where the antiques dealer living there now instructed the maid to show me in and where it took too long for me to orient myself because I had spent thirty years there in photographs in which I was standing *outside* the picture. I did not paint the fascinating number 38 in rue Saint-Vincent, which I photographed rising up, eerily, out of the Cemetière Saint-Vincent, fascinating enough to build a novel around, which I did. I did not paint the workweary high-heeled step on the stair that I heard every night at 6:30. I did not paint God with a Gladstone bag creating the heavens and the earth. I did not paint the Arab Quarter, Château Rouge, where a real estate agent told me that the allegedly egalitarian communist assholes never wanted to rent. I did not paint the florist in the Marais who assaulted me for taking a piece of cardboard that looked like garbage and whose fury took forever to pacify. I did not paint the world's most dismal nightclub in rue André Antoine where, despite the promise of **AMBIANCE** and **SPECTACLES**, one could not imagine a human form, French or otherwise, entering the grungy doorway under the neon **BEVERLY**, flanked, on either side, by neon Beverly nudes in high neon heels who, because of the way they are wired, look as if they are being hanged.[3] I did not paint the view of Delacroix's garden from Delacroix's window, or the view of Delacroix's window from Delacroix's garden. I did not paint the alluring adolescent schoolgirl who passed me in schoolgirl laughter with a mate as I leaned on an old stone wall making notes in the Passage Saint-Paul by the Lycée Charlemagne and who, doubling back alone, approached me and spoke a few shy words in French, so that I wondered, for an instant, whether she was a prostitute uniformed as a schoolgirl, or a schoolgirl who also walked the streets after class or who at least wanted to grow up a hell of a lot faster than the curricula allowed, but then she lost her nerve and walked away, although I did spot her again, window-shopping in rue Saint-Antoine, sauntering for shoes and a way to make it bearable to go back home. I, because I am not Degas, did not paint the jazzy dancing class that I saw from my window in rue Ravignon as I looked over the steps of rue Androuet and that I used to watch, relaxedly, without prurient intent, as I stood with my plate of sautéed vegetables that I had seen unloaded by long white coats (like mine) that morning in the streets of Montmartre, nor did I paint the motherly crow three flights below in the *passage* to whom I used to call "Merci, Madame!" whenever I saw her convening *les chats des Abbesses* for feeding and gossip at such late hours that it savored of a criminal escapade. I did not paint Père Bénéteau, the curé of Saint-Eustache, who showed me how to properly mix *moutard* into the *soupe de poissons* on which we dined in a bistro on the Île Saint-Louis, and who told me how he joked with the archbishop of Paris that his Notre Dame must be a favorite of the blind because it is so dark in there, and who, when I told him that I'd love to spend the night, alone, in that great old church of his in order to write a sequence in my Matisse novel but that I knew it wasn't possible, said to me, without hesitation: "What do you *mean*? Why *not*? It's *my* church, isn't it? After all that I do there, they'd better *not* tell me what I can and can't do," and then gave me the code and introduced me to the sacristan, who showed me how to work the lights, so that one night I walked to Les Halles with my notebook, I let myself in, and I slept—or, rather, didn't-sleep—wrapped in a coat, gloves, and a cap in a chair over a small heating vent, listening to centuries of stone in a place that had heard the cries of baby Moliere when he was baptized there. . . so that on the next evening, when I met the curé feeding the poor of the neighborhood, he was puzzled as to why I had entered by the front door and hadn't again used my own private entrance, for, as he said, "This is *your* church now." I did not paint the pavilion that had once served the busy French markets next door until Les Halles was transformed, in the 1960s, and the pavilions were obliterated, excepting this one, which was transported in pieces to Nogent-sur-Marne, where it hosted conventions and where a kindly custodian unlocked the doors and allowed me to roam it alone so that I was walking in one of the scenes of Zola's *Ventre de Paris*—*The Belly of Paris*—which indeed it had been when this pavilion was packed every morning with fish, meat, fruit, flowers, cheese and vegetables, and to Zola all the buildings, "steeped in the rising dawn. . . seemed typical of some gigantic modern machine, some engine, some caldron for the supply of a whole peo-ple, some colossal belly, bolted and riveted, built up of wood and glass and iron, and endowed with all the elegance and power of some mechanical motive appliance working there with flaring furnaces, and wild, bewildering revolutions of wheels" (37), while "the everlasting stream of carts and horses stretched away as far as Rue de Rivoli and the Place de l'Hôtel de Ville" (42), and "the great pile of St. Eustache glittered brightly in the sunlight like some huge reliquary" (49). I did not paint the fetching American downstairs who fetched me to open a bottle of wine for her and offered me a glass until her terribly young French boytoy rang the bell, a neat little stunt in which I was glad to be of service and hoped that the evening ended well for her. I did not paint what Kerouac calls *old atomic bomb Atlantis*, which you can find in any town but which is different in Paris. I did not paint the grungy little Chinese joint where I betook myself out of a snowfall, sipped salty soup and slurped dead noodles, gladly, one perfect Parisian Christmas Eve. I did not paint the dogs who were nipping at a little girl who tried to fend them off while the din-ers in Place Contrescarpe looked on placidly, so that I couldn't be sure whether I was seeing a real attack or whether this was how kids played with animals, or they played with kids, on this very very strange planet of Paris. I sketched but I did not paint Hemingway's place, 74 rue de Cardinal Lemoine, although I did go up the stair and tip my cap to his door the way I had gone up the stair to tip my cap to Newton's door in Trinity College, metaphorically trembling and genuflecting as if before a king. I did not paint Modigliani's house, no I didn't, although it was two minutes up the mountain of martyrs from me. Why not? Here's why: because the daycare center, from whose window I wanted to take a shot over the wall that surrounded the house, would not let me in. I did not paint Matisse's apartment on Quai Saint-Michel with crayon drawings taped to the door. I did not paint the beautiful professor who, driv-ing with her mother, picked me up and carried me out of the grounds of Ver-sailles—"You don't want them shutting the gates on you"—and who told me, as other educated Parisians had done when I asked them about the Reign of Terror, that this savage chapter of the French Revolution was a myth and that the great old buildings that were torn down completely or reduced to a rem-nant—like the Église Saint-Jacques, which one could only see as the Tour

Saint-Jacques—were decimated only "because the peasants needed the stone." I painted none of that. But in an energetic and, I hoped, muted concession to the Paris picturesque in which I attempted to do something *un*original and yet in some way my own, I did paint a lonesome corner of Saint-Eustache. . . a sad stoical row of midget chairs in Saint-Pierre de Montmartre. . . the primordial tower of Saint-Germain-des-Prés. . . bocce ball along the Canal Saint-Martin. . . a cobbler's in rue Lamarck. . . a guy reupholstering a chair on the sidewalk in front of the Elie-Fitzo Tapisserie at the corner of rue Ronsard and rue Cazotte. . . Henry Miller and a dog in the Place du Parvis-Notre-Dame. . . a view in both directions along rue Saint-André-des-Arts. . . the view across the Seine from Quai Voltaire—that sort of thing. And so without a formal invitation, the city of Paris worked its way into "Older Professions" (the piece I was writing about *The Stonemason*, which is set in Louisville) and the city of Paris worked its way into these pictures of Cormac McCarthy's house. No one is ever entirely anywhere. Whereness is not that trivial—or submissive, a fact that is understood by David Cronenberg in his film of *Naked Lunch*, where a view of Central Park out of a Tangiers restaurant or, on a narrow Moroccan road (shot in northern Ontario), a businessman with an attaché case smoking under two bright lamps against the rail of an Eighth Avenue subway, fleetingly body forth what Cronenberg calls "the hallucinatory duality that Bill Lee lives in, that he is always partly in New York and partly in Interzone no matter where he is." I have painted the playwright Racine's house, knowing little about Racine except: *this is his house, it would have to be.* The house *becomes* the man, *my* Racine—whether or not Racine even lived here—or, in this case, died here too, for **ICI MOROUT RACINE** is engraved in its stone. I have noticed a resemblance between some of my Racine houses and my McCarthy houses, which have brought the American Southwest to rue Visconti, that narrow, sunless street in Saint-Germain-des-Prés where a community of French Huguenots lived before they were slaughtered, for French Catholicism, on St. Bartholomew's Day, a street that also belongs to Balzac, Bazille, Mérimée, Delacroix. . .[4] and I have seen Racine's house with a beat old Texas pickup beside it. If they are not entirely separate in my mind, why should they be so in my pictures?

When I spent three years writing a piece called "Poe at Ground Zero," I wasn't being a wiseass: Poe was down there with me in Lower Manhattan, with me on

Ann Street, on Greenwich and Cedar, on Broadway, on Nassau, on Newspaper Row. When, in 2008, I started a new series of these houses, a pair of monoliths rose up behind the low stucco building the way the Twin Towers rose up behind the little four-story Church of St. Nicholas, which had served its Greek Orthodox parishioners, at 155 Cedar Street, for over ninety years before it was crushed by the collapse of the South Tower. Now that those looming Rockefellers have emerged in El Paso, grapplers, dumptrucks, flatbeds and cranes might not be far behind. That will not be inappropriate. All the streets of Lower Manhattan are Coffin Avenue, and I see Ground Zero wherever I look. And when, in the future, I reimagine Dickens' house in Tavistock Place, the beautiful five-story dwelling in which he wrote *Bleak House*, *Hard Times*, and *Little Dorrit*, don't be surprised to see clocks set to 9:47, or a blownout bright red doubledecker number 30 London Stagecoach in the foreground.

5.

In the Paris of Flaubert, Zola, Maupassant, bookbinders were not permitted to work in houses of stone because their presses were too tough on them.

During the writing of *Suttree* or *Blood Meridian*, what proseproof substance kept McCarthy from making a ruin of his house on Coffin Avenue? Discussing the "Children of Adam" cluster of poems in *Leaves of Grass*, Walt Whitman told Horace Traubel: "Children of Adam—the poems—are very innocent: they will not shake down a house" (*Camden Conversations*, 88), but Whitman was wrong, for such honest poetry has the power to disrupt or destroy many a house, including his own. Whitman lost a job and a friendship over the poems, and *Leaves of Grass* was suppressed in the city of Boston because of what they could easily do to a Boston house, and because, as William Burroughs says in *Naked Lunch*—a book that was brought to trial in Boston—*all houses in the City are joined*. What's more, the term *stone deaf* is a misnomer. Stone hears everything. I once heard an argument between two brothers walking the floor of the Grand Canyon. As this bottomless rivalry bounced off the ancient walls, walls that had weathered all of time and stood it well, stood it beautifully, I could hear the stone hearing it, there was no doubt, and I was more embarrassed than if it had been a library, a church or a museum. "Sorry, stone," I said. "Centuries, and we are still a pack of jackasses." I wonder at what the stone in or under McCarthy's house absorbed, hearing those books before they were ink on the page. As the Hunchback of Notre Dame, Charles Laughton says to one of its gargoyles: *Why was I not made of stone like thee?* And yet you get the sense that he is halfway there and might as well speak to a statue as to a bell. "Its very nature is stone" (330), the Judge in *Blood Meridian* tells us about the desert in which much of the book is set. It's no wonder. That book is at least as primal as stone—and almost as knowing. For six months I read *Blood Meridian* aloud, distributing its sentences all over the map in a world that did not have a choice but to listen.

And yet, as with people, longevity for a house might be less related to what you know than who you know, or who knows you. Remember this: when, in a year to come, McCarthy's house is bought to be bulldozed for something cardboard and the armchair appreciators who did nothing about it when it was there will say: "Why wasn't something done about it when it was there," no one can ask me that question, for I traveled, I watched, I vigil'd, I shot, I painted, I hanged, I showed, I sold, I spoke, I wrote, I filmed, I published—and once having been, I am never not there. That's enough for one provincial scribbler. Now you get to work.

6.

A few months after that paragraph was written, McCarthy's childhood home at 5501 Martin Mill Pike just outside of Knoxville, where he spent about ten years of his life, burned to the ground on January 27, 2009. This two-story house, which had been built by a member of the Knoxville Garden Club and had fish ponds and rock gardens around it when the McCarthy family moved there from Providence in 1941 (when McCarthy was seven), had fallen into extreme disrepair, and Knox Heritage had listed it as the most endangered historic structure in Knox County. Its owner, who hadn't paid his property taxes in two years, was not in the house at the time of the fire and had shown infrequently before that. My pal Wesley Morgan, whom you have met in other chapters, rushed to the scene during the fire. In Wesley's cellphone pictures the house is only a frame full of flames that are reaching, fiercely, into the black above the forest.

"I was at my office about five miles away when I received the call and ran out there," Wesley told me. "By then the house was fully engulfed in flames. It was the first cremation I have attended. There were four fire trucks, but they had decided, by then, there wasn't any saving the place."

"Were the walls pretty much down by then?"

"No, they were still burning and collapsing."

"Two floors. So it wasn't a little shack."

"O no, it was a *really* nice house. I think five or six bedrooms. I didn't have a camera with me, but I did go out the next morning and take photos of the remains. It was hard to relax. I was run off by the deputy sheriff and was constantly looking over my shoulder. The scene reminded me of the landscape described in *The Road*. I guess houses have a mortality of their own. This place, although special to many, had, in truth, been on its last legs for some time. I had hoped that Knox Heritage might have been able to provide life support—but, alas."

Wesley called me the following day from the site. He was alone in the rubble.

"It's still smoldering," he said. "There's a wet, charcoal, burned-wood smell. I can see smoke drifting up around an old sewer pipe that's sticking up in the air. There are four chimneys still standing. One of them has partially collapsed. It was a *huge* house."

"Well, six kids, right—and two adults at least?"

"That's right. It had some outbuildings as well."

"Are you literally *in* the wreckage, or on the outskirts?"

"I'm at a barrier tape that says 'Fire Line Do Not Cross.' I'm right at the bed of a blue pickup truck. There's debris that has fallen into the truck, and there's a large plastic trashcan in the bed that looks partially melted."

"Are there any walls up?"

"There's one wall that goes almost to the roofline. The roof is all collapsed, except for one gable. You can see a second-floor radiator. There's a chimney just sticking up in midair that has an old television antenna still strapped to it."

"So, if you're seeing a radiator, there must be some flooring?"

"Well, it's actually stuck *on* the wall—kind of suspended. You can see a little bit of tongue-and-groove flooring that's kind of peeled down, hanging over, because whatever was supporting it is burned away. I don't see *a stick* of furniture. There's an electrical meter right in front of me but it's certainly not running anymore."

"If you were passing on the road," I said, "could you see that a house had burned down?"

"You can't see it," Wesley said. "When the house was here you couldn't see it from the road, either. Although you could sure see it when it was burning."

"So the house is now even more of a house that belongs in *The Road* than the house that's *in The Road*?"

"That is *exactly* what I was thinking."

"I realize I'm just kind of chatting with you," I said, "but I'm upset."

"I am too," Wesley said. "In my work in psychology, I've specialized in fetishes—special things—and among the kinds of special things are the attachments that people build up to objects and places. Even though I've never lived here, and didn't have much contact with it, I feel it's a significant loss in some strange way."

"It's consoling," I said, "that someone who feels that way is there amongst the wreckage. I felt that way about my project at Ground Zero—that the place needed people appreciating the details *within* the ruined neighborhood, and to preserve that phase of the event. There was a guy whose job was to tag the ruins for what was *not* to be grappler'd and dump-truck'd away. These were, in his estimation, whatever might be wanted by museums in the future— a twisted bicycle rack, a beam, a sign—and I think of you in that capacity, except that you have to both tag them *and* take them away in your car because no one else will."

"I think once I get to muck around in these ashes," Wesley said, "that's what I'll do."

Afterward, I couldn't shake one of the ordinary phrases that Wesley had used: *when the house was here.* Already, the past. These things we take for granted we one day wake up to find have disappeared.

Disappeared, but not entirely. Once the property had been legally investigated, Wesley returned to it and took more pictures.

"Then a funny thing happened," he told me. "When I got home a few minutes ago, I noticed a yellow firebrick sitting on the passenger seat of the car. Wonder how *that* got there."

Over the following two weeks there were further developments. When Wesley suggested that I adapt an old song about a fire to the McCarthy situation, I responded by writing a fresh tune, "Wesley's Song," that I recorded with an old Martin Shenandoah and sent to him. A week later I received a manila envelope from Knoxville. Within it was a Ziploc sandwich bag in which he had placed a piece of burnt wood from the house. The odor was strong. This, to me, was more than a gift: it was an assignment, as much an assignment as the Knoxville trolley token that he had given me and that I had written about in a piece called "Suttree and the Brass Ring: Reaching for Thanksgiving in the Knoxville Gutter."[5] All right, so I had put the old McCarthy house into a song—easy enough. But how to get the ruins, the fire, *the odor* into the new McCarthy houses going up in my studio? Some things are easier to do literally than any other way. . . so, for starters, I ground up some of the charred and stinking wood, stirred it into my paints (which are often house paints in every respect), and brushed it into some of the new houses with an old-century sash brush. If the Amazonians could have their *terra preta*—anthropogenic soil made of mulch, charcoal, shards of pottery *and ash*—surely I can have mine. I also stirred the ash with my moist, gluey fingers and finger-painted a little, so that it entered the pores of my skin as it entered the pores of the paper. Thus did the conflagration in Knoxville directly contribute to the building of a brand new home for Cormac McCarthy on Coffin Avenue in El Paso, Texas.

CHAPTER THREE

Collaborating with God

1.

There is a lyrical brutality to much of McCarthy's work that may be seen to lend itself to my own rather crude, often hostile line. . . and with respect to McCarthy's compassion for the downtrodden, the outsider, one could say of my style as a painter that it is downtrodden, outsider. . . but this is incidental. The traits in McCarthy's work to which I am most attracted—the masculine lungpower of his prose and its trapdoor phrases that, as in Shakespeare, drop you into the infinite. . . his diabolical sense of humor. . . his vocabular afflu-ence. . . his indifference to popular trend and its boring menus of narrative confections. . . his refusal to write a novel as if he were writing *a grant* to write the novel. . . his Dickensian authority in populating the worlds of his invention (and, even, his need—also Dickensian—to represent the world as an insane asylum, for which task both writers tapped into the subconscious deeper than Kafka or Joyce)[1]. . . his ability to synthesize, even to imitate authors who were geniuses before him without self-consciousness (so that, like Picasso, McCarthy could say: *I don't borrow—I take*). . . the undauntable willfulness of his protagonists and the sociopathic (or, better to say, sophis-topathic) strain that informs them—are beyond my capacity to tribute in paint—which is to say, in verse. And if a picture is painted in prose there is no point painting it.

Have I mentioned Picasso? Picasso told a story of painting a sideboard in a bistro. Next day it was gone. This made sense to Picasso (as it might have done to the Judge in *Blood Meridian*): once he had painted it, it was point-less for it to exist elsewhere. Can it be that once a house has hosted a great piece of writing, it may as well dilapidate? If so, perhaps it vanishes into painting.

2.

I have painted, over the years, a few of McCarthy's characters. Robert Mc-Evoy limping toward murder in Graniteville. . . two of the Bens laying stone, both of which I modeled on an old photograph of a stoneworker, white, on the WPA. . . John Grady riding a horse as if he were an Indian. . . Suttree rowing the Tennessee as if he were on the Grand Canal. . . but I am not the man for the job. I don't know who is, but some remarkable portraits have already captured a flavor of McCarthy's dramatis personae and they are among the finest of the last century. They were painted, before McCarthy was born, in the studios of Paris, mostly in Montparnasse and Montmartre. I am thinking of Modigliani.

For Robert McEvoy, try Modigliani's 1918 *Léopold Zborowski*, which could also serve the Kid. . . or try his 1915 *Chaim Soutine*, which could also serve Blevins. . . never mind that Soutine was a Russian-Jewish painter and Zborowski a Sorbonne-educated Pole who patronized Modigliani's work. Forget the sitters. Mostly forget their clothing as well. Clothing can be more important—more a portrait—than a face, but here it is in the faces that you can find your McCarthy.

For an alternate take on Bobby McEvoy or the Kid, try *The Little Peasant* (1908).

For a stimulating alternate of Blevins, look at *Boy in Short Pants* (1918).

If you think that *Oscar Miestchaninoff* (1917) is too disorienting (or degenerate) a take on the Kid, assign him to somewhere else in *Blood Meridian* and he will fit. So will *Pierre Reverdy* (1915), for although Reverdy was one of the premier poets in Paris—a pal of Picasso and Matisse who later became what amounted to a monk—Modigliani has rendered a one-eyed brute with about as much vision in his Adam's apple as in the look on his face.

For the Captain in *All the Pretty Horses*, *Dr. Devaraigne* (*Le Beau Major*) of 1917 even resembles Julio Mechoso, the actor who was so right for the Captain in the film.

For the Dueña Alfonsa snugly and smugly conversing with John Grady, try Modigliani's 1916 *Portrait of Hanka Zborowska*, or his second portrait of her from 1917, although in the latter she is not sitting with John Grady, only deflecting and destroying him.

For Alejandra's plain and equally neurotic sister (not disclosed in the novel), look at *Paulette Jourdain* (1919); and for a middle-aged misery of Oedipal Alejandra reflecting, deadly, on how she threw her life into a trashbin and married a wealthy, controlling surrogate for Rocha, try *Young Lolotte* (1918).

For Wanda in *Suttree*, try Modigliani's *Seated Nude* of 1916. For Joyce, try *Nude on a Blue Cushion* (1917). . . or if you would like her dressed and a little hungover, fed up or fuckedout, try *Ritratto di Ragazza* (1916). . . or if you want her in between, look at *Portrait of a Young Woman* (1916–1919), a picture that, oddly enough, could almost be Rinthy on her visit to the doctor in *Outer Dark*.

Modigliani's *Paul Guillaume* of 1915 could fit into several places in *The Crossing*, as would three other portraits from that same year (a big year in Paris for *The Crossing*): *Moise Kisling*, *Antonia*, and *Juan Gris*. Modigliani's 1913 *Paul Alexandre in Front of a Window*, his 1918 *Seated Man with a Cane*, and his 1919 *Roger Dutilleul* could also illustrate that brilliant, infuriating novel.

La Fantesa (1915) could be Martha of *The Gardener's Son*, and she would also fit well into *Outer Dark*.

Leon Indenbaum (1916) could easily be cast in *Blood Meridian*, as could the male half of *Jacques and Berthe Lipchitz* (1916), perhaps as the ex-priest Tobin.

Modigliani's *Seated Man with Orange Background* (1918) looks as if he is paus-
ing between secret and perverse homicides, so we can easily book him a space
in *Blood Meridian*.

What is it in these drowsy creatures that makes them say the name of
McCarthy?

Is it partly the way that they show the wear and tear of life?

Is it the way Modigliani risks the appearance of madness by making them
crosseyed to avoid the falsehoods of the ordinary?

Is it their odd ocular dimness or lack of eyelight altogether?

Is it something to do with the fact that they are often either being born, soon
to die, or dead already, and that some of them exhibit all three traits together?

Have a look. Perhaps you will tell me that I have been hallucinating. In
which case, congratulate Modigliani.

3.

During the exhibition at the Centennial Museum, where the walls were dou-
ble-hung, framelessly, with sixty-five houses attached by lengths of twine that
were molded into the fabric of this unusual Mexican paper (which is why I
stated earlier that the walls were *strung* with houses), one of God's less appreciated creatures, a scorpion, made its way into the gallery and crawled onto the
wall of one of the houses and died there.

For sweet Florence Schwein to accommodate these houses, a gallery of
arthropods was bumped to another slot, so perhaps this scorpion—eager to
see, or steal, or eat the show—had not been notified. Having inserted itself as
a character, the scorpion had turned this double portrait into a triple. Despite
a distaste for collaborating with God—the touch of the scorpion, I thought,
was a little obvious (the picture was better without it)—I left it on the stone.
In the matter of these houses I am large enough to give God a break, which
is more than he had done for me lately. At least, so I was thinking at the time.
Having written two books and having handmade a film about the destruction of the World Trade Center that entailed trying to build broken houses
everywhere in a neighborhood where people were burned alive, pulverized,
asphyxiated, or had fallen a hundred stories and exploded, I can see, now, that
everything I do is a break.

CHAPTER FOUR

Because the Easel Rocks

1.

With the curator of the Centennial, Scott Cutler, I was hanging the exhibition in the second week of August 1998 when one of the volunteers at the museum had a conversation with Scott about McCarthy's house, which she knew only from seeing the Josyphs going up.

"Does it *really* look like that?"

"Well. . . more or less."

"No wonder he moved."

Shortly after the exhibition opened, a woman looked at a few of the pictures and said: "I wouldn't want to live in *that* house." Which is a way of saying she wouldn't want to meet me—a sentiment to which I can relate, for I wouldn't want to meet me either, which is why I want paint to turn me into another man. Some artists work in order to find their own voice, their fingerprint, their genetic code, their artistic signature: self-expression. God help us. In theatre I would say to my actors: "If you're interested in self-expression, the bathroom's across the hall."

When a pretty young woman named Elizabeth asked her mother to buy her a house and the mother consented, Elizabeth asked me to talk to her about it. We stood together in front of the picture, but I have learned to let others explain my pictures to me, especially when they want to buy one.

"You picked a good one."

There were three front doors and walls made of green leafy vines, freestone, and larger blocks of limestone, as in a cathedral. Arrows and crosses. Writing that reads **COME TO EL PASO HOME OF CORMAC MC CARTHY THE GOOD WRITER** and **HIS HOUSE LOOKS LIKE THIS ALWAYS.**

"But why this particular house out of all the others?"

Elizabeth, who had not read McCarthy, said: "When I'm married, that's *exactly* the house I want to live in."

Hoping I had not set too high a standard for the husband to be, I wondered whether Elizabeth might not be more in the house now than she would be as a wife—but of course I didn't say it. I was hoping that the house would be a talisman for her and would carry a little magic for her life wherever she went with it—or that the luck would come from somewhere whenever she needed it.

If, like the writers of memoirs I have known and have read, I were willing to pretend that lying is an accepted or acceptable technique in the art of the memoir—as if the reader of nonfiction expects to be lied to, or ought to be lied to, and so there is no dishonesty—I would combine the older women in these two anecdotes so that the lady who declined to live in my McCarthy houses had, in the end, to buy one for her daughter. But that would be a short story, not a remembrance.

In the world of paint, the trap to be avoided is not the picture lying to you; it is, as I've suggested, the painter trying to snow his own picture. In Zen, the artist enters a state of grace before achieving his or her effect in a swift series of gestures. I don't know about grace (if this was Zen, it was punk Zen—earthquake Zen), but often I would stand motionless in front of a house, or poke around a canvas, a sentence, a meal, or walk through the historic Mills Pond House where I was lucky to have a studio, or sit on the steps and look at the ancient trees until I had, somehow, upset myself sufficiently to finish a picture—or, in some cases, *un*finish a picture that was becoming too finished and, by taking a step backward, take it a step beyond, into the *un*formed. It is really a matter of turning yourself into another person for long enough to fuse into the paper enough paint—enough of *the right paint*—to make a little magic and to do it without tricks, even without knowhow—better yet, without know*you*: without the you that you would love to strip away for the sake of the picture. Phrased a little differently, the question becomes: Can you cut the crap for long enough to do this right?

In one of Kerouac's fliptop pocket notebooks from 1959, the entry for January 27 lists, "roughly," the tenets of his theory of painting, "worked out as I strolled after supper," a list that concludes with number 5: **STOP WHEN YOU WANT TO "IMPROVE"—IT'S DONE** (*Departed Angels*, 142). This neatly correlates to *First thought, best thought*, Allen Ginsberg's summary of Kerouac's essentials for spontaneous composition. If I were to follow either of these tenets without revision, I wouldn't exist. For me, a page that is lively and clear is the beginning of an endless coddle and tweak, and often a finished picture will have to defend itself until it is, finally—to borrow a phrase from Picasso—*the sum of its destructions.* Only this afternoon I bought an old steel horse comb and an old misshapen leather hammer with an **M** in its red handle, for you never know when a picture will need a knot stroked (or streaked) out of it, or a rough spot pounded into submission. The **M** on the hammer, which looks as if it were carved over a century ago—feeling the hard mangled condition of the leather, one can believe it—serves as a reminder that a painting is there to be manhandled. Better for you to beat it than for it to beat you. If it turns out well, I can use the horse comb on myself.

In speaking about the ideal of art that James Joyce, working with Thomas Aquinas, conceived for Stephen Dedalus and himself, Joseph Campbell said: "And now comes the mystery: When the rhythm is fortunately achieved, you are held in aesthetic arrest."[1]

This sounds splendid and highly civilized, especially when you hear the way Campbell pronounces the word *for-tunate-ly,* so that it conveys all the charm, the finesse, the radiance and, too, the lack of strain, even of effort that appears to characterize the more refined and revered of our performances in art. Who could argue with a rhythm *for-tunate-ly achieved*? Such coherence in tone. Such harmony of parts. *Achieved,* yes, but never announcing *process.* On the contrary, looking as if it had never not existed. No ridiculous failures were balled up and tossed in composing this sonnet. . . no curses were hurled when this concerto was born in the keys of a Steinway. . . no principals were bossed and no love was lost in mounting this ballet. . . there is no blood in the red of this magnificent canvas. And maybe there isn't. But maybe there is. Maybe it was achieved after the studio became a war zone, a detention center, a charnel house, a brothel, an insane asylum. Cocteau's observation that Picasso proceeded by accidents and showed them to us without sweeping up is more than a brilliant remark, it's a work of genius in itself, worth more than a shelf of criticism, for it captures the essence of art that does not seek to cover its tracks. . . and the remark presages—and sharpens our understanding of—the rest of Cocteau's artistic century, including abstract expressionism, action painting, neo-Dada and Pop. But one should remember that some of Picasso's accidents were meticulously arranged or at least arranged for; that some of his not cleaning up might have taken him months to realize; and that Cocteau (or any of us) could never know for certain whether a *leaving alone* or *leaving in* wasn't really a *putting back*. It is probably a healthy thing to conceive that art criticism, history, biography, are all speculative; indeed, are categories of fiction. However much we know about a painter before and after he or she enters the studio, one can only guess at what he or she might have had to become in order to make that stroke, or keep from making it, or obliterate it after it was made.

When Hamlet and Edgar in *King Lear* try on madness and wear it awhile— albeit north by northwest, so that they are, as Hamlet says, *mad in craft*—in attempts to navigate impossible passages in their lives, it is more than a disguise to protect their wounded and fragile psyches: it has a liberating effect, as does any mask, so that they are urged into realms of discovery and expression of which a socially acceptable Hamlet or Edgar might not have been capable, or under the influence of which these men might have broken. Similarly, some pictures are nonnegotiable—you would have to be crazy to bring them off. Often I have said: "I'd hate to be the person has to finish *this* picture," and the truth is that I *cannot* be that person. Often I have scolded my own hand for moving the way I have trained it to move. The hand then shrinks and sulks like a dog under a whack or a yank of the leash. One is tempted to put it out of the room. This is why I drove the winding wooded road to my studio with no thought for painting but, instead, listening to sentences taped in the morning and jotting alterations on a pad I had attached to the dash of my car. . . or rehearsing lines for a play I was in, or a film I was shooting, rehearsing as if a word out of place could lead to incarceration. . . or listening to Conrad, Pepys, Churchill, Achebe, Hemingway, Le Carré, Matthew, Mark, Luke, John, Virgil, Joyce, Hugo, Donne, Feynman, Sacks, Kerouac, Faulkner, Wells, Adams, Woolf, Homer, Carroll, Caro, Foote, Burgess, Burroughs, Wharton, Waugh, Galsworthy, Keats, Forster, Hardy, Melville, Trollope, Poe, *Bird Flight* on the radio—whoever or whatever it took to *not* arrive as a painter but as a writer, a reader, an actor, *a driver*—or, ideally, an assassin, anything to keep me from looking at the work with fond anticipation, but rather with a sense that it all has to stop—the *all* being one's way of working—the illusion that this is art on the wall, the lie that the best you can do is nothing to be ashamed of—no. Smother it all with washes of gesso that blot out your past, your charm, your talent, your technique, the hug from your mother, the kiss from your lover, all of which are enemy if you take them seriously. . . or else silence it with renegade attacks of oilstick with which you stab yourself in the throat. In Oxford I saw *The Merchant of Venice* with Leo McKern as Shylock. After Shylock's daughter, Jessica, ran away from home with a sackful of his ducats and a Christian, Mc-Kern tore open his robe and sent the buttons flying downstage in my direction, setting an example for the kind of disinheritance/disownment for which I, as a painter, should be prepared the moment I button my lab coat.

Should we not disregard (or discard) *technique* altogether? Fine: here is a technique I have employed to great effect. Call it *The Gunslinger*. You turn out the floods in the studio, you walk to the door, you start into the hallway, and as you are going to lock the door you open it up again and dart back into the dark room to catch the night's work by surprise. All alone, dimly lit by a drift of moon or a bulb in the hall, trapped in your stiletto sights. If it can't defend itself, shoot it down.

2.

When another visitor to the Centennial exhibition said about the artist: "He must have been in Vietnam," it didn't sound strange to me. For that viewer, my McCarthy houses *were* Vietnam—the one with the war.

3.

For me, every house is an attempted suicide. Without annihilation nothing is revealed.

4.

If you do finish the picture, don't finish the house: every house should present as a question—a house posited, never a house confirmed. In this regard, remember Elvis: *Well, sir—you take the wiggle out of it, it's finished.* And yet every day there is this challenge: how do you bring this house alive without making it too interesting? A picture in any style can be too full of *appearance*.

5.

Hard work is easy. Impossible work is what's difficult to achieve.

Late one night I was working with Kevin Larkin on a series of found-object assemblages, *Lives of the Saints*. I was stifling sobs of shame, lowing and mewling in front of a piece of "finished" work. It was a part of the one saint, *St. Jerome in His Study*, that was not an assemblage but a thirty-five-foot altarpiece. We were collaging and painting it on shaped pieces of canvas, mounting it on matching foamcore, and hanging it forty feet over the altar in Church of the Advent on Broadway and 91st Street in Manhattan, a nice old place from the turn of the Lutheran century with authentic Tiffany windows. The pastor was imitating a church in Cologne that had invited artists in—not into the vestibule or into the basement, but directly into the precincts of the Lord. Kevin—who told me later that he had been hanging back, allowing me to do most of the work on this piece, because he hadn't chipped in on the cost of the paint (insane)—asked me what was wrong. I told him that in managing the problems in this part of the mural, I had taken the easy way. We both liked the solution, liked it very much, and that was the problem: it was comfortable. A sad reckoning. Stunted growth from masturbation of the brush. At any age, paint youngly *but not too nimbly*. Will you look at how I have foxed myself? On a track of Jack Kerouac reading, with Zoot Sims tooting, Kerouac said: *All day wearing a hat that wasn't on my head.*

After a night without relief one summer at the artists' colony Yaddo, in Saratoga Springs, I was walking back to my room in the old-century mansion of the Trasks—the husband and wife Victorians who had bequeathed this place for artists to do their work—when the novelist Jerry Badanes, sunning himself in starlight, asked me how the work was going. "Working on a difficult canvas," I said, "is like stepping behind a barn in order to go ten rounds, barefisted, with some tough son of a bitch who is twice your size and beats the shit out of you," although the image in my head when I recall this sensation is of Terry Malloy getting the beans beaten out of him behind that little shack in *On the Waterfront*. To quote the primadonna in *The Crossing* again: "To be killed night after night. It drains one's strength" (229). But of course being killed night after night is what gives you your strength to begin with. At least that was honest

work. This? My father was honester with scratches on the sheet (slang for racing form), making book on the ponies, waiting on results from Hialeah, hand on his tortured stubble of neuralgic jaw, mercy of Benson & Hedges helping his heart into the grave. Honester me Ma, who was doing a radium dance at Jimmy Kelly's on MacDougal Street before she married the handsome MP. *What kind of an act was this?* Corot hoped with all his heart that there would be painting in Heaven—because, he might have added, there is heaven in painting. But there is hell in it too, to which one is sentenced by these two traitor hands.

As an act of contrition, I eradicated all my misdemeanant solutions for *St. Jerome.* Somewhere Hemingway said: *All the outs are too easy, and the thing itself is too hard to do, but you have to do it.* The lateness of the hour, the pressing deadline (tomorrow) for trucking the work into Manhattan, the lack of supplies (at one point I stole a squeeze of yellow, my only theft of paint)—none of these considerations could keep me from destroying the good work on *St. Jerome.* If I had left it there I would never have made it home; or, if I had, the key to my apartment would not have opened the door.

6.

Don't be fooled, and don't let the viewer be fooled, by the Southwest-suburban-adobe motif. Grenades of every type can be tossed from the safest of houses. Even a house of haiku is permitted its apostrophes. No harm for a house to be quoting Hamlet:

> For, though I am not splenetive and rash,
> Yet have I in me something dangerous. (5.1.)

For a house to be a house, it must be sufficiently precipitate. So must I. In discussing the English art in the Paris exhibition of 1855, Dickens denounced the works as having *a little, finite, systematic routine in them*, and thus identified the enemy of anything I have tried to do as a painter.

When, in 1833, John Constable showed *Englefield House, Berkshire, Morning* in the annual exhibition of the Royal Academy in London, he was approached by the president of the academy, Sir Martin Archer Shee, an author and portraitist with a reservoir of what Constable called self-devotion. "It is only a picture of a house," Shee told Constable about *Englefield*, "and ought to have been put in the Architecture Room" (Leslie, 221).

Constable's reply, that *Englefield* was "a picture of a summer morning, *including a house*" (Leslie, 221), was a defense on which one is tempted to expand, for it seems to say something about the issue of what exactly constitutes the subject or the focus of a painting, and what, or who, determines that. One is tempted—until one looks at the canvas: *very weak John Constable.* The house itself, Englefield—still standing about ten miles from Reading—is an Elizabethan manor with a typically long list of occupants and restless renovations. It was sometimes a seat of Catholic recusancy, starting with its titular owner, Sir Francis Englefield, who supported Mary Tudor and lost the house in exile under the reign of Elizabeth when, like now, it wasn't enough to be on the side of the angels unless you were on *the right side*, and the angels of Angel-field were not. Constable's *Englefield* was commissioned by Benyon de Beauvoir, a very landed gentleman who made his own major alterations on the house. He also made alterations on the picture. At the suggestion of

Constable's friend and Boswellian biographer, Charles Leslie, the painting was embellished with a graze of cattle in the wide foreground, to which de Beauvoir objected, causing Constable to turp out the cattle and replace them with a herd of deer. We should not, however, assume that if the commissioner were happy with the picture he would not have expressed disfavor over the cattle, for when a gentleman pays a fair price for a painting, we cannot be surprised if he does not want cows on his wall.

That the house was a commission is seemingly not the problem here. The problem is that the painter was more inspired by the commission than by the house or by the sketches he made in Berkshire. De Beauvoir liked seeing his house, but it is the house that ruins the picture and the slaughtering of cattle was hardly more than a local anesthetic. For one thing, Englefield is so well lit that one is a little embarrassed at Constable's attempt to make it the center of an atmospheric drama—Constabular clouds, Constabular light bathing the house in a glory of importance, etc. One sees at a glance that *the painting needs less house*, or less *houseness*, not more. . . needs to be seen, perhaps, portionally through hedges in the snow or over the shoulder of a gamekeeper. Sir Martin might have been a blowhard—he was certainly a prick for having strolled up to Constable with a mind to insulting his picture—but he was right about *Englefield*, for the attempt to integrate or contrast the elements of Nature with an unexceptional mound of domestic architecture fails. When you look at *Englefield* you see a rich man's home lit strangely for no earthly reason in the middle of nowhere.

This is why I have said that the commission is *seemingly* not the problem. It might have been. Do you imagine that de Beauvoir was paying for a partial view of his home through a snowy hedgerow? Constable, on assignment, could not have made the painting more important than the house, whereas a painting is always more important than a house. A house! What is that to a work of art? As I have suggested, when a painting is no longer interested in a motif, neither can you be. But Constable was being paid to render an acquisition, a measure of standing and privilege represented by shapes of clean white stone. That is why I refused to paint a poster for a Cormac McCarthy conference and, instead, insisted on painting an exhibition. I needed to lose as much of McCarthy's house as might be necessary, perhaps to lose it all—lose McCarthy as well—if the momentum of the paint demanded it. I needed to make room for art. To rehabilitate Sir Martin's disparagement of *Englefield*—"It is only a picture of a house, and ought to have been put in the Architecture Room"—we could translate it into three words: *It's not art.*

One of the easiest things to notice about McCarthy—something so salient that one might not remark it consciously—is that his entire work ethic is geared toward making way for art. This would not be worth saying were it true for more of his contemporaries, but it is true for few of them. What we might call *the tradition of security* in the reader means nothing to McCarthy when he is at the top of his form. One way of understanding the depth of McCarthy's genius is to identify the writerly concerns, attributes, responsibilities on which he has turned his back. Whenever there is a conflict between, say, narrative cohesion and art, character development and art, arc of story toward satisfying conclusion and art, it is the potential for art that McCarthy can taste on his tongue: everything else is meaningless. You cannot paint for your mother, cannot write for your mother, you must give yourself permission (because no one else will)—more, you must assume the obligation—to be a worthless son of a bitch to everybody. Then you might be doing something. Probably not. Making way for art is not the same as making art. But essaying or settling for less is a waste of life.

But look here: my use of the phrase *making way for art* has me shifting uneasily. Along comes Degas to help me out. In a letter to his young friend Albert Bartholemé, Degas wrote: "I was afraid of bronchitis, everything was shaping for it, it was avoided" (150). That phrase, *everything was shaping for it,* is more what I mean. In McCarthy's studio, *everything is shaping for art.*

7.

Van Gogh once explained, in a letter to his friend Émile Bernard, why Cézanne's artistic stroke visibly wavered. The work fluctuated between a sure and a clumsy hand because the fierce wind of the south, the mistral, must have been blowing. "It's because his easel rocks," van Gogh said (*Letters to Émile Bernard*, ed. Lord, 50). After all, van Gogh had battled against the mistral himself, and in one of his letters to Bernard he had illustrated his method for securing his own easel with two-foot iron stakes and cord. "Like that you can work in a wind," he told Bernard (39).[2]

But this business of the easel was not why Paul Cézanne was uneven. Cézanne was an amateur who slowly worked up to the level of genius. A moving attribute of Cézanne's early work is the way that it fights its own incompetence. Gross imperfection—really bad painting—can be spotted everywhere in the young Cézanne. Time and again he bungles a picture, or *in* a picture, but Cézanne soldiers on until his pictures are astounding. But van Gogh's phrase, *It's because his easel rocks*, could be the impulse for a spirited improvisation around the themes in McCarthy. I had hoped that you would do it. *It's because the easel rocks* would ring like a gong and illuminate the genius of the novels, especially *Suttree*, according to the fierce wind of the South, south of what being open to reverie. Having invoked Henry Miller, it would be nice to have Miller take the lead in such a riff. *Of course* McCarthy's easel is rocking, he would say—that's what's wrong with literature: no one's easel is rocking enough—*if at all*. The artist *needs a mistral*—some unmerciful force, nameless, primeval—to shake up his easel, blow his canvas into the trees, slam the old boy hard—*not* so that it merely *shows in the work*, but *so that it ruins the work*, making it readable. Does it shake the hand? That's what we *want* of our geniuses—*may their hands tremble forever*! Is the artist not to be disturbed at his devotions? That is because he must disturb them himself.

Of course I am also discussing the work of lesser artists—mine, for instance—and of course the easel is me, for an easel made of wood is something I think of for students, Sunday painters, Churchills and housewives—or a painter who is so far down on his painter's luck that he can't afford a wall to work on. Luckily, most of these pictures of walls were painted on walls, the very old plaster walls of the Mills Pond House, once the home of the Mills family, which was tied by marriage to the Long Island Smiths of Smithtown, who lived in the house until the last of the Smiths to inhabit the place—tall and quite Smithy old gentlemen, two of whom once walked around with me and reminisced about the olden days—departed for more practical housing and the Mills Pond House was given to the town to which they had given their name. Although most of the house dates from 1824, the kitchen retains features from the 1700s. Foraging in the woods, Kevin and I found a timber from an icehouse that was that old—and used it in an assemblage to give it new life. Outside my second-floor studio it was treeful and quiet. A driveway circled a broad lawn. Beyond the hedge, across the road, there was a farm. There was a farm next door that kept a llama. Sheltering the grounds in the back, one of the great trees in all of Long Island presided over weddings and once had models in slinky skirts climbing into its branches for a magazine spread. I was told that my studio had been the bedroom of a spinster aunt. In the attic I stored some of my work in servants' quarters where slaves might have lived, a fact that was not emphasized in the literature, any more than the fact that there was one in my studio. There were shelves and boxes of books from the previous century, recruiting posters from World War I, a spinning wheel, a set of watercolors from the 1920s, *Harper's Magazines* dating back to the Civil War including one in which *Great Expectations* concludes. Around and beneath me there were gallery spaces. The architect Stanford White, who had married one of the Smiths and lived in St. James at nearby Box Hill, had dined and smoked cigars in these rooms in which, as the Smithtown Arts Council's artist in residence, I walked every day and had the pleasure of showing my work.

For a film called *Cormac McCarthy's House*, I shot my houses on one of the gallery walls and then, having two nights and a day in which to achieve it, I taped to this wall a sheet of paper the size of a mural, covered the floor in plastic, filled a table with supplies, and painted the biggest of all the McCarthy houses as the camera followed me.[3] By *biggest of all* I mean that I went from 24" × 32" to 8' × 12'. Painting big and fast was easy for me then. The larger the surface, the easier it seemed. This big and this fast—and with the camera rolling—I had never done that, but the worst that would happen was that I would paint a bad picture that would have to be repaired before the clock ran out. I worked for thirty hours with one brief break. King Cormac counseled against playing on a cliff, but I was living, literally, a few feet behind a broken cliff above the Long Island Sound ("If it rains," an engineer told me, "go out to a restaurant"), and so painting on the edge of a metaphorical cliff was nothing to me. If you slide into the water, that'll rock the easel, no? And on film. As for pulling a pair of allnighters, approaching the zero hour—that moment in which you are a cripple, mindless, dying to sleep, the stifled groans of a broken back inserting into the soundtrack—will seldom hurt the work, and it might stimulate those moments of madness—or, at least, of uncontrol—that are needed.

I have not much seen the big McCarthy house, for after hour number thirty it was rolled out of sight, unrolled again only to shoot two boys reading from

Blood Meridian in front of it. I have had to watch it on film, in which it is hard for me to recognize the sureness of the brush. The film begins at seven o'clock on a Sunday night; by 12:30 a.m. I am drunk on fatigue. It is one of the few times that I speak—most of what you hear is the brush in the cup or on the surface of the paper. Later there is the mystic sound of the Long Island Railroad passing through the St. James station—for me, the stamp of eternity. Attempting to cut the paper, I set aside the T square. "It's better to be ten inches off than to use that goddamn T square," I say. "It's like some torture from the second grade. Midnight and I'm supposed to use a T square. . . Sure. . ."

The house looks sound on camera, but all I have to say, at the end of the shoot, is: "That blue on the top really helps, doesn't it?" Looking at this big picture a decade later, I see that I was right: the blue at the top helps, and the line is a fair representation of what it is to work as an artist and, too, of why it is that most films with or about artists have nothing to do with art. *That blue on the top really helps* is exactly the way the work is done—but it lacks the ring of romance, passion, adventure, creativity—*self-expression*. I recall a line of Aldous Huxley: *There are no artists, only men at work.* I like to change it to *men and women at work*, and of course there are *a few artists* and Huxley knew that, but *That blue on the top really helps* is what he meant by *at work*. *That blue on the top really helps* is what you see when you rummage the archive in San Marcos and locate the interesting changes McCarthy is making in his manuscripts. *That blue on the top really helps* is how most art, in any medium, is accomplished. It might be interesting to roll the big picture out again and take a shot of it—but let's not be precious about any of these houses. Wasn't it my initial intention to burn it on camera? After a hundred of these houses, I said to Kevin: "I feel as if I've done the warmup. Now is when I ought to start, and now I have to stop, ship it, and hang it."

8.

Thinking tonight about this fine Mexican paper (*papel hecho a mano*) from the De Ponte mill with the twine (*mecate*) molded through it about three and a half inches from the edge on each side, I realize something I hadn't noticed. The houses I first painted on other paper—sheets of good quality, sheets even thicker and pleasanter to work on—do not have a problem holding their own as works on paper, but *as houses* they tend to be neglected, even excluded. I couldn't write about them as houses—couldn't write about them at all—for, it seems, the houses need the paper from Mexico. And the converse is true: the Mexican paper needs *Cormac McCarthy's House*, for I have never been able to paint much of anything else on these peculiar, twiney sheets. Having kept a stash of them, empty and waiting, I discovered that, even after a decade, the case of *McCarthy's House* was still open.[4] Hadn't I told Kevin that I was running the scales? Right, then—round two. Recently, I painted another big house—by accident. A complicated canvas was not going well, I turned around and saw a *McCarthy's House* on the wall, I turned back around and converted the big mess into one of the best houses. Either I don't yet know, or I have forgotten, what a house looks like.

9.

Let's go back, for a moment, to the young woman, Elizabeth, who bought one of the houses. I mean that literally: let's find her and ask her whether the house has held up for her, whether she still owns it, whether it mightn't have been sold or consigned to the cellar or a closet.

I did not know Elizabeth's address so I wrote to her mom, Margie, who passed along the query to her daughter. Elizabeth is now a lawyer with a firm in El Paso: Mounce, Green, Myers, Safi, Paxson & Galatzan, P.C. "I am looking at it as I type, in fact!" she wrote to me about the house. "It hangs in my office at work, and truly makes me very happy. I tell people that it is my 'law degree,' as that is what most people in my law firm have hanging in their office. I, instead, have my Peter Josyph painting. . . people will just have to trust that I have a degree (it is still in its tube at the back of a closet somewhere). ☺

"My *House* painting started out above the couch in my first home," Elizabeth told me. "A tiny adobe house out in the middle of a cotton field in New Mexico, right outside of El Paso. It has traveled with me to law school, hung on the walls of a handful of other homes I have lived in, and now hangs in my office, along with photos of my husband and two sons. Thank you!"

This came as a message in a bottle to me. I try to make a picture to last—to support itself and its owner—and one hopes for the best. . . but I have never *presumed*. . . and whenever I visit a place where my pictures are hanging I am like a health inspector (an honest one), examining every article to find out whether it will pass, and sometimes I say: "It'd be nice to bring paints. . . maybe a trace of red on the right. . ." It doesn't make a difference how many pictures have "held up," doesn't matter that this "holding up" is perhaps the one assurance I can make about a picture and to me is the true professionalism. It always takes me by surprise when I see it for myself, or hear it from another. So I was warmly pacified—and encouraged—when Elizabeth ended her letter by saying: "Thank you for asking how the *House* has held up. . . perfectly!"

She also said: "I am sad, as were many, that Cormac left El Paso."

CHAPTER FIVE

San Jacinto Plaza

I am sitting on a bench in San Jacinto Plaza in El Paso, reading André Gide's *The Counterfeiters*. I am dressed in white linen, for which the day is too hot. *Bound to be a dignified gent there in whites*, but no, that's me, the only lounger in a coat of any cloth. A girl is preaching the Bible in shrill Spanish, sawing the air with that crazy old book of which I have had a bellyful. How I grew up with it—whispered to the Father and the Son, murmured, hymned, intoned indecipherably in that Roman tongue. . . but there was none of this theatrical passion, this medieval minstrelsy, at St. Gregory the Great. This woman is battery powered by the Holy Ghost to save the border communities. A man with a chart on an easel is demonstrating the hazard of crossing the border either way without Jesus, apparently forgetting that a man who didn't make it past thirty-three would not be the best of guides to longevity. But let's leave this impossible girl, the guy with the chart, and even the Holy Trinity alone without further provocation because, although the plaza is named for the battle in which Sam Houston defeated Santa Anna in less than twenty minutes, Jacinto is the Polish Saint Hyacinth—another indefatigable evangelist—who preached himself to death in the thirteenth century. Known as the Apostle of the North for his work in Denmark, Sweden and Norway, Jacinto is the patron of those in danger of drowning, a suitable saint for a place down the street from the *rio* in which thousands of escapees from lands of the forgotten, some of them children, have died on the journey to Texas.

These nifty old benches are made of cast iron with redwood planks and festooned medallions for back support. Fashioned more for craft than for comfort, the cameo backrests—painted flowers in relief surrounding Millet-type farmers—are not restful. At least I have this bench, the only one without shade, to myself.

It is one in the afternoon, a busy time for a place where nothing is meant to happen, but I am not busy, and in me, too, nothing is meant to happen.

An assortment of South Texans, all dark of complexion, are reading the paper, eating, smoking, chatting, daydreaming. A few flies reconnoiter me. Trucks airbrake or signal as they back into deliveries. Flap of a black pigeon. Sparrow at my feet. This hour of our death. This time in my hands. This light on the page. This ash in my hair from a giant yet to be blinded and burned. That a simple pair of shoes should have such meaning. (Like teeth, haven't they the right?) What ventures have I toed them into, they me, now at the bottom of America, hanging until dead or until sold. What such fellows as I do, crawling in between. All these miles of loneliness. And all this against the law, which, as Thomas More says to Richard Rich in *A Man for All Seasons*, amounts to this: *Be a teacher*, not this ends-of-the-earthing with your stacks of decorations and manuscripts.

Those houses had better sing in that space. *Don't* be another art bozo bristling paint into the eyes of the innocent.

As I button my cash into the flapped back pocket of my trousers, there is a three-way conversation behind me.

"A quarter."

"Don't give her *nothin*."

"I'll pay you back."

"Have you got a match on you? Have you got a lighter on you?"

"You want *every*thing. Why you want *every*thing?"

For me it is enough to receive the June day and for the meeting at the Centennial to plan the exhibition called *Cormac McCarthy's House* to come off smoothly. After taking this dictation, I return to *The Counterfeiters*, Chapter 4, a conversation between the troubled Vincent Molinier and the well-to-do Robert de Passavant. Then I do an odd thing: I begin to transcribe into my notebook the dialogue in Gide the way I have taken down the banter in the plaza. It's where the brash and wealthy Robert tells Vincent to go gambling with his, Robert's, money at a place called Pedro's.

"Be off with you now."

"But your father?"

"Oh, yes; I forgot to tell you; he died about. . ." He pulls out his watch and exclaims: "By Jove! How late it is! Nearly midnight. . .. You must make haste. Yes, about four hours ago."

All this is said without any quickening of his voice, on the contrary with a kind of nonchalance.

"Aren't you going to stay to..."

"To watch by the body?" interrupts Robert. "No, that's my young brother's business. He is up there with his old nurse, who was on better terms with the deceased than I was." (36–37)

This has never happened to me, it won't happen again, but two categories of perception or experience—overhearing a live conversation vs. reading a book—have folded into one.

"I'm hungry."

"Tell her to kiss your ass."

"Kiss my ass."

"I'll give you an IOU."

This plot of ground, really Mexican territory, a haven for travelers of every account and for those of none at all, has welcomed, harbored, or at least signified to men with oxdrawn carts, covered wagons, Jefferson Davis's camel corps, stagecoaches, sixgun shootouts, a little more law and a little more order, lots of preaching and drinking and thieving and drugs and a multitude of city buses, lost lives like mine and a rarefied genius like McCarthy. Useless to wonder why he would "want" to live here. You are living here. Why would Henry Miller, knowing Paris the way that he did, "want" to live in Pacific Palisades? Why would Whitman "want" to live in Camden, New Jersey? Why would John Wesley Hardin, a doublebreasted gunslinger, the Terror of Texas, "want" to live in El Paso? To practice law on the third floor of the Wells Fargo Building a few blocks from here—and to write his memoirs? Perhaps these are all men who, like Thoreau at Walden, wanted to transact some private business with the fewest obstacles. For McCarthy, like Thoreau, it worked out well: you can read the results. Hardin never finished his book, and the law done him in. "You have four sixes to beat," he said (allegedly) before he was shot in the back of the head in the Acme Saloon by a sort of constable in the summer of '95 and was buried, for $77.50, in Concordia Cemetery.

Pairs of Levis don't mean the same in a storefront here as they do in Lower Manhattan. In the windows of Chelsea Jeans on Lower Broadway, blue jeans were white from the clouds of 9:59 and 10:28 that turned them into texts on international business, religious dementia, sexual sublimation, political corruption. Here, displayed in a shop that has stood for a century, they are a text on the Old West. Above the parkinglot along the side of the old Hotel Cortez, corner of North Mesa and Mills, there used to be billboards announcing **RODEO** with as much anticipation as *The Sunset Limited*. A brief doze into the verbal—what I call *a drowse* of dream language—generates this in the subconscious: *What happened was, when he died her blood was sufficient to cover this thing called sin.* Seeing a sign that reads

NO TIRAR BASURA
AVISO MULTA NASTA DE $1000
POR TIRAR BASURA

I refuse to litter this historic plaza with even the trash of dreams, so I close *The Counterfeiters*, stand up in the heat, and make a small ink sketch of the bench, then I go to meet old Florida Rick and dear Florence at the Centennial. When the business of art is afoot, the length of a sit in the Texas sun is a precise calculation for which you factor in the weight of your jacket, the coordinates of the appointment, the strength of your deodorant, and whether there is some in your case or in the jacket, the issue of whether you care to keep *any* appointment *any*where for *any* good reason ever again, and the feasibility of returning to the hotel as it is weighed against the risk of being late. As I depart, there is anger and sarcasm, but not in my direction: "Thank you *very much*, sir, *I appreciate it!*" And a voice of sexual laughter over an offer to do something with the mouth: "Why should I pay a dollar when I can get one for free?"

It will take me exactly a decade before I see that my reading of Gide this afternoon is the end of reading the book for me, not because *The Counterfeiters* cannot hold its own in or against San Jacinto, for it has done so beautifully in the way that the plaza has held its own against Gide. I can recall thinking: *This is not Paris, but neither is it the opposite, for people are retreating and recruiting in this square the same as I have seen in all the best places.* I believe, now, that when I thought that I was stopping myself from entering *The Counterfeiters* into my notebook, I did not succeed, and *The Counterfeiters* became the notebook, where it waited to become *Cormac McCarthy's House.* That moment on the bench—that was the book for me, as is this moment that is keeping me awake in the middle of the night on the second floor of an old B & B on Western Avenue in Albany, New York ten years later. Whether or not I ever read it to the end, I will never be able to "finish" *The Counterfeiters*, not unless we agree that it concludes at Chapter 4. Nor could I ever return to San Jacinto to "finish" the novel or to read those pages again. To do that would be to bury myself, to step on my own life. A truth that I have accepted over the last year or so is that I cannot bear *not* to be living in the past because I am still there: it is the ever-present for me—nothing that has happened is ever not happening—and in the present, I am reading Chapter 4 of *The Counterfeiters* in San Jacinto Plaza. I also have to accept that I am myself a counterfeiter—or a counterfeit—or an imitation of one as I sit here in the plaza, for it could be that I have taken *The Counterfeiters* in order to read these pages of Chapter 4 on the bench forever and to be able to tell you, honestly, that I am sitting on a bench in San Jacinto Plaza reading *The Counterfeiters*. . . the counterfeit, or presumed counterfeit, being exposed or suggested by the thought that *perhaps* I came to the plaza in order to write the first sentence of something that doesn't exist, not yet, not even in speculation, but has required me to do this thing for when it does. . . and, in thus coining myself, I have written a sentence of a very different order.

If I ever want to leave this bench with this book, I shall have to create a new forever for this combination and inscribe it in another black Scottish notebook. That will never happen. For a guy like me there is not enough room for that many forevers with Gide's *The Counterfeiters*.

It is hard to render this without sounding esoteric or downright silly, but there is no paradox. Let's call it a singularity of psychological space. I feel the same way about the very beautiful whore who shimmered the atmosphere when she gave me the glowing eye in a doorway along El Paso Street, where I was walking toward the Santa Fe Street Bridge to Juárez. El Paso is another street of martyrs but it is not rue des Martyrs. Such a doorway is seen only once and forever. If only *la belle dame sans merci* could know that she has not aged a day, that her looks and, beyond that, the unsounded sadness of her beauty are intact, that—beyond and despite the Seven Sorts of Sorrow in her life— part of her mission is accomplished for good, and when Mark Twain said that *words are painted fire but a face is fire itself*, he was talking about her, and that the sight of her in Spanish is better than the sound of the Bible, unless she is reading it to me and all my belongings with *The Counterfeiters* on the bedtable and I am praying for her deliverance from the legions of welcome abusers, from the stained wallpaper, from the abortions of Dr. Benway, from the needle, from the knife, from AIDS, from poor Mexico, and from too much time (more than a minute) on the street.

Counterfeiting. . . In Shakespeare's day, portraits were known as shadows, images, dumb shows, likenesses, even tables (after the boards on which they were painted). They were also known as counterfeits. When the poet in Sonnet 16 importunes his friend to marry and bear children, he says:

> Now stand you on the top of happy hours,
> And many maiden gardens, yet unset
> With virtuous wish would bear you living flowers,
> Much liker than your painted counterfeit.

Such a designation would make a portraitist of Cormac McCarthy's house a counterfeiter—which we know that I am, but I am one thrice over, for it often feels as if I am counterfeiting a counterfeit, really not painting the image and likeness of his or any house, and these walls are not built to hold up a roof or shut out the world, these windows are not to be seen through in any direction and have more to do with the fascination of squareness, rectangularity—more to do with the interesting things that happen whenever you choose a color, paint a shape.

Now let me contradict myself. When I refer to the meeting at the Centennial in which I ironed out the dates of the exhibition and the reception; the number, cost, and ETA of the postcards and what they needed to say; the press-pack to be circulated; agreements to be signed; how the pictures would be shipped; what it would cost; when they needed to arrive; how they might be hung and by whom, without frames, from the twine that is woven into them; how many inches of space were available; where the mounted text would be displayed; and whether we had to build a fence for kid-protection, it could create the impression that *Cormac McCarthy's House* is about my own work, and so could these soundings in San Jacinto Plaza. But this is not the case. Whatever moves I might have pulled on *The Counterfeiters*. . . whatever moves it might have pulled on me (I am still disturbed to think that it gulled me, for even a moment, into taking it down as if I were hearing it in the plaza, as if its characters—Gides to the bone—had joined the population of El Paso). . . the point is that everything—traveling to El Paso to shoot the house, painting the work, planning the exhibition, hand-lettering the poster, having it turned into four-color separations and all the back-and-forthing with the production house ("I can't promise you that iridescent red is going to pop the way you want it—I've never *seen* a red pops like that") and with the printer ("The first ten or twenty are *never* as deep as the rest because it takes that long *to get the ink up*"), the talking to Michael Hall from *Texas Monthly* and to sweet Betty Ligon, hanging the show with Scott, where we planned and diagrammed like surveyors staking a bridge, then delivering a talk at the crowded reception— all of that, including the self-educated gallery assistant who was reading the Tibetan Book of the Dead and *Finnegans Wake*, the Alwych notations in San Jacinto Plaza, and even this thing now a decade later and speaking to Senator Shapleigh and hearing from dear Elizabeth about her "law degree" and every permutation of the life I have led in relation to this project—including my travels to Warwickshire, to Norrbotten, to Berea, Kentucky—and including the title of this book—all of it exists because a man sat down in solitude to place one sentence after another and thereby to build his own house, a house that will separate the quick from the dead, a house that will last and into which all the generations will go.

CHAPTER SIX

Cormac McCarthy's House

Cormac McCarthy's house has an improvised history that I have not yet traced with completion, but it includes at least one previous author or coauthor. This is Captain D. A. Spina, who was the professional consultant on Franklin W. Dixon's *The Hardy Boys' Detective Handbook* (1959) and who retired here after he left the Newark, New Jersey police force. The actor Claude Akins, a large man with a forceful hand that I had the pleasure to shake in a Shaker village (seriously) up in the Berkshires (not far from Edna St. Vincent Millay's house, Edith Wharton's mansion, and Melville's Arrowhead), resided here for half a year; and the filmmaker-adventurer Karl Denham, who later caught King Kong, slept here for three weeks after shooting an action picture in Mexico. Orvan Autry took lemonade directly across the street when, as a fledgling musician (before he became Gene), he was touring with the Fields Brothers Marvelous Medicine Show. And it was here that, hitching up from Mexico City, Blind Lemon Jefferson had been staying a week before Sam (Lightnin') Hopkins and his brother John Henry heard him playing at a church social in 1920. The earliest tenant of note, Ranse Stoddard, was the United States senator who, for much of his life, was thought to have been the man who shot Liberty Valance.

Cormac McCarthy's house. Its verdure springs from a source of its own, respecting no latitude or season.

Clouds blow from it in all directions.

It has its own bestiary.

It is *not* a nest.

It becomes a fortification. It becomes a cathedral, leaning. It becomes a celestial city with sheep grazing its streets of cotton. Worn. Sad. Noble. Christless.

It becomes a Tuscan town, and in the road there is a burro that carries the Virgin on its back. It becomes Lester Ballard, wide-eyed observer in a Memphis anatomy lab, flat out and bloodless for surgeon-barbers of the long coat, scholars of the long face—and for Rembrandt. It becomes the gardener's son, Bobby McEvoy, posing in a waistcoat and jacket, gazing into a world beyond the lens or walking to Graniteville with a revolver in his belt and a knife in his wooden leg. It becomes a city of the plain with Blevins on a palfrey as Billy walks the reins. Papaw is lifting a chunk of freestone. McCarthy, long hair in a headband, is holding a paintbrush. Suttree's getaway car gets away.

There are pickups around it. They don't look too bad. They don't look too good.

It pays no attention to you.

Wrestlers are joined in the grass.

Lizards converse.

No mail is delivered.

There are fistfights and firelights in front of it.

Two guys are floating.

A strongman lifts it.

Its surplus population is as much at home here as its lawful owner, its collective face and its posture calling up deeds of equal weight.

There are always arrows in it (lots of feathers at the end).

There are crooked crosses on it.

There are big, Texas-size stars above it.

There are bars over the bars over the windows.

Chamfered corners are angled again.

A hooded man with a rifle guards the door.

Rude phrases hover in the sky, creep around corners, crawl out of the dust. *No women.*

It might look beat but it is never indisposed.

No lobsters will ever be cooked in it.

Eisenhower passes it in a dream—not his.

It smells of the odor of odorless mineral spirits, foreign oil, leathery skins of acrylic slashed by a stiletto.

It catches the wind in its chest.

Tall black leather boots bearing a skull and crossbones lead up to a leg leading up to a red dress leading up to the center of the earth.

Gary Cooper's signature endorses Chesterfields. Someone smokes one on a boulder, watching blue horses and palm trees.

A dead mule is dragged out of the livingroom, clearing the way for a visit from McCarthy's brethren. The car engine'll stay: they can tool it together with the radio on or they can ignore it and reminisce tall times in Knoxville.

St. Jerome in a skullcap crouches under a bare bulb, but if it is monastic it is van Gogh's Rule: leave it not for a brothel more than twice a month.

In the floodlit crater in *2001*, the monolithic Tycho Magnetic Anomaly sends the *Discovery* to Jupiter, but the film develops differently for those who watch it here.

It tells you how the West was won, how the rest was stolen.

Ralph Fiennes, inhabiting Beckett's *First Love* in a brown suit and hat, scuffed shoes and a beige trenchcoat, shuffles off the stage into it.

One day, the day on which it ceases to exist, everything about it is labeled and numbered.

Like the shepherd shacks in Thomas Hardy, Cormac McCarthy's house rests on wheels so the author can roll it in and out of the desert at his convenience.

Two Hemingways

In another day I had a landlord, Tom Hogue, who wrote overseas for the Associated Press during World War II, where he used to see Hemingway, of whom he was resentful for his highfalutin attitudes and privileges—not, we are certain, for any other reason, such as his genius.

"There was this Mercedes and he wanted it reserved for himself for whenever he needed it," Tom said about being with Hemingway in France. "He was always with the fists out, ready to fight with anybody, fight over nothing all the time. Tough guy, you know?"

I was not impressed with Tom's account, in which Hemingway was, in the consensus, a belligerent asshole and a braggart. Not because I couldn't take Tom at his word, but because I shouldn't have had to hear it from Tom, for by the time Tom encountered him, Hemingway had written some of the war's most astonishing journalism, such as: "Voyage to Victory" for *Collier's* (July 1944), a piece that can take your breath away... not to mention *The Sun Also Rises*, *A Farewell to Arms*, and *For Whom the Bell Tolls*, a novel that was published just before the war... a novel without which McCarthy would not be McCarthy... a novel that, when it introduced me to Hemingway at the age of fourteen, was one of the factors in making me a man... a novel that, when I read it after forty-six years, made me see that, as with bad things that are truly insufferable and make you want to die, some works of art are unbearably beautiful, the force of the sentences driving me to tears and a kind of despair that was close to suicide, for how can you live in a world with something that fine and majestic? Merely the lining up of sights on Robert Jordan's *machina* is a thing more worthy than a continent of Hogues—meaning, of course, that in *For Whom the Bell Tolls* there is no *merely*... so that if Hemingway had taken a swing at Tom and flattened him, stolen his hat, his deck of cards, his cigarettes, his whiskey, his girl, and maybe his boots and his typewriter, I would feel that it was all for the greater good and that Tom should have come around, jaw stiff, head blazing, and said, as Maria says to Robert Jordan: *Inglés, how can I help thee with thy work?*

I will go a step further. When I met a poet-revolutionary from South America—a guy who had fought with power weapons in the jungle and had been through hell—who told me that he didn't think much of Hemingway, as if his work were more or less tourist trade, I pretended to take it in stride because he was a swell guy and his English was small and—well, for Christ's sake, he had fought *For Whom the Bell Tolls* in the flesh. So I drove him up to Lake George, where we walked around the fort. . . but I wasn't *thinking* in stride, I was thinking: *On whose side were you fighting if you shrug Hemingway—and will you tell me the geniuses with whom you are in love?* As the answer to that, I knew, was, for example, Joseph Conrad, a choice with which neither Hemingway nor any sentient being would want to quarrel, I have had to content myself that in matters of revolutionary taste there is no disputing.

When I reported Tom's trash to a woman, Irene, whom I had met on the Bayville Beach and who worked the library in nearby Oyster Bay, a woman after whom Mr. Tom dearly lusted, for he would ask me about her, tell me what he thought of her, and hated when she didn't come around for a while (sodden wretch that he was, dripping at the window), Irene told me her own Hemingway anecdote.

This is peculiar, I thought: *two Hemingway anecdotes in the same little Long Island town—and within a week of each other. . .*

I was living in a one-room apartment attached to Tom's house like the quarters of a servant. I slept on the floor. It was there that I learned that one could sleep on anything—or, sleep on nothing—except when one is sick, when, unless you are an Arab, a bed is more than a luxury. For the first few months my bookshelf was a Hefty bag spread out at the foot of the "bed." Then it was two. The property was one block from the Long Island Sound and only a few paces from a peaceful body of water called Mill Neck Creek, so close that one morning after a storm I awoke to find a boat had been washed up on the lawn. The water opened out the apartment into a wonderful place to live, not small at all if you looked outside. I could see the Bayville Bridge from my writing table and from the seat in the bathroom and it always relaxed me to see and to hear the cars and trucks rolling over it, especially whenever I composed myself for sleep, for it reassured me that there would be a world outside even when I closed my eyes, even when I slept, for I never assume a sunrise. I was not a painter yet but I painted my first canvas in that little hut of a house, and it was there that I finished my first novel, which I called *Midnight Peninsula* because it was based on the nightlife of dreams and the nightlife of performing in clubs. As I typed its closing pages, a storm of birds gathered slowly in the creek across the drive. I could see it clearly as I worked: it was directly in front of me, and I could hear it, too, for this variety of bird, such as I had never seen, was squawking and chirping and screeching at a volume that I had never known. As soon I typed the period on *Midnight Peninsula*, the riot began to disperse, and within ten minutes the birds had disappeared. It was a rare sensation of being joined by what we call *nature* (as if we weren't joined to it with every cell), and this exceptional experience gave me the start of my third Matisse novel, *Matisse in the Street of Flowers*, in which it happens to Matisse in his quarters on Quai Saint-Michel as he finishes his first major canvas, and it gave me the opening sentence of the book: "The birds have always known what I'm up to."

At the time that I met her, Irene had been newly liberated from her sloth of a drunken husband. A chief of police in a nearby town, he slapped her, punched her, kicked her, threatened to kill her (often), and he used to, as she told me, "rattle his gun in his holster" whenever he felt that she was hard to control. . . until one winter day he kicked her out of the house—literally: threw her down a flight of stairs and kicked her out the door in a heavy snowfall, locking the door and leaving her in the snow with broken bones and a bruised face for which she was hospitalized for weeks. This police chief was not so macho in all things, for he was ashamed of his body, never revealed his private sector to her, hid behind a door when he undressed for bed, and didn't do much of anything when he arrived, so that even after decades of marriage his wife was still a child and utterly a stranger to ecstasy. He knew nothing about women or sexual relations. She too, in her way, was ashamed of her body, which she had been led to believe was "too flat-chested" and "cold."

"When did you know that it was a mistake?" I asked of the marriage.

"After a week."

She had been married for exactly twenty-one years before he kicked her out of the house, a house to which she was inordinately attached and of which she sued for possession until she saw, over time, that I was right in saying—in *promising*—that she would not miss the house for five minutes, not once she gave up the ghost, moved out of her parents' house and took a little place of her own, and that she would wonder, the rest of her days, that she had not abandoned it twenty years and fifty-one weeks sooner.

At first even to speak to me in public was a furtive thing for her. Yes, the Chief had kicked her out, but he was having her followed, police style, to be sure she wouldn't connect, in any way, with another man—a thing that he had done during the years of her marriage. In fact he made sure she didn't connect with *any*body or any*thing*, including her poetry, for which she used to have to sneak out of bed in order to jot down a few hidden lines. Now a shout or a siren or the sight of a patrol car could jolt her upright, widen her eyes, and turn her to stone. "Talking on beach with hippie" was one of the notes in the Chief's logbook about her life beyond the law, leaving us to wonder who the hippie could be until we realized the hippie was me. This surveillance heightened her hunger to break the taboos in her life, even in yours, and she broke them with me as often as she could, for I was the first and only man and she wanted revenge on the time she had lost in the house of a slob of a cop with a gun.

In the lives of everybody that we know there are at least a few facts or incidents that will strike us as strange and for which we will never receive, and never concoct, adequate explanation. For me, there is this about Irene: She had a copy of Sartre's *Being and Nothingness* on her night table. Even the Finnegans of *Finnegans Wake* would admit that *Being and Nothingness* is one of the least readable masterworks in literature, and how it could have served as Irene's pillow book will never be clarified. At first she told me that she had read it all, but when I pressed her about it she admitted that wasn't *quite* true, but that she had read much of it. For her to have read or to have wanted to read even a part of it mystified me then, and mystifies me now, although now, as I write this, for the first time it occurs to me that maybe Sartre's *title* had an appeal to her because it named, perfectly, both the after and the before of her separation.

At the time that I knew her, Irene was *an older woman* to me but, as I have suggested, older only in age, and she herself knew it. In fact, she was the youngest woman I had ever met. As she was nonetheless years younger than I am now, this is an old story. . . although I no longer know what "old" really is when everything that seems like yesterday is more like now. At the time of the Hemingway anecdote, in 1953, Irene was a teenager, on vacation in Tampa with her sister and a friend of her father's. I mentioned that it would have been okay with me and with the universe if Hemingway had stolen Tom's girl. To the degree that Irene was Tom's girl in fantasy, Hemingway had, in fact, made her his own, even if only for a song.

They were sitting in a bar. Across the room was Hemingway, whose gray-bearded visage was one of the most easily recognizable in the world. Hemingway, who was there by himself, could not resist the attraction of this creature and her sister. Even Irene, now a separated wife in the depths of her demeanment, admitted that she was "once" a beautiful girl. After staring at—better to say appreciating—the sisters for a while, Hemingway came to their table, introduced himself, and asked whether he could dedicate a song to them. He went to the bandleader and told him to play "My Wild Irish Rose." Which they did, with Hemingway smiling and Irene having a thrill. Then he left.

What does Irene's anecdote have to do with Cormac McCarthy? Nothing, but I have always wanted to pass it along, and fearing I will never find the right place for it, I have decided to do it here. In Cormac McCarthy's house he would rather you tell a story, even an anecdote, than talk to him about his own work, so don't be so certain that Irene, Hemingway, and "My Wild Irish Rose" are out of place.

NOTES

PART 1

Judging *Blood Meridian Or The Evening Redness in the West* by Its Cover

1. In Paulo's correspondence with McCarthy, Paulo pointed out that the biblical town of Jedda was misspelled "Jeda." When Vintage International published a twenty-fifth-anniversary edition that incorporated minor corrections/alterations by McCarthy, some misspellings were retained from the original, but the correction of "Jeda" to "Jedda" prompted me to congratulate Paulo on expanding the novel by one letter.

2. Rick Wallach's Picador paperback of the novel is a fascinating object. It has been Rick's study and his notebook for twenty years, and there are only a few pages that have not been highlighted and scratched with layers of marginalia in every available space. It needs the critical equivalent of a geological survey, one that I shall perform myself if I can pry it loose from him for long enough. When I proposed it as a project, Rick's response was positive, but he concluded by saying: "I'll have to consult a therapeutic shaman who can help me through the exercise in nonattachment." In talking about the fact that practically every inch of the book has been filled with notations, Rick quoted something he was told by his friend the mythologist Joseph Campbell: "If you want to go deeply into a text, act like a German."

3. When Wesley Morgan and I visited the Southern Railway Depot, we could see that McCarthy's window was clearly not for buying tickets.

4. The building that used to be Draper Books is now a travel agency but the sign for the bookstore has not been removed. When the door is open, one can see it behind the sign for the new business. Draper Books was at 205 Mohican Street, a short walk from the Colony Motel on the same side of the street.

5. St. John Chrysostom, who decided that the Devil would be more terrified by a martyr's severed head than the head when it was speaking, doesn't appear to have imagined that severed heads might not necessarily shut up. There are many cases of religious post-ignition, gruesome in ways that, as with gargoyles on a cathedral, remind you that religious fervor reaches as well toward the ugly and the absurd as it does toward the sublime. . . such as the head of St. Paul, said to have chanted "Jesus

Christus" fifty times before subsiding into silence. . . or the head of St. Denis, said to have preached a sermon during a six-mile walk to what is now the *commune* of Saint-Denis, a crime-ridden suburb of Paris. . . or the nine-year-old head of St. Justus of Beauvais, said to have asked his father—or do you say *its* father—to take him/it to his/its mother to be kissed a farewell. I have known several people—martyrs in their own rooms for putting up with me—for whom the urge to preach to me would not be impaired whether their heads were on their necks or in their hands or elsewhere. We can also assume that both the priest and the blind man encountered by Billy Parham in *The Crossing* would not be silenced by something as benign as a beheading. In the history of cephalophores, St. Denis is the most famous due to the founding of a church on the site where he was beheaded—thus Montmartre, the mountain of the martyr—but cephalophoric stories attach to St. Nicasius of Rheims, St. Aphrodesius of Alexandria, St. Valerie of Limoges, St. Ginés de la Gara, who tossed his head into the Rhone, and St. Gemolo, who managed a ride on horseback to his uncle, a bishop who will have to be forgiven if he displayed mixed emotions about the devotion of his nephew. Of course the real horror is that centuries of real heads have rolled because men have doubted or disputed the doctrines and dogmas attaching to these frightnight fictions.

When I was delving into de Born, I was also rereading Michael Herr's Vietnam memoir, *Dispatches*, published eight years before *Blood Meridian Or The Evening Redness in the West* in 1977, and I realized I was reading about the subject of *Blood Meridian_Or The Evening Redness in the West*. Not war per se, not the Vietnam referenced in Barcley Owens' *The Western Novels of Cormac McCarthy*, but quite specifically Michael Herr's Vietnam—in other words, another man's art. Herr's Vietnam exists in *Dispatches* and in the parts that he wrote for *Full Metal Jacket* and *Apocalypse Now*, although certainly veterans of Vietnam have recognized their own nightmares in Herr's. At the time Mark Morrow was photographing McCarthy, I was playing Ben Franklin in a two-man play while sentenced, during the day, to proofreading retail copy at an ad agency where I shared a small office with an ex-CIA spook, a man named Glenn who extracted from the briefcase that seldom left his side a loaded semiautomatic that he called an "antipersonnel device," making me glad that Glenn and I were getting along. Glenn's father was a five-star general with whom he liked to attend air force maneuvers, and I saw in the son all five of the father's stars when a long-legged receptionist stood in our office in one of her many miniskirts discoursing on the perils of nuclear armaments while Glenn, unconsciously, drummed on his desk the percussive prelude to "The Marines' Hymn." At a time when no one like Glenn was in Cambodia, Glenn was in Cambodia doing aerial reconnaissance photography to implement the war where there wasn't any war for a country that wasn't there. The two of us shared such an energetic liking of *Apocalypse Now* that one afternoon Glenn phonied up an excuse to watch it with me on a VCR while the rest of the agency was generating ads for Lenny's Clam Bar and electronics stores managed by manic Israelis. I told Glenn that I loved the film as a rare case of high art in cinema; also because, as I sat there and watched it at the movies, I was finally at home and at ease. "How so?" Glenn asked. "Because," I said, "to me, it felt like daily life." Glenn told me that when he watched it for the first time alone, he wished that he could have had everybody he knew in the theatre with him so that he could say to them: "*This* is *exactly* what it was like." Part of that was Francis Ford Coppola, John Milius, and—although shamefully uncredited—Joseph Conrad; and part of that was Michael Herr.

It would have been interesting to hear Glenn's reaction to *Blood Meridian Or The Evening Redness in the West*. We know Michael Herr's response to the novel through the blurb that he wrote for it—"A classic American novel of regeneration through violence"—but it would be interesting to know whose idea it was to ask for Herr's comment. I do not mean to ascribe any influence on McCarthy, who might not even have read the book (he probably did). But with passages in *Dispatches* like: "Our machine was devastating. And versatile. It could do everything but stop" (71), or: "'If you kill for money you're a mercenary. If you kill for pleasure you're a sadist. If you kill for both you're a Green Beret'" (257), or: "I told him about the colonel who had threatened to court martial a spec 4 for refusing to cut the heart out of a dead Viet Cong and feed it to a dog" (204), or: "the war gave it urgency and made it a deep thing, so deep that we didn't even have to like one another to belong" (224), or: "There was a lot that went unsaid. . . but just because it was seldom spoken about didn't mean that we weren't very much aware of it or that, in that terrible, shelterless place, we weren't grateful for each other" (224), or: "There was no way of thinking about 'who we were' because we were all so different, but where we were alike we were really alike" (224), or: "you felt you were being dry-sniped every time someone looked at you" (14), or: "the saturating strangeness of the place which didn't lessen with exposure so often as it fattened and darkened in accumulating alienation" (13), or: "PRAY FOR WAR was written on the side of his helmet" (25), or: "even the dead started telling me stories, you'd hear them out of a remote but accessible space where there were no ideas, no emotions, no facts, no proper language" (31), or: "inspired saints and realized homicidals, unconscious lyric poets and mean dumb motherfuckers with their brains all down in their necks" (30), or: "'My *best* tour we'd go through and that was it, we'd rip out the hedges and burn the hootches and blow all the walls and kill every chicken, pig and cow in the whole fucking ville. I mean, if we can't shoot these people, what the fuck are we doing here'" (29), or: "some reporter asked a door gunner, 'How can you shoot women and children?' and he answered, 'It's easy, you just don't lead 'em as much,'" (35), or: "In Chu Lai some Marines pointed a man out to me who swore to God they'd seen him bayonet a wounded NVA and then lick the bayonet clean" (35), or: "The colonel in command was so drunk that day that he could barely get his words out" (12), or: "'We had this gook and we was gonna skin him'" (66), or: "Going crazy was built into the tour" (59), or: "only heavy killing could make them feel so alive" (58), or: "[they] followed the black light around the bend and took possession of the madness that had been waiting there in trust for them for eighteen or twenty-five or fifty years" (58), I felt as if I were reading about the Glanton gang, to such a degree that after copying out relevant passages, I noticed that the citations were reading like this: 13, 13, 14, 15, 15, 15, 16, 17—in other words, I was copying out half the book. Concentrating on a single motif—even a far-out one like the collection of ears—didn't change the situation, not with bits like: "He pulled a thick plastic bag out of his pack and handed it over to me. It was full of what looked like large pieces of dried fruit. I was stoned and hungry. I almost put my hand in there, but it had a bad weight to it. . . . Someone had told me once, there were a lot more ears than heads in Vietnam" (34), or: "a picture of a Marine holding an ear or maybe two ears or, as in the case of a guy I knew near Pleiku, a whole necklace of ears, 'love beads' as its owner called them" (119). Herr's insightful evocation of how he and his fellow correspondents were observed in their observing reminded me of the Kid being watched in his watching and of the fact that the prototype for the Kid, Samuel Chamberlain, was a writer himself and thus a kind of war reporter. In perhaps the least likely place, I found a flavor of Judge Holden. The photojournalist Tim Page, an English orphan who roamed the globe dangerously before he was wounded many times in many places in Vietnam and who, in Herr's view, was erudite and at times an aristocratic snob, reacts to a proposal by an English publisher to write a book that will finally take the glamour out of war:

> Take the glamour out of war! I mean, how the bloody hell can you do *that*? Go and take the glamour out of a Huey, go take the glamour out of a Sheridan. . . . It's like trying to take the glamour out of an M-79. . . Ohhhh, war is *good* for you, you can't take the glamour out of that. It's like trying to take the glamour out of sex, trying to take the glamour out of the Rolling Stones. . . . I mean, you *know* that, it just *can't be done*! The very idea! Ohhh, what a laugh! Take the bloody *glamour* out of bloody *war*! (248–249)

Rereading *Dispatches* made me wonder whether it wasn't perhaps necessary to reread *everything* after one has read *Blood Meridian Or The Evening Redness in the West*, for what Herr says about the war in Vietnam applies equally to McCarthy's masterpiece: "The thing had transmitted too much energy" (49).

6. On the back of the anniversary edition of the novel published in paperback by Vintage, there is a recent photograph—taken by Nerissa Escanlar—of McCarthy sitting in front of two tall shelves full of books in the library of the Santa Fe Institute. The photograph is peculiar for several reasons. McCarthy's eyes are not visible, as he is

leaning forward in the far left of the frame, looking down. His broad forehead is overlit, but the brightest thing in the photograph is a shaded table lamp that is nearly at the center of the frame. It is thus a photograph that is chiefly about a lamp and a forehead. At least his face is well lit, and carries the suggestion of strength and reflection.

7. After Paulo Faria and I breakfasted with McCarthy in Santa Fe, I told Mark that McCarthy was a prince of a guy. "You are correct," Mark said, "he is a prince of a guy, and of all the impressions I had of him so long ago, that is the strongest."

A Walk with Wesley Morgan through Suttree's Knoxville

1. Wilma Dykeman's review of *The Orchard Keeper* (Random House, $4.95) is interesting, especially in its original format, bearing the headline CORMAC McCAR-THY'S BOOK IMPRESSIVE, above which there is an underlined kicker: *E-T Scenes Sharp, Clear.* There are two mentions of the fact that McCarthy's father was a lawyer with the TVA: in the review, and in a biographical addendum: "Cormac McCarthy is the son of Mr. and Mrs. Charles J. McCarthy, Martin Mill Pike. The father is chief counsel for TVA. The book brought the 32–year-old author a $5000 fellowship from the American Academy of Arts and Letters for travel abroad." In the photograph of McCarthy, with the cutline "Knoxville author," McCarthy is dressed in a jacket and tie. The picture does not hint at the career ahead of him, whereas an image I have seen of him in elementary school does indeed do that, or at least allows for that. The name "Dykeman" is given as almost the nom de plume of Mrs. James R. Stokely of Newport, Tennessee. She was introduced to Stokely, son of the president of Stokely Brothers Canning Company, by Thomas Wolfe's sister Mabel. In 1957, Dykeman wrote an important book with Stokely, *Neither Black Nor White*, but her first work of nonfic-tion was *The French Broad* (1955), for which she won a fight with her publisher over a chapter on pollution. In 1962 she published the first of three novels, *The Tall Women*. She was a columnist for the *Knoxville News-Sentinel* from 1962 to 2000, a position out of which Dykeman published two collections. She was an early feminist, integration-ist, and environmentalist.

Already in 1965, Dykeman made observations about McCarthy's work that are per-tinent today. After delineating the three main characters in *The Orchard Keeper*, Dyke-man says: "Around these three the author weaves an intricate pattern of flash-backs in language that is sometimes more tortuous than clear. Violence is rampant. In fact, it becomes the most commonplace thing in the book before we reach the last page." Depending on how you read it, Dykeman's prognostic conclusion about McCarthy either makes no sense at all, or is at least interesting for how it distinguishes between two paths that have not turned out to be separate for McCarthy. "He may become a coterie writer, refining his keen and original sensibilities into ever more elegant and abstruse prose," Dykeman wrote, "or he may become a richly endowed observer of the human scene with much to tell us about ourselves." See George Brosi's excellent appreciation of Dykeman in his editorial "This Side of the Mountain."

2. For Wesley's photograph of this fire, see page 91 of the Winter 2011 *Appalachian Heritage* (vol. 39, no. 1), an issue featuring five articles on McCarthy. For Wesley's photograph of the post-fire fireplace and chimney, see page 25. A map of downtown Knoxville is on page 20. The issue is illustrated with several of Wesley's and my images of Knoxville, including John "Big Frig" Hannifin (who appears in *Suttree*), and the interior of Lester's hideaway that we visit in Part 3 of this chapter. For a detailed discussion of the fire and the remains of the McCarthy family home, see Part 6 of Chapter Two, "Finding the Where," in Part Two of this book, "Cormac McCarthy's House: A Memoir."

3. See Josyph, *Adventures in Reading Cormac McCarthy*, 21–22.

4. See Morgan, "Thematic Apperception Test Images." The test, known as the TAT, was first published in 1935 out of Harvard, where Murray was a major figure for decades and developed a holistic theory of personality known as personology.

5. Although Murray told Melville biographer Lewis Mumford in 1928 that he expected to finish his own work on Melville in eighteen months, he persevered—or perseverated—for more than a decade before abandoning it in 1940. His preface and introduction to *Pierre; Or, The Ambiguities* were published in a scholarly edition by Hendricks House in 1949. Murray's style is often antiquated but he is capable of insights, such as: "Melville was not writing autobiography in the usual sense, but, from first to last, the biography of his self-image. These identifications and self-dramatizations should not be dismissed as inconsequential shadows; they constitute the very core, the mythological and religious core, of personality" (xx). In his correspondence with Mumford, collected in an interesting book called *"In Old Friendship,"* Murray, less pretentious in tone, improvises gems of observation and speculation, such as this about Melville's relations with Nathaniel Hawthorne: "I think Hawthorne was a kind of untouchable separate one who held a mirror before Melville, that he might see Ahab glaring out of his own bloodshot eyes" (56).

Melville was not the only historical figure Murray analyzed. In a joint report on the psychology of Adolf Hitler commissioned by the OSS in 1939 and published in 1943, Murray (and his colleagues) predicted Hitler's suicide and suggested a suppressed homosexual side to Hitler's personality. Thus Murray had the distinction of analyzing, simultaneously, Herman Melville and Adolf Hitler.

6. When Suttree Landing Park opened in 2012, Wesley was underwhelmed. The photos he sent me support that reaction. "It is located on the south side of the Tennessee River along Langford Avenue," Wesley said, "probably not far from where Suttree launched the police department's 'Car Seven' (441–442). The 'park' seems to consist

of about a quarter of an acre of largely gravel-covered ground surrounded by a second-hand chain-link fence and with a boat-launch ramp currently blocked by large stones. Not exactly a spot that I would pick to spread a blanket for a picnic lunch, but at least it's a start and perhaps it'll be improved."

"You went in?"

"The gates were open. I was the only one there."

Now there is also Suttree's High Gravity Tavern at 409 South Gay Street in Knoxville, where one of the bartenders is the actor Steven Dupree, who played Black in a production of *The Sunset Limited*. Co-starring Greg Congleton as White, directed for the Actors Co-op by Travis Flatt, the production ran from February 21 to March 1, 2008 in the Carpetbag Theatre's Black Box Theatre at 5213 Homberg Drive near the former location of Draper Books (see n.3). Dupree can be said to personify the title of this book, for he has inhabited several houses that McCarthy has built—Black's Harlem apartment, the play in which it appears, the small theatrical company devoting itself to McCarthy, the black box in which the show was staged, the theatre that owned it, and the tavern or public house named in tribute to McCarthy's great novel—and he is reading the author by going to work on and in his play, and by tending bar where *bar* is both the counter at which refreshment and conversation are served to Knoxville, and the wider premises in which a twice-fictional Suttree invites you to partake.

7. See Morgan, "McCarthy's High School Years."

8. The passage in *Suttree* is the following: "He found the story on page two. Yeggs last night boarded the River Queen, popular Knoxville excursion boat, in what was apparently an unsuccessful robbery attempt. He smiled and finished the milk and laid his dime on the counter and pushed back the paper" (235). The deleted manuscript version of the story is in the Cormac McCarthy Papers, Southwestern Writers Collection, Alkek Library, Texas State University at San Marcos, box 19, folder 13, 392–400.

9. See Morgan, "Death and Epidemic Violence." The dead body of a homeless Iowa man named Paul David Shields, age fifty-one, was found in exactly the same spot on November 30, 2010. See Jacobs, "Body of Homeless Man Recovered from Fort Loudoun Lake."

Believing in *The Sunset Limited*

1. In the audio commentary for the DVD of *The Sunset Limited*, McCarthy speaks of Beethoven as the greatest composer, and says: "I think Mozart's violin concertos are just—they're just poetry."

2. On the DVD of *The Sunset Limited*, the audio commentary features Samuel L. Jackson congenially drawing out McCarthy on various issues. An anecdote reported by Pat Jordan in the *New York Times Magazine* suggests another facet of their working

relationship. "When Jackson was making a filmed version of the play *The Sunset Limited*, with Tommy Lee Jones," Jordan writes, "the play's author, Cormac McCarthy, complained about his line readings. Jackson said: 'It sounds better my way. I'm not trying to make this [expletive] worse!'"

3. See Monk, "'An Impulse to Action, an Undefined Want.'"

4. In the spring of 2006, when Austin Pendleton played White in the Steppenwolf production of *The Sunset Limited*, he was asked whether he found thematic connections between the play and McCarthy's prose. "I've read four or five of his novels," he said, "and *The Sunset Limited* doesn't remind me at all of any of them. . . . I wouldn't ever have known it was the same writer who wrote *Blood Meridian* and *Suttree* and *All the Pretty Horses* and all the other things of his that I've read. I never would have guessed it, except that it's passionate and beautifully written and it's about issues of life and death." As I have suggested, Pendleton's familiarity with, and admiration for, McCarthy's fiction is typical of performers involved in his work. The quotation is from a feature of Steppenwolf's website called "Watch & Listen," http://www.steppenwolf.org/watchlisten/, under "News & Articles," volume 3 (2005–2006), "Storytellers."

5. During the introductions to the audio commentary for the DVD of *The Sunset Limited*, McCarthy says simply: "I'm the playwright."

6. These issues are also discussed in the next chapter, "'Now Let's Talk about *The Crossing*.'"

"Now Let's Talk about *The Crossing*"

1. See, for example, Marty's delightful "Games in the Border Trilogy."

2. In Josyph, *Adventures in Reading Cormac McCarthy*.

3. For a fascinating discussion of this issue in Montaigne, see Chapter 8 of Hugo Friedrich's *Montaigne*. The chapter, called "Montaigne's Literary Consciousness and the Form of the *Essais*," is a model of balanced, informed, and compelling analysis of an author's approach to composition.

4. In Josyph, *Adventures in Reading Cormac McCarthy*.

5. Here is Christian Kiefer's response: "I recall our discussion then, and my adherence to the notion that *the rest* of *The Crossing* was superior to *The Wolf Trapper*, and I will admit that I've changed my mind some about that. I've come to realize how beautifully *structured The Wolf Trapper* is, and what a shamble is the rest of the novel. Nonetheless, there are such moments of beauty, horror, and philosophical prodding in the remainder of the book that I can't help but feel that *The Crossing*, as a whole, is not so failed as some might believe. It's true that the novel fails to cohere as well as *The Wolf Trapper* promises, but there is a fair amount of philosophical searching in the rest of the book. Perhaps it's not hollow searching, although it certainly seems less intellectually deep as it did when I was in my 20s. The questions about history, memory, and

violence that are present in *Blood Meridian* are present in *the rest* of *The Crossing* too, but somehow the questions have become more muddled, and what answers are suggested in the storytellers' tales are not real answers in the end. But then, do we expect concrete answers from McCarthy's fiction? I hope not. Does that mean *The Crossing* is, as a novel, a kind of failure? Perhaps. I certainly wouldn't have said that twenty years ago. I guess that means my perspective *has* changed. Maybe I owe you a beer!"

6. This observation by McCarthy is quoted in an editorial sidebar to *The Wolf Trapper* in *Esquire*, 95–104. The sidebar is on 97.

7. Marty's suspicion is correct. The rumor that *The Wolf Trapper* was written originally as a separate entity has been proved untrue.

8. In the poet H. D.'s memoir of therapy with Freud to which I referred in my first chapter, there is this: "I did tell the Professor of a great-grandmother who heard her son calling to her. She ran out in the garden to meet him (in Pennsylvania). Her son was in the West Indies. It was some time after that news reached them that her son had died at the exact moment she had rushed into the garden to welcome him home" (173).

9. Wesley Morgan wrote: "Good eye. You are correct about the p. 16 description of a theatre in *The Road* being pretty generic, and yet, when I first read the novel, I too made a marginal note: '?Tennessee Theatre?' The things McCarthy mentions— 'listening to the music,' 'gold scrollwork and sconces,' 'columnar drapes,' are all consistent with the place and somewhat characteristic of it. The Tennessee has a large theatre organ that was most often played between movie features as well as in dedicated concerts. I believe the theatre was the home of the Knoxville Symphony. Thus there was plenty of opportunity to hear music there."

10. In May 2006, the Steppenwolf Theatre Company in Chicago premiered *The Sunset Limited* at the Merle Reskin Garage Theatre, directed by Sheldon Patinkin, starring Freeman Coffey as Black, Austin Pendleton as White. Marty saw this production in Chicago. I saw it that fall, with the same cast and director, at the 59E59 Theaters in Manhattan.

11. This quotation from a letter to Albert Erskine around the time of *The Orchard Keeper* is in box 29, folder 3 of the Albert Erskine Collection at the University of Virginia Library. The letter is undated. The folder is dated 1962–1964.

12. In Santa Fe I asked McCarthy where he bought the interesting boots he was wearing, a narrow-toed pair of clay-toned ostrich, a taste that he shares with Chigurh. "Where I buy all of my boots," he said. "El Paso."

13. In the audio commentary for the DVD of *The Sunset Limited*, Jones says this about the coffee insert: "There's a shot coming up that I stole from Jean-Luc Godard. That one. . . . I just wanted to put the world in a teacup. Or a coffee cup in this case. That accounts for the echoing dog barking."

14. The stew that was used on the set, which was made by the mother of the property master, Keith Walters, included hot dogs. Both actors enjoyed it.

15. On November 28, 2011, a man was killed by a southbound C on the tracks of the 155th Street subway station at St. Nicholas Avenue. This is a different station from the one at 155th Street and 8th Avenue that is depicted at the start of the HBO film. The two stations are in very different neighborhoods of Harlem. The 8th Avenue station, which exits in front of a housing complex, the Polo Grounds Towers, and is close to the Harlem River, is difficult to reach from the west side of Harlem (it took me four separate trips to locate it), for one version of 155th Street turns into a bridge into the Bronx while another version resumes in Manhattan underneath it. Neither the play nor the screenplay specifies at which of the two 155th Street stations White attempted suicide. It is an eerie feeling to walk down the steps of either station with White's ambition even notionally in mind, and once a train enters the station you tend to drive White out of your consciousness and step back farther toward the center of the platform.

16. On an edition of NPR's *Science Friday*, in a discussion at the Santa Fe Institute between Werner Herzog, Cormac McCarthy, Lawrence Krauss, and Ira Flatow, Herzog said: "By dint of declaration, Cormac McCarthy creates a whole landscape that has been unknown to all of us, even though it seems to exist like, let's say, Faulkner and others invented and described the Deep South; someone like Joseph Conrad describes the Congo and the jungle and the mysteries."

17. *Freud's Last Session*, written by Mark St. Germain, directed by Taylor Marchant, starred Martin Rayner as Sigmund Freud and Mark H. Dold as C. S. Lewis. It ran from July through November 2010 at the Marjorie S. Deane Little Theatre at the West Side YMCA on West 64th Street in Manhattan, then it resumed performances in January 2011. In October 2011, it transferred to New World Stages on West 50th Street.

18. When I discussed *The Gardener's Son* with Kevin Conway, who played James Gregg, we touched upon the nightmare of cutting *All the Pretty Horses*. "I don't understand these guys," he said of its producers. "In terms of the audience, two hours and forty-five minutes is excruciatingly long if you're not enjoying the film. Another fifteen or twenty minutes, if it brings it all together, makes the time go like *that*." More of my discussion with Conway appears later in this chapter.

19. In "Games in the Border Trilogy," Marty writes: "Almost nothing that happens in the last volume is not foreshadowed by something that happened in the first two" (270).

20. Myers, *A Reader's Manifesto*.

21. After I shared this discussion with Stacey Peebles (editor of the *Cormac McCarthy Journal*), she said this about Bobby's response to Gregg's offer of the coin: "I have always thought that Bobby reacts to the coin more or less as a symbol of everything he hates about industrialization: the mill, class divisions, etcetera. I never thought that Bobby needed to know about Gregg's offer to Martha in order to be angered by the coin. Buy sex, buy privilege, buy people—what's the difference? For Bobby, the coin represents all the corruptions of capitalism at its worst."

PART 2

Chapter One

1. I am not alone in this feeling of needing to paint something in order to see it. In his delightful book about working in watercolors, *The Waters Reglitterized*, written in Paris in 1939, Henry Miller says: "For, as you well know, you can look at things all your life and not see them really. This 'seeing' is, in a way, a 'not seeing,' if you follow me. It is more of a search for something, in which, being blindfolded, you develop the tactile, the olfactory, the auditory senses—and thus *see* for the first time. One day, odd as it sounds, you suddenly see what makes a wagon for example. You see the wagon in the wagon—and not the cliché image which you were taught to recognize as 'wagon' and accept for the rest of your life as a time-saving convenience. The development of this faculty, for an artist in any realm, is what stops the clock and permits him to live fully and freely" (38).

2. That Henry Miller understood the balance of respect and contempt for one's media is suggested by a passage in *The Waters Reglitterized* in which he refers to his crayons as "the axe," an axe with which he "swung into" a picture "with all my muscle and will" to produce "a terrifying piece of insanity" that is nonetheless "a very tender piece of portraiture" (40–41).

Sometimes a mere shift in style can evoke a response that suggests the actual use of new media when in fact it is only a shift in attitude. When Cecil Beaton went to photograph Picasso at Notre-Dame-de-Vie in Mougins after an absence of thirty years, at a time when Picasso said that it took him a long time to become young, Beaton, whose photographs are pristine, was unpleasantly disturbed by the new young Picassos, telling his diary that his work "seems to have lost exactitude. The line is not good, the brush stroke so coarse and rubbed" (44), so that he wondered whether Picasso were painting with a cork. "I noticed no brushes," (44) he says tellingly, judging that much of the work was unfit to be seen "and probably will never be exhibited". . . . "Some were wild blobs and smudges of a ruthlessness that was really very unpalatable. Sad that someone who can draw with the exactitude of Ingres and the freedom of a Japanese master now does thick smudges that have no apparent drawing" (47). But Beaton is smart enough to doubt his own evaluation. "But no doubt I am wrong again," he says (47).

In early April 1888, van Gogh wrote from Arles to his friend Émile Bernard: "I don't keep to any one technique. I dab the color irregularly on the canvas and leave it at that. Here lumps of thick paint, there bits of canvas left uncovered, elsewhere portions left quite unfinished, new beginnings, coarsenesses; but anyway the result, it seems to me, is alarming and provocative enough to disturb those people who have fixed preconceived ideas about technique" (*Letters to Émile Bernard*, ed. Lord, 24). In June, still in Arles, he summarized the approach this way: "It's more the intensity of thought than the tranquility of touch we are after" (50). In the same letter, van Gogh commits an interesting linguistic inversion in which the painter himself, not the canvas, is the victim of attack. "After all," he says, "it's rather like being suddenly assaulted by a rapier" (50).

3. In the Wittliff Collections at the Albert B. Alkek Library of Texas State University at San Marcos, the Woolmer Collection of McCarthy materials contains a letter from McCarthy to the book collector Howard Woolmer that sheds light on McCarthy's use of the term "little project." In referring to the Border Trilogy, McCarthy writes: "Anyway I'm still at work on my little projects I've finished rough drafts of 2 novels and started a third. They are all three connected. . ." (McCarthy to Woolmer, November 17, 1988, quoted in "A Guide to the Woolmer Collection of Cormac McCarthy, 1969–2006, Collection 092," 14).

4. My profile of Robert Antoni and his extraordinary novel *Divina Trace* was published as "A Gift of Voices" in the *Bloomsbury Review*, May/June 1995. My conversation with him, "Walking Down the Trace," can be found at robertantoni.com.

5. Quotations from the Texas Senate are from its proceedings for February 7, 2001, at www.journals.senate.state.tx.us/sjrnl/77r/html/2-7.htm.

Chapter Two

1. McCarthy to Howard Woolmer, January 26, 1977, quoted in "A Guide to the Woolmer Collection of Cormac McCarthy, 1969–2006, Collection 092," 6.

2. For Danchin's edition of Artaud's letters, see *Artaud et l'Asile*, vol. 2.

3. This club is now Le Solitaire, advertising BOOGIE NIGHT MIX MOVE, but the pair of high-heeled neon Beverlys are still hanging there, so she must be within, and a visit could not be all that solitary.

4. After I gave my friend Harry Guest—an English poet, novelist, and translator—a picture of Racine's house in rue Visconti, Harry added to my memory of this historic street—called in one guidebook dilapidated, dark, and dirty, but to these eyes perfectly beautiful—a reminiscence of his own, referring to "the vivid evocation of that street in Paris where a girl I knew in 1955, when I was studying Mallarmé at the Sorbonne, had a dorm and wove incredible tapestries for international exhibitions. Her studio rang with LP's of Sidney Bechet or works by Bach." Having given Blaise Cendrars a mistress in this street in one of my Matisse novels, I can no longer separate my character Cendrars from my friend Harry, or Harry's girl friend from Cendrars' mistress. It is as if, in two sentences, Harry wrote me a novel in code.

5. In Josyph, *Adventures in Reading Cormac McCarthy*.

Chapter Three

1. Recent rereadings of *Barnaby Rudge, Oliver Twist, Great Expectations, A Tale of Two Cities,* and *The Uncommercial Traveller* have confirmed my opinion that McCarthy has at least as much in common with Dickens as with Faulkner, Hemingway, or Joyce.

Chapter Four

1. Campbell, *Wings of Art.*

2. For van Gogh's sketch, see *Letters to Émile Bernard* (plate 21, page 46), a real lifer of a book that I recommend highly. (It is also in a newer, more readily available edition of the letters called *Vincent Van Gogh, Painted with Words: The Letters to Émile Bernard* (59). This lavishly illustrated edition includes facsimiles of all the letters, but it is annoying to read, and I have not used it for my citations.)

In another of the best books about a painter, Brassaï's *Conversations avec Picasso,* translated as either *Picasso and Company* (by Francis Price) or *Conversations with Picasso* (by Jane Marie Todd), Maurice Raynal takes Brassaï with him to revisit the Bateau-Lavoir in rue Ravignon. Brassaï: "Raynal plucks through his memories, calling up pictures of the box mattress with no legs, the round folding table, Picasso's old deal armoire and the rickety, creaking easel he still has with him at the rue des Grands-Augustins" (Todd, 269). In Price's translation, the easel was "groaning" (199).

3. The portion of the film *Cormac McCarthy's House* in which I paint the large house is viewable at http://www.youtube.com/lostmedallion.

4. It is my custom to tear up corrected pages of my work before throwing them out. While working on the new series of *Cormac McCarthy's House*—in which I incorporate a great deal of collage—I rescued from the trash a handful of this manuscript confetti and kept it in one of the pouches where I store my materials. As the scraps were from *Cormac McCarthy's House*—this book—and as they made their way into paintings called *Cormac McCarthy's House,* one can say that, in the most literal sense, the writing and the painting are building blocks of each other.

WORKS CITED

Allen, Woody. "My Philosophy." In *Getting Even.* New York: Warner, 1972.

Appalachian Heritage. Vol. 39, no. 1 (Winter 2011).

Aristotle. *De Somniis* and *De Divinatione per Somnum.* In *The Basic Works of Aristotle.* Edited by Richard McKeon. New York: Random House, 1941.

Arnold, Edwin T., and Luce, Dianne C., eds. *Perspectives On Cormac McCarthy.* Revised ed. Jackson: Univ. Press of Mississippi, 1999.

Baldwin, James. *The Fire Next Time.* New York: Dell, 1970.

Balzac, Honoré de. *Gillette; or, The Unknown Masterpiece.* Translation of *Le Chef-d'oeuvre Inconnu* by Tony Rudolf. London: Menard, 1988.

Beaton, Cecil. *Beaton in the Sixties: The Cecil Beaton Diaries as He Wrote Them, 1965–1969.* New York: Knopf, 2004.

Bible. Authorized King James Version. Edited by Robert Carroll and Stephen Prickett. New York: Oxford Univ. Press, 1997.

Bloom, Harold. *Genius: A Mosaic of One Hundred Exemplary Creative Minds.* New York: Warner, 2002.

———. *Novelists and Novels.* New York: Chelsea House, 2005.

Brassaï. *Conversations with Picasso.* Translated by Jane Marie Todd. Chicago: Univ. of Chicago Press, 1999.

———. *Picasso and Company.* Translated by Francis Price. Garden City, N.Y.: Doubleday, 1966.

Brosi, George. "This Side of the Mountain." *Appalachian Heritage,* Spring 2007. http://community.berea.edu/appalachianheritage/issues/spring2007/sideofthemountain.pdf.

Burgess, Anthony. *Re Joyce.* New York: Ballantine, 1966.

Burroughs, William. *Naked Lunch.* 1959. Reprint, New York: Grove, 2004.

Campbell, Joseph. *Wings of Art: Joseph Campbell on James Joyce.* Audiocassettes. St. Paul, Minn.: HighBridge, 1995.

Campbell, Neil. "Liberty beyond Its Proper Bounds: Cormac McCarthy's History of the West in *Blood Meridian.*" In *Sacred Violence: A Reader's Companion to Cormac McCarthy,* edited by Rick Wallach and Wade Hall. Revised ed. 2 vols. El Paso: Texas Western Press, 2002.

Cleary, Thomas. *The Counsels of Cormac*. New York: Doubleday, 2004.

Cox, Brian. *Salem to Moscow: An Actor's Odyssey*. London: Methuen, 1991.

Danchin, Laurent, ed. *Artaud et l'Asile*. Vol. 2: *Le cabinet du docteur Ferdière*. Paris: Nouvelles Éditions Séguier, 1996.

Deas, Michael. *Portraits and Daguerreotypes of Edgar Allan Poe*. Charlottesville: Univ. of Virginia Press, 1989.

Degas, Edgar. *Letters*. Translated by Marguerite Kay. Oxford: Cassirer, 1947.

Dillard, Annie. *Teaching a Stone to Talk*. Revised ed. New York: Harper Perennial, 1988.

Dykeman, Wilma. "Cormac McCarthy's Book Impressive." *Knoxville News-Sentinel*, May 30, 1965.

Ellis, Jay. *No Place for Home: Spatial Constraint and Character Flight in the Novels of Cormac McCarthy*. New York: Routledge, 2006.

Esquire. "American Fiction, Summer 1993: The Beginning and the End of Everything." July 1993, 74–104.

A Family Thing. Directed by Richard Pearce, 1996. DVD. MGM, 2001.

Faria, Paulo. "Na Estrada de McCarthy." Photographs by Peter Josyph. *LER*, September 2010, 41–43, 86–88.

Faulkner, William. *Light in August*. In *Novels, 1930–1935*. New York: Library of America, 1985.

Fitch, Noel Riley. *Anaïs: The Erotic Life of Anaïs Nin*. New York: Abacus, 1996.

Friedrich, Hugo. *Montaigne*. Translated by Dawn Eng. Berkeley and Los Angeles: Univ. of California Press, 1991.

Genet, Jean. *L'Atelier d'Alberto Giacometti*. Photographs by Ernest Scheidegger. Paris: Marc Barbezat, 1963.

———. *Letters to Roger Blin: Reflections on the Theater*. Translated by Richard Seaver. New York: Grove, 1969.

———. *The Studio of Alberto Giacometti*. Translated by Richard Howard. In *The Selected Writings of Jean Genet*, edited by Edmund White. Hopewell, N.J.: Ecco, 1993.

Gide, André. *The Counterfeiters*. Translated by Dorothy Bussy. New York: Knopf, 1927.

Gideon's Trumpet. Directed by Robert E. Collins, 1980. DVD. Acorn Media, 2007.

Ginsberg, Allen. *Howl*. Edited by Barry Miles. New York: Harper and Row, 1986.

Gogh, Vincent van. *Letters to Émile Bernard*. Translated and edited by Douglas Lord. New York: Museum of Modern Art, 1938.

———. *Vincent van Gogh, Painted with Words: The Letters to Émile Bernard*. New York: Rizzoli, 2007.

Hall, Michael. "Desperately Seeking Cormac." *Texas Monthly*, July 1998.

Hart, David Bentley. *The Beauty of the Infinite: The Aesthetics of Christian Truth*. Grand Rapids, Mich.: Eerdmans, 2003.

Hass, Robert. "Travels With A She-Wolf." *New York Times Book Review,* June 12, 1994.

H. D. *Tribute to Freud.* Manchester, UK: Carcanet, 1985.

Hemingway, Ernest. "Voyage to Victory." In *By-Line: Ernest Hemingway.* Edited by William White. New York: Scribner's Sons, 1967.

Herr, Michael. *Dispatches.* New York: Knopf, 1977.

Hustvedt, Siri. *A Plea for Eros.* New York: Picador, 2006.

Jacobs, Don. "Body of Homeless Man Recovered from Fort Loudoun Lake." *Knoxville News-Sentinel,* December 1, 2010. www.knoxnews.com/news/2010/dec/01/body -recovered-near-rail-bridge.

James, Elizabeth. *Charles Dickens.* New York: Oxford Univ. Press, 2004.

Jordan, Pat. "How Samuel L. Jackson Became His Own Genre." *New York Times Magazine,* April 29, 2012.

Josyph, Peter. *Adventures in Reading Cormac McCarthy.* Baltimore: Scarecrow, 2010.

———. *Cormac McCarthy's House.* Directed by Peter Josyph and Raymond Todd. Lost Medallion Productions, 1999. www.youtube.com/watch?v=10O-sX8fvyM.

———. Liberty Street: *Encounters at Ground Zero.* New York: SUNY Press, 2012.

Joyce, James. *Letters of James Joyce.* Edited by Stuart Gilbert. New York: Viking, 1957.

———. "A Portrait of the Artist." In *A Portrait of the Artist As A Young Man: Text, Criticism, and Notes.* Edited by Chester G. Anderson. New York: Viking, 1969.

Kerouac, Jack. *Big Sur.* New York: Penguin, 1992.

———. *Departed Angels: The Lost Paintings.* New York: Thunder's Mouth, 2004.

———. *The Kerouac Collection.* CD. Rhino-Atlantic, 1997.

Klein, Mason, ed. *Modigliani: Beyond the Myth.* New Haven, Conn.: Yale Univ. Press, 2004.

Langewiesche, William. *The Outlaw Sea: A World of Freedom, Chaos, and Crime.* Portland, Ore.: North Point, 2005.

Laporte, Nicole. "True Gruff." *Newsweek,* February 6, 2011. www.newsweek.com/2011 /02/06/true-gruff.print.html.

Leslie, C. R. *Memoirs of the Life of John Constable.* Ithaca, N.Y.: Cornell Univ. Press, 1980.

Lewis, C. S. *The Cosmic Trilogy.* London: Pan, 1990.

———. *A Grief Observed.* New York: Harper and Row, 1961.

Ligon, Betty. "Even McCarthy Should Appear at This Show." *El Paso Inc.,* Aug. 23–29, 1998.

Luce, Dianne C. *Reading the World: Cormac McCarthy's Tennessee Period.* Columbia: Univ. of South Carolina Press, 2009.

McCarthy, Cormac. *All the Pretty Horses.* New York: Knopf, 1992.

———. *Blood Meridian Or The Evening Redness in the West.* New York: Random House, 1985.

———. *Blood Meridian Or The Evening Redness in the West*. Revised ed. New York: Vintage, 2010.

———. *Child of God*. New York: Vintage, 1993.

———. *Cities of the Plain*. New York: Knopf, 1998.

———. *The Crossing*. New York: Knopf, 1994.

———. "A Drowning Incident." *Phoenix*, March 1960, 3–4.

———. *Meridiano de Sangue Ou O Crepusculo Vermelho No Oeste*. Translated by Paulo Faria. Lisbon: Relógio D'água, 2004.

———. *Meridiano de Sangue Ou O Crepusculo Vermelho No Oeste*. Revised translation by Paulo Faria. Lisbon: Relógio D'água, 2010.

———. *The Orchard Keeper*. New York: Vintage, 1993.

———. *The Road*. New York: Vintage, 2006.

———. *The Stonemason*. Hopewell, N.J.: Ecco, 1994.

———. *The Sunset Limited: A Novel in Dramatic Form*. New York: Dramatists Play Service, 2006.

———. *The Sunset Limited*. Directed by Tommy Lee Jones. DVD. HBO Films, 2011.

———. *Suttree*. New York: Random House, 1979.

———. *Suttree*. Translated by Paulo Faria. Lisbon: Relógio D'água, 2009.

———. *The Wolf Trapper*. *Esquire*, July 1993, 95–104.

Melo, Filipa de. "Knoxville O Território de McCarthy." Photographs by Peter Josyph. *LER*, May 2009, 46–52.

Melville, Herman. *Pierre; Or, The Ambiguities*. New York: Hendricks House, 1949.

Merton, Thomas. *The Wisdom of the Desert: Sayings from the Desert Fathers of the Fourth Century*. New York: New Directions, 1960.

Miller, Henry. *The Waters Reglitterized: The Subject of Water Color in Some of Its More Liquid Phases*. Santa Barbara, Calif.: Capra, 1973.

———. *Tropic of Capricorn*. New York: Grove, 1961.

Miller, Henry, and Anaïs Nin. *A Literate Passion: Letters of Anaïs Nin and Henry Miller, 1932–1963*. Edited by Gunther Stuhlmann. New York: Harcourt Brace Jovanovich, 1987.

Monk, Nick. "'An Impulse to Action, an Undefined Want': Modernity, Flight, and Crisis in the Border Trilogy and *Blood Meridian*." In *Sacred Violence*, vol. 2: *Cormac McCarthy's Western Novels*, edited by Rick Wallach and Wade Hall. El Paso: Texas Western Press, 2002.

Morgan, Wesley G. "McCarthy's High School Years." *Cormac McCarthy Journal* 3 (2003): 6–9.

———. "Origin and History of the Thematic Apperception Test Images." *Journal of Personality Assessment* 65 (1995): 237–264.

———. *Searching for Suttree: Photographs by Wes Morgan.* http://web.utk.edu/~wmor gan/Suttree/suttree.htm.

———. "A Season of Death and Epidemic Violence: Knoxville Rogues in *Suttree.*" *Cormac McCarthy Journal* 4 (2005): 195–209.

Morrow, Mark. *Images of the Southern Writer.* Athens: Univ. of Georgia Press, 1985.

Mumford, Lewis, and Henry A. Murray. *"In Old Friendship": The Correspondence of Lewis Mumford and Henry A. Murray, 1928–1981.* Edited by Frank G. Novak, Jr. Syracuse, N.Y.: Syracuse Univ. Press, 2007.

Myers, B. R. *A Reader's Manifesto: An Attack on the Growing Pretentiousness in American Literary Prose.* New York: Melville House, 2002.

Naked Lunch. Directed by David Cronenberg, 1991. DVD. Criterion Collection, 2003.

On the Road With Duke Ellington. Directed by Robert Drew, 1967. DVD. Docurama, 2008.

Owens, Barcley. *Cormac McCarthy's Western Novels.* Tucson: Univ. of Arizona Press, 2000.

Partisan Review. America and the Intellectuals: A Symposium. New York: Partisan Review, 1953.

Priola, Marty. "Games in the Border Trilogy." In *Myth, Legend, Dust: Critical Responses to Cormac McCarthy*, edited by Rick Wallach. Manchester, UK: Manchester Univ. Press, 2000.

Rimbaud, Arthur. *"A Season in Hell" and "The Drunken Boat."* Translated by Louise Varèse. New York: New Directions, 1961.

Russell, John. *A Lost Leadership.* New York: Museum of Modern Art, 1975.

Russian Proverbs. New York: Peter Pauper, 1960.

Science Friday. "Connecting Science and Art." NPR broadcast with Werner Herzog, Cormac McCarthy, Lawrence Krauss, and Ira Flatow. April 8, 2011. www.npr.org /2011/04/08/135241869/connecting-science-and-art.

Sepich, John. *Notes on* Blood Meridian. Austin: Univ. of Texas Press, 2008.

Shakespeare, William. *The Complete Works of William Shakespeare.* Edited by David Bevington. Glenville, Ill.: Scott, Foresman, 1980.

Shimpf, Shane. *A Reader's Guide to* Blood Meridian. Gainesboro, Tenn.: BonMot, 2008.

Smythe, Barbara. *Trobador Poets: Selections from the Poems of Eight Trobadors.* 1911. Breinigsville: General Books, 2009.

The Song of Roland. Translated by Patricia Terry. Indianapolis: Bobbs-Merrill, 1965.

Sontag, Susan. *At the Same Time: Essays and Speeches.* New York: Farrar, Straus and Giroux, 2007.

St. Germain, Mark. *Freud's Last Session.* New York: Dramatists Play Service, 2011.

Twain, Mark. *A Connecticut Yankee in King Arthur's Court.* New York: Webster, 1889.

12 Angry Men. Directed by Sidney Lumet, 1957. DVD. Criterion Collection, 2011.

Walker, Dale. "'Best Unknown Major Writer' Seeks and Receives Privacy in El Paso." *Rocky Mountain (Denver) News,* April 26, 1992.

Wallach, Rick, ed. *Myth, Legend, Dust: Critical Responses to Cormac McCarthy.* Manchester, UK: Univ. of Manchester Press, 2000.

Wallach, Rick, and Hall, Wade, eds. *Sacred Violence: A Reader's Companion to Cormac McCarthy.* Revised ed. 2 vols. El Paso: Texas Western Press, 2002.

Whitman, Walt. *Walt Whitman's Camden Conversations.* Edited by Walter Teller. New Brunswick, N.J.: Rutgers Univ. Press, 1973.

Woodward, Richard B. "Cormac McCarthy's Venomous Fiction." *New York Times Magazine,* April 19, 1992.

Zola, Emile. *The Belly of Paris.* Translated by Ernest Alfred Vizetelly. Los Angeles: Sun and Moon, 1996.

ACKNOWLEDGMENTS

Thanks to Rick Wallach for instigating and encouraging my adventures in reading Cormac McCarthy; to Paulo Faria, Wesley Morgan, Mark Morrow, Tom Cornford, and Marty Priola for their invaluable contributions to this book; to Florence Schwein, formerly director of the Centennial Museum of the University of Texas at El Paso, and Scott Cutler, curator of collections and exhibits at the Centennial; to Nick Monk and Susan Brock at the CAPITAL Centre in Coventry, England; to Svenolof Halveres and Ingela Ölgren Weinmar at the Kulturens Hus in Luleå, Sweden; to George Brosi, Chris Miller, Samantha Hall, and Chad Berry at the Loyal Jones Appalachian Center in Berea, Kentucky; to Raymond Todd, who helped me shoot *Cormac McCarthy's House* and *Acting McCarthy*; to Miriam Colon, Anne O'Sullivan, Brad Dourif, Kevin Conway, Jerry Hardin, Fred Murphy, Robert Morgan, and Andrew Sarris for discussing *The Gardener's Son*; to Kevin Larkin, fellow painter and friend; to Norma Cohen, formerly director of the Smithtown Township Arts Council in St. James, Long Island, at the Mills Pond House; to Winfried Heid, my dealer at Galerie Signum Winfried Heid in Heidelberg for two decades; to Winfried, Elizabeth Ruhmann, Harry Guest, Paulo Faria, Stacey Peebles, and Christian Kiefer for permission to quote from their correspondence; to Senator Eliot Shapleigh of the Texas Senate for an informative conversation; to Steve Davis, at the Southwestern Writers Collection at Texas State University–San Marcos; to the University of Texas Press; to Dr. Richard Soden for eyes; to Dr. Arthur Miller for teeth; to Dr. Butch Purslow for spine; to the hospitality of the Gratz family; to the hospitality of the Sandler family; and to the hospitality of the Stanke family. Special thanks to Tim Hagans, Michele Brangwen, and Barbara Mann.

INDEX

Page numbers in italics refer to photos.

Concordia Cemetery, 240
Congleton, Greg, 261n6
Conquest of the Air, The, 153
Conrad, Joseph, 116, 224, 250, 257n5,
  264n16
Constable, John, 228–230
*Conversations Avec Picasso / Conversations
  with Picasso / Picasso and Company*,
  267n2
Conway, Kevin, 15, 175–176, 264n18
Cooke, John R., 22
Cooper, Gary, 247
Cooper, James Fenimore, 107
Coppola, Francis Ford, 75, 257n5
Corleone, Fredo, 75
Corleone, Michael, 75
Corleone, Vito, 75
Cormac McCarthy's House (series/
  exhibitions), 5, 114, 151, 185–200, *200*,
  201–212, *212*, 213–227, *227*, 228–239, *239*,
  240–248, *248*, 249–253, 267n4; film,
  232–233, 267n3; poster, 190
Cormac McCarthy Journal, 127, 264n21
Cormac McCarthy Society conferences,
  8, 52, 61, 89, 190; Ballarmine College
  (Louisville, 1993), 52, 93; CAPITAL
  Centre, University of Warwick (UK,
  2009), 61; Texas State University–San
  Marcos (2010), 3, 94–95; University of
  Texas–El Paso (1998), 24, 190, 193, 229
"Cormac McCarthy's Venomous Fic-
  tion," 79
Cormac McCarthy's Western Novels, 7
Cornford, F. N., 62
Cornford, Francis, 62
Cornford, John, 62
Cornford, Tom, 61–88, 148, 161
Coronado Country Club, 192
Corot, Jean-Baptiste-Camille, 227
Counterfeiters, The, 237–244
Cowley, Malcolm, 110
Cox, Brian, 62
Crane, Hart, 107
Cranly, 20
Critic as Artist, The, 84

Cromwell, Oliver, 178
Cronenberg, David, 211
Crossing, The, 44, 68, 79, 89–139, 143, 155–
  156, 158–159, 165–166, 168–174, 178–181,
  219, 256n5, 263n5
Cumberland Hotel, 42–43
Cumberland Street, 42–43
Cuomo, Governor Mario, 113
Cutler, Scott, 221, 243
Cutty, 79

Dali, Gala, 10
Dali, Salvador, 9–10, 24, 188
Dalton gang, 29
Damon, Matt, 164–165
Danchin, Laurent, 206, 266n2
Dante Alegieri, 19, 23, 143, 173, 199
Darwin, Charles, 34–35, 62
Davidson, Hazel, 11, 53
Davis, Jefferson, 239
Davis Mountains (TX), 99
Dead, The (film), 128
"Dead, The" (story), 100
Deas, Michael, 16
"Death and Epidemic Violence," 261n9
Death and the Ploughman, 84
Death of A Salesman, 78
de Beauvoir, Benyon, 228–230
de Born, Bertran, 19–22, 24, 256n5
Dedalus, Stephen, 20, 223
Degas, Edgar, 198, 209, 230
De Gaulle, Charles, 207
Delacourt Theatre, 142
Delacroix, Eugène, 208, 211
DeLay, Rep. Tom, 196
DeLillo, Don, 10, 130
DeLisle, Annie, 48
Democritus, 126
Denham, Carl, 245
Departed Angels, 222
De Ponte Mill and paper, 201, 220,
  233–234
Depot Street, 14
Derrida, Jacques, 6
Descartes, René, 173